DIGITAL MEMORIES
Scrapbooking
with your computer

Carla Rose

que®

800 East 96th Street
Indianapolis, Indiana 46240

Digital Memories: Scrapbooking with Your Computer

Copyright © 2004 by Que Publishing

International Standard Book Number: 0-7897-3147-9

Library of Congress Catalog Card Number: 2003116907

Printed in the United States of America

First Printing: April 2004

07   06   05   04   4   3   2   1

Executive Editor
Candace Hall

Development Editor
Kate Small

Managing Editor
Charlotte Clapp

Project Editor
Matthew Purcell

Copy Editor
Kezia Endsley

Indexer
Chris Barrick

Technical Editor
Jennifer Burke

Reviewers
BethAnn Buehler
Alice Tumey
Annette Williams

Publishing Coordinator
Cindy Teeters

Designer
Anne Jones

Page Layout
Stacey Richwine-DeRome

Trademarks

Warning and Disclaimer

Bulk Sales

Que Publishing offers excellent discounts on this book when ordered in quantity for bulk purchases or special sales. For more information, please contact

U.S. Corporate and Government Sales

1-800-382-3419

corpsales@pearsontechgroup.com

For sales outside of the U.S., please contact

International Sales

1-317-428-3341

international@pearsontechgroup.com

Contents at a Glance

Part I: **What You Need to Get Started**   **5**

1   Starting a Scrapbook   7

2   Traditional Scrapbooking Tools   19

3   Digital Tools: Hardware   35

4   Digital Tools: Software   51

Part II: **Building Your Scrapbook**   **75**

5   Page Layout and Design   77

6   Creating and Using Backgrounds   95

7   Working with Old Photos   107

8   Working with Digital Photos   135

9   Turning a Photo into Art   169

10   Adding Type   197

11   For Web/CD-Based Scrapbooks   217

Part III: **Appendixes**   **235**

A   Other Uses for Digital Art   237

B   Glossary of Computer Graphics and Scrapbooking Terms   245

C   Manufacturers, Web Sites, and More   261

Index   267

Table of Contents

Introduction 1

I What You Need to Get Started

1 Starting a Scrapbook 7
What's It About? 7
    Organization 8
    Style Is More Than Fashion 9
    Color Schemes 10
    What to Include on a Page 11
What's Your Format? 12
What's the Difference Between a Scrapbook and a Journal? 14
Books and Book Covers 15
    Binding Your Own Book 16

2 Traditional Scrapbooking Tools 19
Storage 19
Taking Stock 20
Booking It 23
Sticky Stuff 24
Don't Run with Scissors 26
Finding the "Write" Tools 28
Stamping Grounds 30
Embellishments 31
Ephemera 32

3 Digital Tools: Hardware 35
The Computer 35
Resolution? I Resolve to Explain… 36
Digital Cameras 38
    Why Go Digital? 39
    When You Go Camera Shopping, Consider… 40
Scanners 42
No Camera? No Scanner? 45
Printers 47
CD or DVD Writer 49
But I Don't Have a Computer! 49

4 Digital Tools: Software 51

Choosing Your Program 52

Scrapbook-Specific Programs 53

    HP Creative Scrapbook Assistant 53

    Art Explosion Scrapbook Factory Deluxe 55

    Print Explosion Deluxe 57

    Photo Express My Scrapbook 59

    Hallmark Scrapbook Studio Deluxe 61

    American Greetings Scrapbooks & More 62

    YM Diary 64

Photo-Editing Software 64

    Adobe Photoshop Elements 65

    Jasc Paint Shop Pro 66

    Jasc Paint Shop Photo Album 67

    Adobe Photoshop Album 68

    Microsoft Picture It! 70

    ACDSee PowerPack 71

Page Layout Programs 72

Programs for "Sharing" Pages Electronically 73

    Portable Document Format (.pdf) 73

    Web Pages 74

II Better Pages with Your Computer

5 Page Layout and Design 77

Working in Layers 77

Working with Templates and Grids 82

Composing a Page 84

    The Importance of Whitespace 84

    Eye Leading 85

    The Rule of Thirds 85

    Coherent Pages 87

Design Elements 88

    Adding Textures in the Computer 90

    Textural Objects: Ribbons, Fiber, and Fabrics 92

    Clip Art for Scrapbookers 92

    Online Sources 93

6 Creating and Using Backgrounds **95**

Using Premade Backgrounds 95

Backgrounds from the Scanner 99

Papers: What's Available 100

Other Materials You Can Print On 103

7 Working with Old Photos **107**

Getting a Good Scan 108

Basic Photo Corrections 109

Adjusting Levels and Contrast 110

Dodging and Burning 111

Cleaning Up Dust Spots with the Clone Stamp Tool 113

Other Touches 114

Retouching in Paint Shop Pro 114

Moving Paint: Blurring, Sharpening, and Smudging 115

Smudges 115

Focus Tools 116

Removing Dust and Scratches 118

Rescuing a Badly Damaged Photo 118

Vignetting a Picture 123

Photo Tinting 126

Correcting Off-Color Photos 128

Correcting Color Cast 128

Using Fill Flash 132

Selective Color Adjustments 132

8 Working with Digital Photos **135**

Shooting for Scrapbook Pages 135

A Better Crop of Pictures 140

About Face! Flipping Images 144

Resizing 145

Blurring Backgrounds 147

Applying Color Correction 151

Correcting Perspective 153

Removing Unwanted Items or People 155

Little Touches Mean a Lot 157

Fixing Red Eye 157

Eliminating Skin Problems 162

Going on a Digital Diet 164

9 Turning a Photo into Art **169**

   Applying Filters and Effects 171

      Faking Oil and Watercolor Painting 173

      Simulating Oil Painting 176

      Creating Line Art 179

   Posterizing 185

   Drawing on Photos 187

   Making Composites and Collages 188

   Making Panoramic Photos 191

      Considerations When You Shoot a Panorama 192

      Photomerge 192

10 Adding Type **197**

   The Language of Typography 197

   Putting the Words on the Page 199

   Choosing Fonts 203

   Adding Drop Shadows 205

   Using Masked Type 208

   Embossing and Other Special Effects 209

      Creating Metallic Effects 209

      Warping Text 210

   Journaling 212

   Online Sources for Clips and Quotes 214

11 Creating Web/CD-Based Scrapbooks **217**

   Understanding the World Wide Web 218

      HTML—You Can't Pronounce It but You Can Learn to Love It 218

      Are You Being Served? 219

      The Right Address 219

   How To Get On the Web 220

      Free Web Sites 220

      Web Sites for (Almost) Free 220

      Be Master of Your Own Domain 221

   Assembling Web Pages 221

      For the Do-It-Yourselfer 223

      Can This Page Be Saved? 225

How HTML Works 226

Enhancing Your Site with Sound and Video 229

    File Formats and Sizes 229

    Copyright Issues 230

    Creating Sound and Video Files 230

    Putting Your Audio/Video Creations on a Web Page 231

Creating CD-ROMs and DVD-ROMs 232

III Appendices

A Other Uses for Your Pictures .... .237

    Iron-On Photos 237

    Printing on Fabric 239

    Printing on Frosting 241

    Trinket Boxes and Other Tchotchkes 241

    Stationery, Calendars, and Cards 242

    The End, or the Beginning? 243

B Glossary of Computer Graphics and Scrapbooking Terms .... .245

C While You're Wandering the Web... .... .261

Index .... .267

About the Author

Carla Rose started her photography career at the age of eight with a Brownie Hawkeye. A graduate of the School of the Museum of Fine Arts in Boston, she was a TV news photographer and film editor, as well as an advertising copywriter and graphic artist, before discovering the Macintosh. She has written all or part of about 30 computer books, including *Maclopedia, Adobe InDesign for the Mac, Sams Teach Yourself Digital Photography in 14 Days, Sams Teach Yourself Photoshop 4 in 14 Days, The Whole Mac, Managing the Windows NT Server, PageMaker 6.5 Complete, Sams Teach Yourself Photoshop 4, 5, 5.5, 6, 7, and CS in 24 Hours, Mac Online, The First Book of Macintosh, The First Book of PageMaker 4 for Macintosh, It's a Mad, Mad, Mad, Mad Mac, Turbocharge Your Mac,* and *Everything You Ever Wanted to Know About the Mac.* Her books have been translated into more than 15 languages. She is a contributing editor to *PhotoshopUser* magazine and has also written for publications ranging from the *Atlantic Fisherman* to *Adobe Magazine* to *The New Yorker.* She lives near Boston, with her husband, audio guru Jay Rose, and three large, friendly cats. She welcomes email addressed to author@graphicalcat.com.

Dedication

This one's for Pink, and maybe for Fred.

Acknowledgments

No project this big could ever get started, much less completed, without help from a lot of wonderful people. I'd like to thank the folks at Que, especially Candace Hall, who had the great idea to do this, Jennifer Burke for a thorough tech edit, Kate Small for a really good job of development, and of course, Kezia Endsley, who cleans up my words without stepping on them, something very rare in a copy editor. Major thanks to the unflappable Matt Purcell, who holds everything together and picks up the pieces. Thanks to the manufacturers who provided hardware and software for my use. Big thanks to the people who supplied photos, ephemera, and/or their own faces for use in the illustrations, including Carole Harrison, Don Maynard, Judy Storgaard, Suzanne Hecker, Judy Blair, Ann Cartee, Linda Standart, Josh and Melissa Rose, Dan Rose, Kara Marzahn, and Jay Rose. (Please note that any photographs not otherwise credited are my own.) Profound apologies to anyone I forgot to mention. As always, thanks to my friends in the ABCs for their moral support as I worked 20-hour days to meet the deadlines.

Apologies and a hug to everyone I had to ignore or chase away while I worked, especially the cats and the kids. And the biggest hug and deepest gratitude of all is to my wonderful husband, Jay, who always does what needs to be done.

Tell Us What You Think!

As the reader of this book, *you* are the most important critic and commentator. We value your opinion and want to know what we're doing right, what we could do better, what areas you'd like to see us publish in, and any other words of wisdom you're willing to pass our way.

You can email or write me directly to let me know what you did or didn't like about this book, as well as what we can do to make our books stronger.

Please note that I cannot help you with technical problems related to the topic of this book, and due to the high volume of mail I receive, I might not be able to reply to every message.

When you write, please be sure to include this book's title and author as well as your name, email address, and phone number. I will carefully review your comments and share them with the author and editors who worked on the book.

Email: feedback@quepublishing.com

Mail: Candace Hall
Executive Editor
Que Publishing
800 East 96th Street
Indianapolis, IN 46240 USA

For more information about this book or another Que Publishing title, visit our Web site at www.quepublishing.com. Type the ISBN (excluding hyphens) or the title of a book in the Search field to find the page you're looking for.

Introduction

The Lure of Scrapbooking

As Simon and Garfunkel said, "Preserve your memories. They're all that's left you."

A scrapbook is, literally, a book full of scraps. The main content is usually photos: weddings, baby pictures, and travel photos. Of course, scraps are all kinds of things, not just photos, but ephemera of all kinds—ticket stubs, pressed flowers, menus, pamphlets, post cards, souvenirs—whatever helps you to remember the places, events, and people they're tied to.

A scrapbook can also be a journal, a way of displaying your thoughts, as well as your favorite things and pictures. Scrapbooks are about people, places, pets, or whatever tickles your fancy or tugs your heartstrings.

Scrapbooks have been around in one format or another for many years, but the concept of creating them digitally is new and exciting. With even a simple digital camera or scanner and some inexpensive software, you can jump right in and have reasonably professional-looking pages in a couple of hours.

If you love scrapbooking, you're not alone. About 20 percent of households now have scrapbooks compared to 13 percent two years ago. The current craze is thought to have begun in 1981, in Utah. Mormons, always big on genealogy, started gathering family photos to go with the family tree. Scrapbooking really started back around the turn of the 20th century, as photographs printed on paper became readily available. Prior to that, photos were made on glass plates, elaborately framed with embossed metal edges and tooled leather covers.

Grandma's scrapbooks were nothing more than large books with black or manila construction paper pages holding neat rows of photos, sometimes labeled, unfortunately sometimes not. Pictures were inserted at each corner into small triangular pockets, or were too often glued in place with anything from wheat paste to mucilage or even rubber cement. These glues destroyed most of the pictures to which they were applied. They stained. They cracked. It was usually impossible to remove the picture from the page without tearing it. The acids in the papers mixed with the chemicals in the photos and inks to bleach out the pictures or even eat holes in them.

Today, we have better adhesives that can be peeled off if you want to move a picture and are free of acids and chemicals that might eat the images right off the page. We have acid-free papers, better photo materials, and we can even save our scrapbooks on CD/DVD discs or send them out into cyberspace for the ultimate in long-term storage.

Scrapbooking brings people together, not only to enjoy the finished scrapbook but also to help create them. Scrapbooking parties, called "croppings" for the picture cropping or trimming that's a necessary part of the craft, are much like old-fashioned quilting bees. Groups of family members or friends get together to share snacks and memories as they work on their pages. It's fun, and there are always a few experienced scrapbookers in the crowd to give advice on making pages more interesting. There are even "cropping weekends" held at fancy resorts and "cropping cruises" to allow scrapbookers some working time while their spouses and kids have something else to do.

Just as the scrapbook originally evolved as a place to show off the then-new art of photography, our current obsession with digital photography led to digital scrapbooking. It's the next logical step forward. A digital scrapbook can even contain film and music clips, spoken journal entries rather than written, animation, and whatever else you can think of.

There are other virtues to digital scrapbooking as well. Unlike regular film photography, it's very easy to retouch a digital picture. You can remove anything that shouldn't be there, including dead tree branches in a landscape or Uncle Harry's tacky girlfriend. If the photo is crooked, you can straighten it. You can use the same picture as often as you want. If it's in black and white, you can color it; or you can remove some or all of the color from those overly bright 1960's Kodachrome prints.

If you make up the pages on the computer instead of with scissors and glue, you can set the type for captions, quotes, or journal notes right on the page. There are thousands of typefaces available, and you can make the type any size you like, knowing it will look professional. You can choose from all the millions of colors your computer screen displays, and you can, if you have access to an inkjet color printer, print copies of your pages to put in a "real" (non-digital) book.

Digital scrapbooks are easy to share. You can put them up on a Web site for family and friends. Use password protection if you don't want to open your scrapbook to the public. You can send your scrapbook as a CD-ROM with sounds and movies, for less than the cost of an annual Christmas card. Distributing copies of your scrapbooks digitally is good insurance against losing all those precious memories in a flood, fire, or other catastrophe.

Why has scrapbooking become such a hot topic? In an interview in the *New York Times*, Deidre Bullock, a consultant for the Minnesota-based Creative Memories, the largest nontraditional retailer of scrapbooking products, says simply, "It keeps the art of storytelling alive." Even beyond that, sociologists have noticed a trend towards "cocooning" that started somewhere in the 1990's. Home and family are more important to us now than in the wild and crazy years that came before. Scrapbooking is a great family activity, as well as a good excuse to get together with friends for cropping parties and to teach each other new techniques.

Finally, in the time since that awful day we call 9/11, it's become even more important to all of us to try to hold on to our relationships with friends and family. Sharing the scrapbooks is one good way to bring people back together, and to remember those who won't be coming home again.

"Memories," said Bullock, "are priceless."

What you Need to Get Started

You've already got the most important thing—your pictures and the memories that go with them. The next four chapters will help you turn them into scrapbook pages you'll be proud of. First, you need to develop a **theme** and a "look" for your scrapbook, and then you need to locate and **assemble** all the stuff you've thought about putting into it. If you're going to build your pages on paper, you need such **basic tools** as scissors and glue, paper stocks, rubber stamps, and embossing powder, charms, stickers, glitter, and more to "fancy up" the pages. You need a comfortable well-lit workspace, ideally one that can be kid- and animal-proofed, and doesn't need to be packed away between cropping sessions. Next, we'll look at the **hardware** you need: a computer, a color printer, either a scanner or digital camera or both, and a CD or DVD reader/writer. Finally, there's **software**: You need a photo-editing program (like Paint Shop Pro, Adobe Photoshop Elements, or MS Picture It) and a layout program (a scrapbook-specific page-assembly program, a Web page or desktop publishing program, or a versatile word processor such as AppleWorks, or MS Word).

Got all that? If not, you get to do some shopping, once you know what to look for. Get ready to have some fun.

Starting a Scrapbook

If you have been scrapbooking for a while, you already know how important it is to plan ahead. If this is your first scrapbook ever, or even your first digital scrapbook, though you're eager to start work, you need to stop and think first. Maybe even make a few notes.

What's It About?

Does your scrapbook have a purpose? Or are you just collecting your old pictures to save in one place? Scrapbooks look best when they're telling a story, rather than just displaying pictures on a page. What kind of story will yours tell? A scrapbook about your baby's birth tells a story. So does one on your wedding, or your kids in general. You can scrapbook your family vacations. Building or renovating a house is a fun topic, with lots of opportunities for comments and progress pictures. You can make a scrapbook of recipes, with photos and/or comments about the people who gave them to you. You can even include a digital photo of the finished dish, or of the family enjoying it. When you're telling a story, you don't skip the punch line. Similarly, plan to end your scrapbook with a photo that sums up the earlier pages. Consider a picture of the newlyweds heading off on their honeymoon, or the baby's first year ending with her first birthday.

Organization

Organization is another aspect to consider before you start. Most scrapbooks seem to be more or less **chronological**. That is to say, your baby book might start with an ultrasound picture and several photos of the expectant mother trying on her first maternity clothes. Several scrapbook pages can be devoted to the preparation of the baby's crib and nursery area, and go on to show family and friends celebrating at the baby shower. When the baby arrives, depending on circumstances, you might be able to capture a few pictures from the labor and delivery room, the doctor or midwife, and of course, several first photos of the baby. You then continue on through baby's first year, and then start a new one for year two, and so on.

Of course, you're not limited to making your scrapbook a timeline. Suppose you want to make a scrapbook about your cat or dog, and you don't have, or can't find, those first kitten or puppy pictures. Start with him now, in a nice pose. Show some of his **daily activities**; perhaps playing ball with the kids, eating, napping, doing tricks for treats. Keep that camera handy, so you can catch him in the funniest or most characteristic poses he takes on.

The point is that your scrapbook needs to be organized in some logical way; otherwise, it's simply a collection of stuff. You might even consider including an **index**. I saw one really neat scrapbook a mom had done for her daughter. It was organized into four sections, each on a different color background. The index page was divided into four sections, each using the appropriate color to identify the categories: family, friends, school, and sports.

I found a unique way to organize the scrapbook that a friend wanted to make of all her favorite 60's and 70's musical groups. She's a pack rat, too, and saved the ticket stubs from every concert she attended. Bingo. There's the unifying factor. I scanned bunches of tickets to make several page backgrounds, and then scanned some of the most important ones by themselves. Now she has a **themed page background** (actually several similar but different ones so that the scrapbook doesn't get boring) and a bunch of embellishments ready to work with. She simply needs to add her photos and possibly some titles and bits of song lyrics. Figure 1.1 shows one of the ticket stub backgrounds.

Figure 1.1

All you really need is imagination. (Ephemera courtesy of Ann Cartee.)

Style Is More Than Fashion

What about style? There are two factors to consider here: your **personal taste** and the **subject** of the scrapbook. Do you love the country look? Are you a Martha Stewart fan? Martha's scrapbook pages reflect a style of elegant simplicity, whereas the country look might have pastel pinks and blues, with flowers and calico or chintz accents.

Did you go nuts for Care Bears, Strawberry Shortcake dolls, or the Hello Kitty line? If so, your style might be "cuteness." Or perhaps you love all things Victorian. Your pages will have lace and lots of the deep mauves and grayed colors so beloved in those days. Dried flowers make nice embellishments for a Victorian-designed book.

The subject of the book might decide the style, too. You can use the Victorian look on a wedding album quite nicely, unless the wedding featured the bride in a decidedly modern mini-dress, or the groom in a polyester leisure suit. In that case, it might be better to try a different, more modern look. Pages featuring really old photos almost demand an antique background. It doesn't have to be elaborate, but consider limiting your colors to some that will not overwhelm the black-and-white or sepia (brown-tinted) photos.

Color Schemes

Once you've decided on a style, your color choices are the next major decision. For each page, you need, at a minimum, one **background color**, a **bright accent**, and a third color that works with both. Choosing colors is easy for some people but difficult for others. I sometimes think "color sense" is something you're either born with or not, like having "perfect pitch." I can look at a piece of khaki colored paper, and know immediately that it will look quite good with a bright turquoise and a related shade of cream. Or I could take a deep cranberry red, combine it with a pale pink and a warm gray, and have a very different looking page, even though the layout might be exactly the same.

Warm gray? Yes, colors have **temperatures**. Reds, yellows, oranges, and even browns, are all **warm colors**. If you were doing a page about a day at the beach, you might want to try mixing red, yellow, and orange to stress the heat of the sun and sand. **Cool colors**, like blues, greens, and violet tones, suggest cooler temperatures, perhaps cool water or leafy forest glades. Warm grays have a touch of one of the warm colors in them. Cool grays include some blue or purple to cool them off. In between is "neutral" gray, which doesn't lean toward either warm or cool.

Colors also have **moods** and even **cultural associations** attached to them. Hot colors are bright, bold, and jazzy. Cool colors are restful and calming. Some colors are associated with particular holidays, and some with moods or places. For instance, purple and yellow together always make me think of Easter. Red and green suggest Christmas. One good way to experiment with color schemes is to drop by your local Lowe's or Home Depot or other store with a large paint department. Grab a handful of those color chip strips. Go for a broad color range from pastels to brights. When you get home, cut them into single colors and then just move them around on a piece of white paper until you find color combinations that please you, or that remind you of moods or places that suggest pages in your book.

Many avid scrapbookers keep a **color wheel** to refer to. I've placed a small one on the first page of the color insert section for you. Here's a diagram (Figure 1.2) to help you see what I'm talking about. Colors on the color wheel are divided into three categories: **primary**, **secondary**, and **tertiary**. The primaries are red, blue, and yellow. These are the "pure" colors. Secondary colors are an equal mix of two adjacent primaries. Red and blue make purple. Red and yellow make orange. Blue and yellow make green. It's fair to say that *any* combination of a primary color and a related secondary color, like blue with purple or blue with green, harmonizes nicely.

Tertiaries are the colors that would be wedged in between the adjacent primary and secondary. For example, blue-green and blue-violet. They harmonize with the colors that make them. So you can happily combine turquoise blue and lime green, because they have green in common, or dark blue and any shade of violet, because they have blue in common.

Figure 1.2

The color wheel in black and white. (See the color insert for the wheel in full color.)

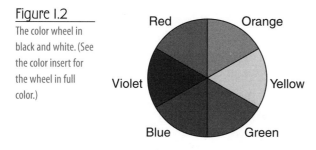

Complementary colors are the ones that are opposite each other on the color wheel, like red and green, blue and orange, and so on. They can also work as combinations, either in their bright form or often more happily as pastels. Red and green can be an effective combination, but come on too strong for some uses. Instead, think pink and pale mint green, or dark blue against tan. Remember that there's more to color than just the color. There are **tints** and **shades** and differences in **brightness**. Think of mixing white with a color to reduce the amount of pure color, giving you a pastel. Mix black or gray with a bright color to darken it or mute it. Grayed colors are particularly effective with a country or Victorian look.

If your photos are in color, make sure that the colors you choose for your pages are similar to the colors in the photo. For instance, suppose you have a picture of your son ready to go trick-or-treating in his purple dinosaur suit, carrying an orange pumpkin shaped candy bucket, and posed against the shrubbery in front of your house. Got those colors in mind? Now, put him on a traditional orange-and-black Halloween page, and you've completely overpowered the photo. Instead, how about using muted shades of the green, orange, and purple together? Sounds rather strange, but it works nicely. See this and some other good color combination swatches on the first page of the color section.

What to Include on a Page

Now that you've done some thinking about your scrapbook in general, you can start putting together a page. Back to square one again. What's the page about? Let's say your daughter's doing a fancy dive off the high board at the pool. What are the colors in the photo? Blue sky, blue water, red swimsuit. Okay, the red's a nice accent for lettering or for an eye-grabbing patch of color behind the photo. The background probably wants to be something in the blue to blue-green range, with a deeper value of the same color to set off a title. Decorations? Maybe a bit of clip art, like a curling wave, or a silhouetted lifeguard's chair or whatever you happen to find. Maybe punched out sunglasses.

While you're thinking about your page, start assembling the stuff that will go on it. Do you have more than one photo? Is one enough? Sometimes it is. If it's a "busy" photo, with a lot going on, you can make several copies of it and crop smaller pieces to use as accents around the big picture. See an example in Figure 1.3.

Figure 1.3
These are all the same picture, cropped to show different scenes.

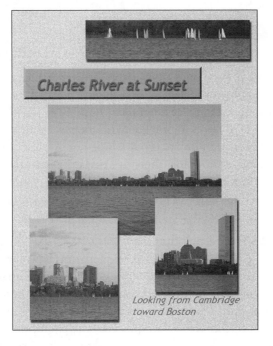

One of the great things about going **digital** is that you can cut copies of your photo and reuse them indefinitely, without risking damage to the original.

What's Your Format?

Once you know what your book is about and why you're making it, the final question is "how?". Will the pages be printed and bound into a book, maybe fitted into page protectors for safety? Will you work on your photos digitally and then paste them on a paper page, or design and print the entire page on the computer?

What about paper? Do you need glossy photo paper to make your prints look more like snapshots? Or do you want to try specialty papers in the printer? What about paper size? Many scrapbookers prefer the **12-inch square pages**, and are therefore limited to printing only parts of the page with a standard printer. You need a wide body printer like the Epson Photo Stylus 1520 shown here, in Figure 1.4, or the

Canon i9100 or Hewlett-Packard CP1700 to make pages wider than 8.5×11 inches. These are a little more expensive; all three are in the $500 range. Your other option is to have your wide pages printed at a commercial copy shop like Kinko's.

Figure 1.4

The Epson Photo Stylus 1520 prints on paper up to 17×22".

If you intend to distribute your scrapbook on a **CD-ROM**, what format will you use? Remember, HTML (.htm) and PDF (.pdf) are the most likely types of electronic documents to be opened by any kind of computer. Unfortunately, every scrapbooking program seems to have its own way of saving pages, and each one is different enough that you can't use one to view another's files. If you know your friends and family use the same scrapbooking software you do, you can confidently send pages in that format. Otherwise, they might not be able to see your work using any other brand of viewer. Alternatively, standard graphic file formats like .tif or .jpg or .png can be read by just about all graphics viewers on both Mac and Windows platforms, assuming your scrapbook program offers any of these file types as a Save option.

Putting your pages on the Web requires that you either have a **Web site** of your own, or that you sign up with a service that offers Web hosting as part of their package, such as Earthlink.net, Comcast.net, or Delphiforums.com. A Web builder service, such as Moonfruit Sitemaker (www.moonfruit.com) or site2you.com, help you assemble your pages online, so you don't need to buy or even understand Web design software. Or, you can ask a Web-savvy friend for some help. I'll discuss this stuff in detail in Chapter 11, "Creating Web/CD-Based Scrapbooks."

If you want to put individual photos on the Web, look into Web sites such as Snapfish.com or ofoto.com (a Kodak company). They will help you get your film photos developed, let you upload your digital photos, and perform minor repairs (such as fixing red eye) and so on. Once you establish an account, they will provide you with a password or specific address that you can send to family and friends. Then, anyone you have shared your photos with can order their own prints or high-resolution digital downloadable photos—for a fee, of course. ofoto.com, for instance, offers prints from wallet size to 16×20". This is obviously not scrapbooking, but it does let your friends see some of your photos.

What's the Difference Between a Scrapbook and a Journal?

The only real difference between a scrapbook and a journal is the ratio of words to pictures. A **journal** goes further than the who, what, and when kind of photo captions we often use in a scrapbook. A journal entry tells a story, describes a place or a feeling, includes a joke or a poem or whatever helps explain to someone else why you made the page. Journaling is sometimes more difficult for the average person than simply scrapbooking, because there's usually more writing involved. Your journal entries needn't be perfect. They should reflect your thoughts and feelings, but it's okay if you want to check spelling before you commit the words to the page. I happen to like to write haiku, a very short and fun kind of poem. To write a haiku, you need to express your idea as a poem in three lines, respectively of five, seven, and five syllables. Here's one:

> *Scraps of old paper,*
>
> *The story of my childhood*
>
> *Stuck down, just one page.*

You can also "borrow" quotes from other people. When my kids were small, I liked to write down in a notebook some of the cute, funny, or profound things they said. That notebook is a wealth of quotes for pages. I especially remember my son Joshua watching Grandma's cat's new kittens.

> *"Look, mommy. They're playing with their chothers."*
>
> *"Do you mean brothers, Joshie?"*
>
> *"No. Chothers, like brothers and sisters both. Each other has their chothers."*

Made sense to me. And it made an amazing quote for the kitten pages. I cherish those little bits of childhood, especially now that both boys are grown up and out of here.

You can put together a scrapbook about anything, if you have the basic materials to use for accents. I am especially fond of **travel scrapbooks**, because I never get tired of seeing new places. One of my friends spent a lot of time in the Middle East, back when travel there wasn't so dangerous. I am very glad that she made scrapbooks of Baghdad, Istanbul, Jerusalem, and other beautiful cities while they were relatively unscathed.

Scrapbooks about **family** members are always a big hit, and become projects that you can keep on adding to as the years go by. For this kind of project, make sure you always have a camera nearby. I've never heard anyone say, "I wish I hadn't taken so many pictures."

Recipe books are a useful and fun kind of scrapbook. Do you have favorite recipes that have been passed along by family and friends? One of my friends used to make a very special apple pie every year on April 1st. It tasted great, but had no apples in it. So I got the recipe, and an old photo, and made a page for Grandma Figg's Mock Apple Pie. Here it is, in Figure 1.5, and it's also in the color section.

Figure 1.5

I've made the pie and it's good. (This figure is also in the color section.)

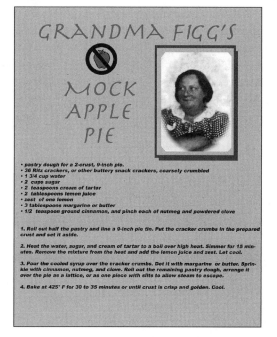

If you have, or know someone who has small children, you can make **"board books"** or scrapbooks specifically for the kids to enjoy. Place your pictures on heavy book-binder's board, and then use sheets of laminating plastic to cover and protect the pages. Make them two sided, and to bind them, punch holes through the sides of the pages and use steel rings from the stationery store. The plastic ones can break and be swallowed, so stick with metal here. These books can be wiped clean as needed, and new pages added after the child has learned all the pictures and words on the first set. Magazine cut outs work well here, as do copies of photos of family members and pets. Don't use any original or one-of-a-kind photos you care about, because the laminating sheets are impossible to remove.

Books and Book Covers

If you check out a large crafts store, you'll be amazed at how many choices you have for **scrapbook covers**. There are premade scrapbook sets with either **ring binders** or binders that **clamp** the pages together. There are **bound** journal-type scrapbooks with a lined page to write on and a blank page to paste on. There are, of course, **book-binding supplies** available to do it yourself, and then there are my personal favorites, the ubiquitous **three-ring binders**. They come in lots of styles, sizes, and colors, but I always look for the ones that have a clear acetate panel on the cover and end spine. What I like about these is that I can customize the fronts and spines by slipping a printed cover page under the acetate. It's also very easy to add pages or change the order if you think of, or discover, something else that can go in there. I also like to use acetate page protectors rather than trusting glue and good luck to hold everything together. On pages that are strictly computer generated, it's not as critical, but I still like to be able to pass the books around and not worry too much about fingerprints or somebody bending a page and popping off my carefully applied decorations.

Binding Your Own Book

If you really want the book to be completely your own, here's a simple way to bind it. At your local art supply or craft store, you can buy what's called **bookbinder's board**. It's a heavy cardboard, almost an eighth of an inch thick. You can cover it with paper or fabric. Putting a thin layer of cotton batting under the fabric gives you a nice puffy cover. Cut the cover material (cloth or paper) about an inch larger than the book cover all around. Turn it face down and, after folding in the corners, glue the material to the inside of the cover as in Figure 1.6. Either miter the corners as you fold them in (as if you were making a bed) or make a "V" cut at each corner to reduce the bulk. Be careful not to cut your "V" too closely, or you might end up with a frayed corner. After that's dried, cut a piece of paper just slightly smaller than the cover and glue it, neatly centered for an inside cover. Marbled papers look really awesome here, especially if yours is a Victorian style or traditional scrapbook. Look for whimsical prints or even nice wrapping paper for a country or "cute" look.

> **tip** Check out online office supply mega-stores like Staples (www.staples.com) or Office Depot (www.officedepot.com) or wholesale clubs such as Sam's Club or Costco for good prices on three-ring binders.

Don't forget to make a back cover too, repeating the steps you used for the front cover. You can make covers out of anything stiff enough to protect the pages. You might need to use a drill on very heavy or thick material to punch the holes for binding, but once the holes are in place, you can assemble the book and bind it with ribbons, heavy yarn, hemp twine, or even those clip-on rings. The crafts stores have plastic ones in a wide range of colors and sizes.

Figure 1.6

Step 1, the basic cover board. Step 2, place cover material under it. Step 3, fold material neatly over inside and glue. Step 4, cover with end paper and glue.

If you're sending out your scrapbook on a **CD-ROM**, investigate label templates. You can design a custom label and j-card (jewel box cover) for the CD, and print them out yourself. Go check out the paper section of the computer store, where you'll find **precut CD labels** that will go through your regular printer, as well as cards to insert into the plastic boxes. The info on the package will guide you to a Web page where you can download the appropriate templates. If you go to www.avery.com, you can find both blank templates to use with your own art or a nicely thought out set of predesigned templates. Insert your own information in MS Word, and print them out. Nothing can be much easier than that.

Got your pictures gathered up, your color scheme picked out, and the ideas flying? Good! Let's go look at some tools.

Summary—What You Need to Remember

The main thing to remember is to have a plan. Know ahead of time what your scrapbook will be about, how you want to organize it, and what photos and other items you want to put into it. Decide on a style that suits the subject and a color scheme that fits the style. Gather your tools and scraps and do it!

Traditional Scrapbooking Tools

Whenever I walk into a scrapbooking store or a crafts store like Michael's or AC Moore, I start to feel like a kid in a candy store. There's so much of everything you can imagine for scrapbooking and paper crafts in general, and of course, I want it all! These places can be very hard on your wallet or credit card, so it's a good idea to plan your project and make up a **shopping list** before you go, and then at least try to force yourself to stick to the list. I also carry a small **notebook** and sometimes a **digital camera** when I shop. If I see something that I like for a future project, I'll make notes or snap a photo for later reference. I don't need to buy it until I'm ready to use it. If it's a patterned paper, perhaps I can re-create something similar on my computer at home and just print it on a light card stock, saving a dollar or so per page, and making my work even more my own. (If you're going to carry a camera with you, watch out for—and obey—signs that say "No Photography.")

Storage

Storing the paper and all the goodies and tools you have gathered for your scrapbooking projects can become a problem. I've learned the hard way that an expensive piece of vellum or handmade paper is a cat magnet, and will become covered in fur and dust in the course of just one afternoon catnap. Sticky-fingered kids are another problem. Your scrapbooking papers and tools seem like fair game to them, and until they're of an age to start their own projects, you might need to declare some things strictly off limits. For households with children, I recommend storing all your scrap-booking supplies in a **locking file cabinet**. Because my own two boys are grown up and gone from the house, I get by with a sturdy plastic three-drawer **rolling stand** (see Figure 2.1), which keeps my tools and supplies organized and keeps the cats out—unless I forget to close a drawer tightly.

Figure 2.1

A good storage container protects your scrapbooking supplies, and can serve as a printer or scanner stand, too.

What sort of scrapbooking supplies do you need most? Well, three things are basic. You need something to put on the scrapbook page, such as photos or other mementoes; something to put these things on, namely paper or card stock; and something to attach them with. Let's start with papers.

Taking Stock

Stock is how designers and printers (the people, not the machines) traditionally refer to papers. It's a question of thickness or weight. **Card stock** is generally used as a basis for scrapbook pages because it is thick enough to support attached items. It comes in a variety of colors, and might be available with preprinted designs. If not, and you want a pattern on your card stock, you can run it through most inkjet printers with no trouble as long as you feed one sheet at a time through your printer. If your inkjet printer is more than a couple of years old, you might want to check the manual to see whether it can handle card stock. If not, you can take your stock and a CD or Zip disk of your pattern file to a place like Kinko's and they'll print it for you.

Text weight papers, such as copy paper or inkjet paper, are often used as layers of a page design, to set off titles or photos or to add some color and texture to the page. If you look in any office supply store or craft store, you'll find tons of preprinted or pretextured papers just waiting to inspire you. These papers might be a bit flimsy to use as a background if you're adding lots of "stuff" to your design. That's why it's best to either back them up with card stock or make sure that your pages go into protective plastic holders. (We'll talk more about those in a minute.)

Tissue papers come in wonderful colors and are great for cutting designs from. They are, however, a real nuisance to attach to the page. I like to use them with thinned out Elmer's school glue to make interesting covers for my scrapbooks and for decorating memory boxes. Building layers of translucent tissue creates a stained glass-like covering. Check out the color insert section to see an example of this kind of tissue work.

Don't neglect any part of the craft or office supply store when you're looking for ideas. I picked up the most amazing **paper doilies**, even some in gold and silver, in the candy-making section of one of the big craft stores. These work beautifully on a Victorian design or on any kind of romantic wedding or Valentine page. You can use the smaller ones, or pieces of a large one, to frame a baby picture too. Figure 2.2 shows some of these.

Figure 2.2

Shops that sell candy-making or cake-decorating supplies are a good source for paper laces.

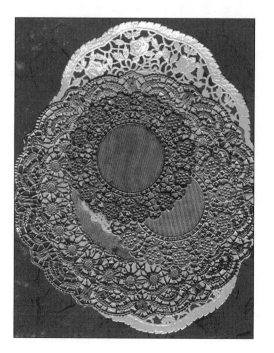

Vellum is a scrapbooking basic. It's a translucent paper designed to resemble the antique parchments that were actually made of animal skins scraped thin. Don't worry. No animals are involved in today's vellum process. It's purely synthetic. Some kinds of vellum have a rougher texture on one side than the other. If you are using vellum with an inkjet printer, be sure to print on the rougher side, and give the ink plenty of time to dry before you touch the printed vellum page. You can speed up the drying time if you need to, with a hair dryer on low or a heat gun purchased from the craft store. If you do use a heat gun, please be careful. They get very hot. Keep it a safe distance from your project. You can actually set fire to delicate papers, according to one of the editors of this book, who's had an unfortunate experience.

The Acid Test

Whatever materials you select to work with, it's very important that you make sure they are "safe" for scrapbooking. After all, you want your scrapbooks to protect your pictures, not destroy them. Many papers are made with a process that uses an acid to help break down the fibers and give the paper a smooth finished surface. Also, wood pulp often contains a natural substance called *lignin* that breaks down into an acid over time. You know what acid does… and it's not pretty. Acid in the paper can react with chemicals present in all photographs, and even in such things as ribbon or dried flowers that you might use for decorations. So you need to avoid direct contact between acid and your photographs whenever possible.

Be sure your papers are either acid-free and/or lignin-free, or at least "*acid-fast*," meaning the acid won't migrate into your photos and other scraps. Hammermill, a paper manufacturer, uses a non-acid process in the making of all its papers, so that brand is generally safe for scrapbooks and other photo preservation projects. If you are unsure whether the paper you have is acid-free or acid-fast, you can get an acid testing pen at the craft store. To use it, just make a tiny dot on one corner of the paper. If it changes color, your paper isn't the best choice for a scrapbook. Use it for shopping lists or something else noncritical.

To make the job even easier, just look for the letters "CK OK" on scrapbook materials that you buy. Creative Keepsakes, one of the better scrapbook and paper craft companies, developed a program to test materials and places their stamp of approval on those that are safe. Other companies are welcome to submit their products for testing, and if they pass, can display the same seal. Creative Memories, another of the leaders in the scrapbooking industry, makes a strong point of repeatedly mentioning that all of their products are acid-free, lignin-free, and chemically buffered to have a neutral acid/alkaline ratio.

Newsprint, used by newspapers and some magazine publishers because it is less expensive, is almost always full of acid. That's why it turns yellow and crumbly as it ages. If you're including newspaper clippings in your scrapbook, copy them onto safe paper, or put them in archival plastic sleeves from the craft store. The sleeves won't stop the yellowing, but they'll protect the rest of your book.

The computer store is another good place to look for papers. In addition to the usual wide variety of **inkjet papers** and **glossy photo paper**, you can find a really cool selection of items like **print-on stickers**, **tags**, **CD labels** in case you decide to distribute your scrapbook as a CD-ROM, some specialty inkjet papers with a canvas, linen, or silk, finish, and even some **art papers**. These are heavyweight textured papers like the ones artists use for pen and ink or watercolor work.

> ## tip
> You can also get iron-on transfer paper to place photos and designs on your t-shirts, caps, or tote bags. (If you try these, remember to reverse or flip the design so it will read correctly when you iron it on.) If you happen to have an item that's difficult to iron on, such as a baseball cap, iron the design onto a small cloth patch, and then sew it on the hat.

Booking It

At some point, you'll need a book to keep your pages in. If your pages are completely printed, you can take the easy way out, by punching them with a three-hole punch and using a **three-ring binder**. If you crave something a bit more interesting, or if your pages are full of stuck-on stuff and you worry about damage, look for a book with **plastic page protectors** included. You can usually buy packs of these page protectors in case the book doesn't come with enough sleeves for all your pages. There are also books that clamp together to hold pages firmly in place. Some are **binding systems** that have you drill holes through the pages and a front and back cover, and then "bind" your book with plastic rings. These can be kind of fun, given the right book. There are also **bound books** with paper or card stock pages that you can paste directly onto. I don't recommend these except for writing journals, because they are small and, I think, too flimsy for heavily decorated scrapbook pages.

If this is your first scrapbooking attempt, I strongly urge you to start with a premade scrapbook. There's time enough to master the art of book binding when you have several books stacked up and you have more experience. **Sleeves** come in several sizes, up to 12×12 inches. If you have a printer that accommodates a wide page, these are fun because you have more space in which to place your designs than on an 8 1/2×11-inch sheet.

Stay far away from **"magnetic" photo albums**. Those were one of the worst ideas to come out of the 1960's and 1970's. Photos that were stored in such albums can sometimes be rescued by scanning the images, without attempting to remove the photos from the album page. But, contrary to the claims made when they were sold, you often can't just peel the pictures out of such albums again. They're stuck in there, and the adhesive might have caused some unexpected and nasty color shifts in some older photos.

Sticky Stuff

Okay, you have a photo and a page to put it on. You need something to attach the picture to the page. First of all, no matter what the men in your life might say, don't use duct tape! Also, don't use super glue, rubber cement, or regular scotch tape. They'll all eventually destroy your pictures.

There are a variety of glues that are "safe" and do the job very well. *Safe*, in this case, means that they are acid-free, and of archival quality. Anything that calls itself **archival** is supposed to be able to be used "without deleterious effect in the conservation or care of important artifacts." Figure 2.3 shows some of the sticky stuff from my work chest. They come in different "styles" according to how they're applied. The simplest is the **glue stick**. It's a tube not unlike a lipstick tube. These are available almost everywhere. I think I bought my current one at the supermarket. They're cheap, not too messy, and stick without lumps or clumps. There are also **liquid glue pens**. You press the pen on the paper, and a dab of glue is released. Press harder and longer for a bigger dab. These are great for gluing small objects, such as buttons or ribbon, because you have good control over where you put the glue. You can even draw or write with a glue pen, and before the glue dries, dust it with glitter or colored chalk powder for some cool textured lettering.

Figure 2.3

Stick with these and you won't get stuck.

You can also buy **bottled liquid glues** for scrapbooking. They come in dispenser bottles with a very small nozzle, like the glue pen, and are also easy to control when gluing small bits of stuff on a page. Some of these liquid glues can be used like rubber cement, in that you can make them form either a permanent or temporary bond between your materials. If you stick the photo down with wet glue, it forms a very strong bond. But if you apply glue to the general area where you want the photo and allow it to dry completely, you can put the picture down, and peel it up again and move it if it doesn't look right. Follow the package directions to make sure you end up with a permanent bond.

Finally, there are **glue dots** in various sizes. They come on a paper backing. Peel them off and stick them to the item you are gluing and then just press it down on the page. These too are moveable. They come in several thicknesses, letting you give a page some dimensional quality by mounting things on thick dots to stand out. **Double-stick tapes** involve the same concept, only in a line instead of a dot. Easily applied with a tape roller, double-stick is often a good way to go. It's ideal if you are scrapbooking with your kids, because it's spill-proof and not messy, and if you drop it, you just pick it up again. Also, look for what's called **photo splits**. They come by the box, and you pull off as many as you need from the dispenser, stick them on the page, and then peel off the protective top layer and stick your pictures on them. Nothing can be easier than that.

The easiest and least destructive way to attach your photos to your pages is the same method that grandma used. Those little **stick-on corners** that hold the photo in place. You can make your own corners or buy them precut. If you had a bunch of envelopes you don't need, you can cut off the corners and recycle them. Because that's rather unlikely, you can make them yourself from whatever scraps are handy. Take a small piece of paper, as in Figure 2.4. This one's a used sticky note. Fold the corners toward the center at a 45-degree angle, making a pyramid shape. Then, cut the pyramid to a nice square corner. Or use scissors with a scalloped or other fancy edge to dress up or add style to your scrapbook page.

Figure 2.4

These work best with glue dots or photo splits.

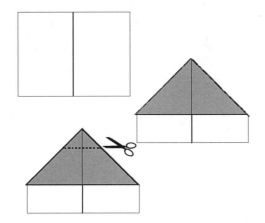

You can buy corners in a range of colors and styles, preglued, too. It saves time, and when you use them, you can be sure that they won't put your precious family pictures at risk. Using corners also lets you pop the picture out of its holder to read the writing on the back, which is important in the case of very old photos that have been handed down through several generations.

Don't Run with Scissors

Scissors are a necessity, unless you're working entirely on the computer. Then, of course, you need a graphics program that enables you to crop your pictures on the screen. I always have at least two pairs of scissors available, large ones for cutting corners or trimming bigger pieces of paper or other material, and a pair of manicure scissors or sharp-tipped embroidery scissors for cutting out small designs or whatever is too difficult with the big ones. Get the best scissors you can, and keep them in a safe place. (Henckels and Fiskars are both good brands.) If you go to classes or croppings and carry your tools in a bag, for heaven's sake, cover your scissors with a sheath. Otherwise, you can damage the tips (or yourself). You can even improvise one by folding a piece of card stock or heavy paper and stapling or gluing it to form a pocket. See Figure 2.5 for an example.

Figure 2.5

This protective sheath was made by cutting a corner from a manilla envelope.

You can also get, as mentioned previously, scissors with fancy edges. They come in all kinds of patterns, from zigzags to scallops to the old-fashioned deckle edges reminiscent of drugstore-processed photos from the 1950's. If that's a look you're trying to achieve, print your photos on glossy paper and trim them with the "photo edge" scissors. The only drawback I've found to this tool is that you do need to carefully watch what you're doing. I make a light line with a pencil and ruler to cut along, and with successive cuts I have to try very hard to match the pattern. Sometimes it's perfect, sometimes it's not. You can always put a sticker or some other little embellishment over a goof, so don't worry too much if you get off-track while cutting a decorative edge. By the way, don't try to use these scissors as pinking shears, if you also sew. They're not strong enough for cloth, and they can't easily be resharpened; so after they are dull, they're gonzo.

In the same general category of sharp stuff, look for a good sturdy **art knife** such as an X-acto brand knife and a cork-backed metal ruler, for cutting straight edges. You will also want a piece of scrap cardboard to cut on, or even better, one of those self-healing cutting mats from the craft store. You'll most likely find them near the scissors and knives. They have a smooth, slightly resilient surface that accepts even very deep cuts and then reseals itself. Pretty amazing technology, if you ask me. Anyway, it's not an absolute must, but a very nice addition to your toolkit that will help to protect the table where you work on your projects.

And then there are **punches**. I can get punchy describing all the different kinds. Seriously. Name a holiday, name a shape, name a critter, and you can find little punches to cut them out of paper. Hearts, dinosaurs, cats and dogs, umbrellas, for when it's raining cats and dogs, I suppose… and so many more you have to see them all to believe it. Don't forget that you can use both the shapes you cut out, and the stuff you cut them from. A strip of hearts punched out of a red ribbon is a cute addition to any romantically themed page. Save the hearts for some other use and mount the punched ribbon on the page as a decorative accent.

Figure 2.6 shows one of my punch tools, and some precut stick-ons, too.

Figure 2.6

Try punching colored papers, ribbons, foils, and even hologram papers.

I'd certainly be remiss if I didn't mention **edge trimmers** and **paper cutters** somewhere in here. You probably remember paper cutters from your school days. I remember being warned to stay away from them, because you can lose a finger in a split second. "Let the teacher do it," we were told. In one dramatic experiment our teacher sliced a potato, just to show us she wasn't kidding around. The good news is that today there are safer ones that won't leave you missing a digit. If you're not good with a knife and straight edge, look for a safety trimmer. The cutter slides back and forth on a bar, and gives you a smooth edge, every time. Some even come with deckle edge and scallop edge cutters that do the same tricks as the fancy scissors, only without your needing to cut extra carefully and line up the patterns.

Finding the "Write" Tools

When you're using a computer to create your scrapbook pages, you won't need as many of the calligraphy pens, markers, and other writing tools used by nondigital scrapbookers. What you will need, though, is a good source of **computer type-faces**, also called **fonts**. There are, of course, tons of free versions on the Web. Some typefaces are more amateur in appearance, whereas others are professionally created by artists and designers. Figure 2.7 shows a single page from one of the many free font sites.

Figure 2.7

To find pages like these, do an Internet search for "free fonts PC" (or "Mac," as appropriate).

You can also find inexpensive, but well-indexed, **CD-ROM collections of fonts** at your local computer store, in the ads in the backs of computer magazines, and so on. Stay away from the professional ones like Agfa, ITC, and Adobe unless you want to pay a lot of money for a single font. Such expensive fonts are intended for professional use and are not a good value for most scrapbook projects. By the way, most of the scrapbooking programs, such as PhotoExpress My Scrapbook by ULead and Art Explosion Scrapbook Factory by Nova Development, come with a collection of fonts. These are generally pretty good ones, chosen specifically to be useful for scrapbooking.

One of the many advantages of computer lettering is that, if you set your type using a word processor or a program such as Photoshop Elements, you can check your **spelling** as you work. Nothing says "amateur" like a misspelled word. It's like a blot on the paper.

The one warning I always give about fonts is not to get carried away. Remember that, first of all, the purpose of putting words on a page is so that they can be read. If the font you choose is illegible, either because it was made that way, or because you've set it in yellow on pink, well... nobody's going to bother to decipher the text. So what's the point of putting it there? If you use more than two unrelated fonts on a page, you'll end up with a different kind of mess, but one that is just as confusing for the viewer. Remember that the words have meaning and the way you choose to display them determines how important the message is. You wouldn't use the same font for a wedding page as for "Billy's Baseball Adventure" or "A Visit from the Great Pumpkin." At least, I hope you wouldn't. Don't feel limited to plain vanilla fonts, either. There's a lot of variety and character or comic fonts, suitable for all occasions. Just use them wisely, and let the message and the reason for the pages help you decide the lettering styles you use.

On the other hand, if you are a master calligrapher, or just someone with really nice handwriting, you can have a lot of fun and make something truly unique by hand lettering your titles, journal entries, and photo captions. My own handwriting is awful. I don't even try. Which means I don't have a good excuse to buy many gel markers, glitter markers, metallic pens, and other kinds of pens, pencils and such found on the shelves of the arts and crafts stores. That hasn't truly stopped me. You can see some of my toys in Figure 2.8.

Figure 2.8
Colored markers and
such are both useful
and fun.

Stamping Grounds

Rubber stamping is a legitimate craft of its own, but it's also a good technique for scrapbookers to have in their bag of tricks. Stamps are one of the best ways for non-artists to get pictures on their pages. Rubber stamps come in just about every imaginable design, from alphabets to art. You can purchase bugs, beasts, butterflies, cats and dogs, Celtic designs, all holidays, drawings and etchings from the Renaissance masters, Victorian art and much more. Do a Web search on rubber stamps or just check out www.rubberstampsclub.com, www.aboutrubberstamps.com, or www.addictedtorubberstamps.com. These are three of the best sites I've found for a good selection of stamps and accessories.

Accessories? Oh, yeah. You don't get away with just the same old standard red or black stamp pad you might use at the office. Serious stampers collect **stamp pads** almost as much as they do the stamps to go with them. There are all kinds of colors and color combinations. Figure 2.9 shows just a tiny sample.

Embossing is a stamper's technique for creating a raised surface from the stamp. First you stamp, using a special pad. Then you dust the stamped design with powder. Shake off the excess, and warm the design with a hot air gun, melting the powder into a slightly raised shiny or matte line that clings only where the lines of the stamp were pressed to the paper.

Figure 2.9
Stamps come in all kinds of sizes and designs.

After you have stamped a design, you can use a variety of markers or watercolor paints to add color to it. Just be careful to stay within the lines and not to let the paper get too wet. Doing your stamping on a heavy paper stock or on watercolor paper will help prevent wrinkling and warping.

The computer version of rubber stamping is called **clip art**, and you can find pretty much the same variety of stuff and probably lots more. Print Explosion and Art Explosion, both published by Nova Development, offer thousands of pieces of art that you can use in your scrapbooks. No matter what you're looking for, it's there somewhere. If you don't want to spend money, look on the Internet for free clip art. Here again, make sure it's free or pay the (usually) small shareware fees. It's not nice to steal.

Embellishments

Embellishments is a big word for little odds and ends of stuff. Do you need them? Not really. Do they add to a page? Sometimes. We're talking now about the items such as charms, ribbons, tags, eyelets, and other goodies you might want to stick on your pages. Some of them, like ticket stubs, and souvenirs of your travels, are entirely appropriate. Others, just stuck on for no particular reason, might not really add anything but clutter to the page. Use them, but use them sparingly.

What should you look for, and where should you look? Well, your jewelry box might be a good place to start. Charms from old charm bracelets are fun. You can pry fake stones from broken junk jewelry. Just make sure it's really junk and not valuable before you use it in your project. Check the notions section of a fabric store for small buttons, spangles, tiny pearls, and of course, rick racks, ribbons, and even things like seam bindings, and odd bits of lace. If the stuff is too thick or sharp-edged to mount on the page, or if you're sticking to computer designed pages, scan the trinkets, and paste them in on the computer. If you use scans, you can also resize them, which you can't do with the real thing.

Military medals, service ribbons, and collar bars and buttons all make nice decorations for a page about your favorite military person or veteran. Scan them, rather than applying them directly, as they can otherwise damage adjacent pages.

Glitter can be messy, but it can also be lots of fun to use. Draw or write with a glue pen, and then sprinkle glitter over the lines. Let it dry thoroughly and then give the paper a good hard shake over a wastebasket to remove the loose bits. Finally, be sure your glittered pages go into a book with plastic sleeves, to keep the shedding down to a minimum.

tip If you scan an object to put on a page, try adding a drop shadow behind it. It will look more 3D that way. Drop shadows are explained in Chapter 6, "Creating and Using Backgrounds."

Stickers are a favorite of many scrapbookers. They are easy to use and add color and character to a page. They are also an easy way out if you want art on the page, and can't draw or paint even enough to fill in a rubber stamp design. Kids started sticker collecting as a craze I think about the same time their parents started scrapbooking, probably about 20 years ago. I certainly remember mine asking for certain stickers, and finding them stuck on everything in the house. Some of the better known sticker companies include Mrs. Grossman's, Suzy's Zoo, Stickapotamus, and Sandy Lion. For one of many good sources, check out www.stickersgalore.com. They have more than 75 sticker brands, plus probably a lot more scrapbooking stuff than you even dreamt was possible. I've found tons of ideas on their pages, too.

Ephemera

Ephemera is a term that describes all the stuff you have collected, in desk drawers, little boxes, envelopes, and wherever your own inner pack rat takes you. A lot of it is surprisingly good for scrapbooking. I love to mix in things like foreign coins and stamps from my trips abroad, and even baggage tags from the hotels I stayed at, and the "collections" I made on my first European trip as a teenager. One such collection included hotel Do Not Disturb signs, another included lumps of wrapped sugar from the various cafes and restaurants, and even the trains we rode on. Those didn't travel too well, so I ended up peeling them and sticking all the wrappers in the back of my travel diary, and they were eventually thrown out. I'd love to have them now. They'd make an awesome page, along with some cups of coffee, tea and chocolate, and perhaps a cutout of a cookie or two and a scrap of poetry about sugar or sweetness, or even lyrics to the "Java Jive." You could add a photo of two people under a Cinzano umbrella in wire chairs at a tiny table, and a (carefully painted) ring from a spilled espresso.

These are the kinds of things that make interesting pages. You must have a ton of them tucked away. Why not dig them out and put them to work for you?

Summary—What You Need to Remember

Here the bottom line is really basic: you need papers, something to put on the paper and something to hold it there, preferably not duct tape or staples. Always look for acid-free or lignin-free supplies. Acid in paper eats pictures. Glues and double-stick tapes are good for keeping your pictures in place; so are corner pockets, which you can make or buy. Once you have the basic page, you can add all kinds of embellishments to make it more interesting. If you have valuable or bulky items, scan them, rather than putting them directly on the pages.

Digital Tools: Hardware

Hardware includes all that computer stuff—the computer itself, with its keyboard, monitor, mouse or trackball, and printer. Chances are you have all that if you're reading this book. You don't need the world's fanciest or most powerful computer to build scrapbooks. And you should know how to make it perform common tasks such as copying, pasting, and saving your work. If you're a real newcomer to the computer world, consider getting a good book on your particular computer and operating system and working through it before you start scrapbooking, or at least have such a book handy for reference as you go along. The *Sams Teach Yourself in 24 Hours* series is a good place to begin. It's not really important whether you use a Mac or a PC. I prefer Macintosh for graphics myself, and you'll find that many of the screen captures in this book have obviously been taken from a Mac, but I have to admit that there's actually a better selection of scrapbooking software available for the PC. Bottom line: Use whatever you have.

The Computer

Let's start here. At its most basic, a computer includes a box called a **CPU** (Central Processing Unit, essentially the brain of the machine), a **monitor** (a video display that lets you see what you're doing), and a **keyboard** (to input text and commands). It can, however, be a lot more than a "smart typewriter." By adding a **mouse, trackball,** or **graphics tablet** with a stylus, you can begin to use the computer as a writing and drawing tool. The mouse or trackball moves the pointer (or cursor) around on the screen, so you can easily edit text, navigate the Internet, draw and paint, and so on. Drawing with a trackball is very difficult, and using a mouse isn't all that much better, so artists often have a graphics tablet and stylus in addition to a keyboard and mouse. The plastic stylus acts and feels like a pen, and is much easier to use than a mouse or trackball for creating and editing artwork or touching up photographs. I strongly urge you to try one at your local computer store and buy it if you like it. I wouldn't use anything else now that I am used to the tablet. Wacom (www.wacom.com) makes high-quality tablets in various sizes.

Computers also need a way to get data in and out, and a place to keep it. These functions are served by an internal and/or external **hard drive** and some sort of **disc reader/writer**. Today most software comes on **CD-ROM** and your computer likely has a built in CD-ROM drive. If not, or if you want extra input, you can usually install another CD reader and writer. You can also add bigger and faster hard drives for more data storage.

Resolution? I Resolve to Explain...

The term **resolution** comes up every time I talk about cameras or scanners, and even monitors and printers. Resolution refers to the quality of the image produced by a camera or scanner, displayed by a computer screen, or created by a printer. Resolution measures the number of dots or pixels (which stands for picture element, the preferred term for dots on the computer screen), per square inch of image. A higher resolution means that the image is made up of more, smaller pixels per inch.

When you look at a picture on your computer or television screen, you're looking at a bunch of relatively large colored dots. (The typical screen resolution for an inexpensive monitor is 72 dots per inch, abbreviated as dpi.) Each dot measures 1/72 of an inch across. Your eye and brain work together to blur the dots into an image. Each dot or pixel has slightly different amounts of the red, green, and blue phosphors that give off light in those colors. They mix visually to make each dot a different color.

If you're familiar with the paintings of Georges Seurat, the famous pointillist painter, you'll remember that he placed tiny, individual dots of color on his canvas. Because you can actually see the little dots and count them, his paintings are at a very low resolution. He was probably working at about 25 dpi, or 625 (25 squared) little dots of paint per square inch of canvas. With patience like that, he should have been a scrapbooker. Figure 3.1 shows a greatly magnified view of a small piece of a Seurat painting. As you can see, every dot is a different shade of color, translated by your eye and brain into a unified image.

Figure 3.1

This is blown up to
show the dots better.
(Georges Seurat,
"Sunday Afternoon
on the Island of La
Grande Jatte")

A similar kind of dot is found on the **sensor**, the "film" part of the digital camera. These sensor dots analyze the light that falls on them, determining its percentage of red, green, and blue. Then the digital camera records this info along with the position of the dot in the captured image. That gets to be a lot to remember. So when you upload the picture to the computer from the camera, all that information is included. The more pixels per square inch you have to deal with, the higher the resolution of the image, and the more memory it takes to hold it all. So, higher resolution means bigger files as well as better-quality pictures. Of course, it takes more time to open and process a large file. It takes more storage space, both on the camera's flashcard and on the computer itself, to save them. You can actually save a little money here by not buying more camera than you need. Think about what you'll want to do with it other than scrapbooking, and whether or not you really need 5-megapixel resolution. If you're going to be shooting outdoors, in a variety of lighting situations, it's more important to find a camera with a flash and a zoom lens.

So, What's a Megapixel, Anyway?

A megapixel is *not* a single pixel that's been super-sized. Megapixel is shorthand for one million pixels. So a 5-megapixel camera captures 5 million pixels worth of information. A 3-megapixel camera captures 3 million pixels worth. You can expect to pay more for higher resolution, but you get photos that will be very clear even when enlarged. If you're not planning to enlarge the photos to a size larger than 8×10 inches, you don't need a 5-megapixel camera. A 2- or 3-megapixel model will do the job.

Digital Cameras

When consumer-level digital cameras first came out, somewhere in the early 1990's, they were more of a gimmick than a useful tool. The resolution wasn't good enough to make a print more than a few inches wide. Photographers weren't ready to give up their film cameras, and computer fanatics weren't into photography except as a way to fancy up their Web sites. But as a relatively short time passed, several things happened. Digital cameras improved and became more affordable, and picture-editing software also improved and became easier to use. Meanwhile, the scrapbook craze was growing bigger and bigger. It seemed logical to combine them.

Today's digital cameras are amazing. Most of them don't look much different from the ordinary 35mm and pocket-size snapshot cameras you're used to. They slide right into your handbag, briefcase, fanny pack, or jacket pocket without weighing you down. They mostly run on AA batteries, which are available anywhere. Most use interchangeable **compact flashcards** for memory, and a single card smaller than a matchbook can hold as many as 90 or more pictures depending on the amount of memory the card has, and the resolution of the camera.

Digital cameras work somewhat the same way a film camera does. Light passes through a lens, but instead of exposing a piece of film, it touches a sensor panel. On both kinds of camera, you can focus the lens and adjust the lens aperture and exposure, or let the camera do it for you. The lens aperture determines how much light is allowed to pass through the lens, and the exposure is the length of time (in fractions of a second) that the light reaches the sensor. One nice feature that most digital cameras include is a **view screen** that lets you see your photos immediately, so you can erase the ones that you consider a waste of film.

Figure 3.2 shows a couple of my favorite digital cameras, along with their flashcards. You can get a camera with a 5-megapixel resolution for what you paid for a 640×480 resolution model only five years ago.

tip

When you shop, look for a camera that uses flashcard memory rather than internal memory. If the camera doesn't have interchangeable memory cards, you'll have to go back to the computer and download your pictures before you can take more. That's a nuisance, especially if you're traveling and don't want to carry a laptop just for picture storage.

Figure 3.2

I really like my Nikons, but there are less expensive cameras that do the job just as well.

Why Go Digital?

The advantages of digital photography are many. Digital cameras are typically **lighter weight** and **easier to carry** around. You don't need to buy **film**, or pay for **processing**. And you're not contributing to the chemical waste the processing plants dump into the sewers, which eventually end up in the water supply.

Digital photography is **faster** than traditional film photography. There's no need to wait for film to be processed into prints and scanned into electronic format. You can look at your digital photos as soon as you've taken them. If there's a TV set handy, you can display your pictures on the TV screen just by plugging in a cable that's included with the camera. Transferring the photo from the camera to the computer takes only a few seconds. All you do is to plug a cable from the camera into the computer (following the instructions included with your camera), open the downloading program that came with the camera, and choose the picture that you want to import.

Most digital cameras also let you throw away bad shots, so they don't waste memory space. The photos you decide to keep last for as long as the hard disk, floppy, CD-ROM, or other storage medium you save them on lasts—virtually forever—without scratching, fading, or color shifting.

Another advantage is the **space** you'll save. Nearly all digital cameras save pictures to a *flashcard*, a piece of plastic about half the size of a business card and only a little thicker. You can pack 20 of these flashcards in the space occupied by just two rolls of 35mm film, and carry as many as 5000 high-quality pictures, instead of the 72 that the film holds. Flashcards aren't cheap, so you might think twice about buying that many, but they are reusable. If you carry only a couple, and have access to a computer, you can upload your pictures and recycle the flashcard to hold more, an ideal situation for the world traveler or roving photo-journalist as well as the family on vacation.

In the long run, digital photography can be **cheaper**. After you're past the initial investment—the camera, the computer, image-manipulation software, and a color printer—your pictures don't cost you anything. You'll never run out of film, and you'll never need to buy any.

Having said that, you won't be paying for film, but you might want to find a place to buy AA batteries by the case. (Costco and Sam's Club have bulk packs at reasonable prices.) Whenever possible, run these cameras from their AC power packs. Lithium batteries give longer service, but because they cost more, it's a toss-up whether you save anything by using them. A few sets of rechargeable batteries and a charger are definitely a wise investment.

When You Go Camera Shopping, Consider...

If you think that you'll need to take several pictures of something in rapid sequence, choose your digital camera very carefully. Not all models can handle **high-speed recovery** between shots. Most require a delay of anywhere from 3–10 seconds or more between pictures while the camera compresses and stores the image it's just captured. A better way to take a sequence of pictures is to use a video camera. It freezes the action every 1/30th of a second, so you can analyze a golf swing or watch the figure skater take off and land the Triple Salchow as well as catch her at the peak of the jump.

Sequential pictures like these are a really cool addition to your scrap-book too. Try running them like a strip of film across two pages.

If you are planning to buy a digital camera strictly to capture images for scrapbooking, any kind of **"point-and-shoot"** camera suffices. You're not going to be worrying very much about image resolution because you're not going to be using big prints. However, after you see how easy digital cameras are to use, and how good the pictures are, even from an older model, you're probably going to want the best one you can find. Digital cameras are sold in camera stores, computer stores, and catalogs. You'll find about the same prices everywhere. You can also usually save a few bucks by shopping on eBay for a slightly older but higher-resolution model. Beware of exceptionally low-priced cameras. They might be "gray market" merchandise brought in from third-world countries and therefore not covered by warranty. Or they might be cheaply made imitations of the good ones. I still remember buying what I thought was a really good calculator for just five dollars on a bargain table, and then getting it home and noticing that the brand name was "Shrap." Not very sharp of me!

Other considerations when digital camera shopping include the **flash** and the **zoom**. Although most experts don't use built-in flashes on cameras, I have found them to be very useful. You simply need to be aware of the shadow that the flash casts, and position the photo subject where a cast shadow won't matter. The built-in zoom lens is a must-have in my opinion. You can't always stand as close to something as you want, but you can zoom in closer on it, or you can pull back for a wider angle shot without moving the camera—and yourself—into a possibly dangerous location. Generally speaking, digital cameras use a **multiplier** (shown as 2×, 5×, or 10×) to represent their capability to "zoom" in on a subject). For example, a normal non-zoom lens shows what you can see with your unaided eye. A 10× zoom is 10 times better, revealing more detail and making a subject appear that much closer to the camera. Always look for the words **"optical zoom"** rather than **digital zoom**. An optical zoom changes the length of the lens, whereas a digital zoom is just a gimmick that makes the pixels bigger so whatever you're shooting looks bigger than it is. It lowers the picture quality in the process.

A **macro, or close-focus, lens** setting is also very desirable, especially for scrapbooking. You can use your digital camera as a quick-and-easy scanner to copy pictures and small objects that you want to put on a page. Because the lens, set to macro and fully zoomed in, lets you make nice clean copies of things at their full size—or larger in some cases—you can enlarge a picture to the point where you can use it as a background for a page. Figure 3.3 shows a quick example of this really neat effect. You'll read more about this later, when you get into designing pages.

Suppose you just want to shoot a few digital pictures and you aren't ready to spend a lot of money on a camera. There's a solution for your problem, a **one-use digital camera**. You can take a picture, view it in the camera, and either keep it or discard it. When the camera's full (it holds 25 photos), you take it back to the store, and they give you—for another 10 bucks—a set of high-quality 4×6 inch prints and a CD-ROM with all your pictures.

Figure 3.3
You can fade the colors of the photo to make it a better background.

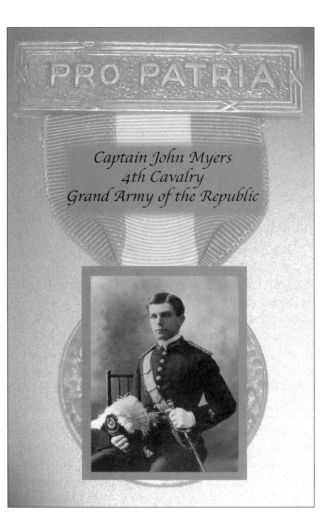

Scanners

The typical desktop scanner looks and acts very much like a photocopier. In fact you can get multipurpose boxes that scan, make photocopies, and also print from your computer. Some can also serve as fax machines. A typical scanner has a **flat glass bed**, and a **lens** inside that moves back and forth to read whatever you have placed on the glass plate. The machine gathers the image, one line at a time, and records the data the same way the digital camera does, but directly to the computer. Figure 3.4 is a picture of my current scanner, a Microtek ScanMaker 5700. I chose this one mainly because it is fast and reasonably accurate color-wise.

Figure 3.4

The Microtek
ScanMaker 5700.

These days you'll find scanners that connect to your computer by **FireWire**, as well as **USB**, **parallel port**, and **SCSI**. Some can even connect via **radio frequency** to an AirPort wireless network (an Apple product). The HP PSC 1350 is typical of the combination scanner, printer, and copiers. For its size, it's remarkably good at both scanning and printing, and is ideal for scrapbookers, because you can plug a camera or compact flashcard directly into it. This helpful device is shown in Figure 3.5. You can print directly from a flashcard, with no computer involved.

Figure 3.5

The HP PSC 1350 and
the Epson CX 6400—
both small, but
effective.

The process of printing directly from a Compact flashcard is really quite simple. First, you plug the card into a slot in the printer. Then, you print a "proof" page that shows all the images on the card. Finally, you simply select the ones you want to print, and run them off in any size from 4×6 to 8 1/2×13. Refer to the owner's manual for your printer to learn how to choose and load different paper sizes, and how to print the proof.

Epson also makes several good combination printer, scanner, and copiers. The CX 6400 does all the same tricks the HP does, and costs about the same. Comparing the same photo printed from both printers, I preferred the Epson version. The color seemed smoother, and the image appeared to have less grain, as if the Epson used smaller ink drops. However, either one suffices.

You Gotta Have Connections

Computers need to be able to "talk" to their printers, scanners, cameras, external drives, and to the Internet. They can make these connections in any of several ways. It used to be that SCSI (Serial Computer System Interface, pronounced "scuzzy") and parallel ports (LPT 1 and LPT 2) were pretty much the only way to do so. SCSI had a lot of problems, sometimes needing a bit of magic to make it work. If the cable was too long, the signal faded out before it got where it was going. If the signal was too strong or not properly terminated, it caused misleading echoes that the computer would try to interpret. That didn't work either. Then came a newer, faster kind of connection called USB (Universal Serial Bus). USB seems to be free of most of these problems and is faster and uses less expensive cable and connectors. Then, Apple gave us FireWire, for PCs as well as for Macs. It's faster than USB, and even more reliable. Finally, there are wireless hubs, such as Apple's AirPort and AirPort Extreme, that connect your keyboard, mouse, and other devices using radio frequency technology. PC users can find similar wireless technology at the computer store or using an online merchant.

Because most of the photos that you'll be adding to a scrapbook are from old paper prints, owning a scanner saves you both money and time. They're not expensive, and using one is about as complicated as making a photocopy. You place the item you want to scan on the scanner's glass plate close the cover and click the Scan button. By installing the proprietary software that came with your scanner, you can begin a new scan, preview the image, and choose how to save data to your computer's hard drive. Image editing programs like Paint Shop Pro, Picture It!, and Adobe Photoshop Elements scan directly into a new document in the program. In fact, the majority of scanners on the market today come with one of these popular picture-editing programs as well as with their own proprietary scanning software.

You can use your scanner to photograph small objects, too. Old jewelry, coins, medals, and other small mementos scan just as well as photos and can then be printed as photos and mounted on foamcore board to give your pages some depth. Figure 3.6 shows a few examples. Notice how clear they are. When you are scanning objects, make sure they don't scratch against the scanner's glass plate.

Figure 3.6

These were all scanned with the Microtek scanner.

In addition to image-gathering software, most scanners also come with software that lets you scan text into an **Optical Character Recognition (OCR)** program and edit it in your word processor. If you have old documents that you want to share via email, such as old family newspaper clippings, this is a good way to transfer the content to your computer. OCR scanning doesn't preserve the "look" of the document, though. It's just for getting the words into the computer without having to retype them. Accuracy depends on how clearly printed the original text is. Typically, OCR software attempts to "guess" at letters that it cannot read clearly, sometimes with unusual or funny results. Newspaper and book print usually come out pretty well. Hand lettering, unless it's in nice clean handwriting, doesn't work for OCR. Sorry, but the program's not quite that sophisticated.

tip

Several scanners, including some Microtek and Epson models, come with special software, which actually repairs damaged photos as they are scanned.

No Camera? No Scanner?

The digital camera and scanner are both great tools for the scrapbooker, but if you can't afford them, don't give up. There are many services, including PhotoQuik, Ritz Camera, and the **photo kiosks** at Wal-Mart, Walgreen's, and CVS and other similar stores that scan your prints or rolls of film and give you the scanned photos on CD-ROM. Kodak offers this service, too, and it's a perfectly good way to get your pictures into the computer.

If you have friends or relatives who have a scanner, ask them to scan your pictures and to email you the scanned photos or burn them onto a CD-ROM. The point is simply to get them into the computer. After you've done so, you can work on them whenever you want. Check with family and friends also to see whether they have already uploaded any pictures that you want to use, such as the annual family picnic potluck, the neighborhood yard sale, or the soccer team's games. Many people create online Web pages, which are a kind of scrapbook, or they upload their pictures to a service such as Snapfish (www.snapfish.com), Shutterfly (www.shutterfly.com), or Ofoto (www.ofoto.com). These services—and there are several more of them listed in Appendix C, "Manufacturers, Web Sites, and More"—not only develop and send back your prints but upload your photos to a password-protected Web site where you can view the pictures, download them to your computer, and order reprints. The storage of your **online photos** is typically free and there's no limit to the number of pictures you can send for posting.

You can take other pictures from the Web, too, and some of them are quite awesome. Anything from the government files can be "borrowed" for free and without even asking permission. Remember those beautiful pictures of Earth from out in space? You can use them. Check out http://nssdc.gsfc.nasa.gov/image/planetary/ earth/apollo08_earthrise.jpg to see one of the most famous, and then scout around that site to see what else you can find. Pictures from the White House? Sure. Go to www.whitehouse.gov and have a look. The Library of Congress has a treasure trove of maps and photos for your enjoyment and use. You can find these at www.loc.gov.

What you can't legally do is use anything that has a **copyright notice** attached. That includes pictures, textures, designs, icons, and other bits of graphic art that you find on other people's Web sites, commercial or otherwise—unless they've posted it along with permission to help yourself. Of course, if your scrapbook isn't going outside your circle of family and friends, you're probably okay anyway. You just can't do anything that makes money for you without the consent of the copyright owner, usually the artist or author involved. If you want to quote some appropriate poetry or a song lyric on a page, you can do so as long as you aren't going to sell the page or make it available for other people to use. The bottom line of fair use is that you can't do anything that might deprive the original creator of making money from his or her creations.

Suppose you're a new bride, putting together a scrapbook of your wedding. "Your song" was "Wind Beneath My Wings." Fine, go ahead and typeset or hand letter that song on a scrapbook page. It's not going to harm the songwriter in any way. But, suppose your scrapbook turns out really well, and you decide to assemble and sell a kit for other new brides to do the same, adding their wedding photos where yours were. Now you're profiting from your work, and you can't do that without the songwriter's permission—which you're probably not going to get without spending some of your own money. You need to find out who the publisher of the song is and send a written request to their permissions department. Depending on how popular any given song is, and how recent, they might ask for a fee or just give you permission and wish you luck. It never hurts to ask.

Printers

If your scrapbook is only going onto the Web, or being distributed on a CD-ROM, you probably don't really need a printer for your projects. However, there are many reasons, aside from scrapbook making, that you might need a printer. Several types of color printers are available, but **color ink jet** is by far the most common and the least expensive. You can also find **color laser printers**, but they tend to be very expensive, and don't give as natural looking results. Ink jets, as the name implies, work by firing tiny jets of ink at the paper. Generally, printers use four colors to create any image: cyan, magenta, yellow, and black. Other printers use a six- or even seven-color system, adding light cyan, light magenta, and light black to improve the reproduction of delicate flesh tones and light sky blue. In addition, some printers now can use either a matte finish or regular black ink. The matte black makes a very definite difference in the quality of any black-and-white work you might need to do, mainly because it looks more dense and black. Color laser printing uses the same process as color copiers. A powdered toner is fused to the paper as it passes over a heated wire on its way through the copy machine or laser printer.

Some printers only take standard 8 1/2×11 paper; others can handle much larger sheets. If you like the traditional 12×12 scrapbook pages and want to create your page layouts digitally, you need a printer capable of handling that page size. In my opinion, Epson makes the best of the **wide-body printers**. Check out the Epson Stylus Photo 1280 at www.epson.com and in Figure 3.7.

It has a six-color Photo Ink System, and gives you **BorderFree photo printing** in six popular sizes. BorderFree means that it can print all the way to the edges of the page without leaving a white margin like some printers do. It's compatible with Windows and Macintosh and includes software. You get both Epson Software Film Factory and Adobe Photoshop Elements 2.0. It's a good buy at about $400. You can find other wide-body printers with four-color inks for a little less money. Check your computer store, and ask to see print samples from any printer you're considering buying.

tip
While you're visiting the Epson Web site, take a look at their section of craft ideas. They have some beautiful photographic backgrounds for your scrapbook pages, as well as templates for pages and tips on how to fix bad pictures. Go to www.epson.com and look on the left side of the screen to explore solutions for craft projects. It's worth the time.

Figure 3.7

The Epson Stylus Photo 1280 is a very good extra-wide printer that can handle 12×12 sheets.

Printers, like scanners and cameras, demand that you install a **driver**. A driver is a simple piece of software that lets the printer communicate with the computer. The driver is what sets up the printer controls and tells the printer how many copies you want to make, the paper size you selected, and any other details it needs to know, such as what kind of paper it's going to print on. Some papers are naturally more absorbent than others, and require different amounts of ink.

Be sure to look in both your computer store and in office supply or art stores for different types of printing papers. There are a great many choices, from basic white **copy weight paper** to **glossy photo paper**, **matte photo paper**, even **textured papers**, **canvas**, **silk**, and **metallic foil**. You can purchase precut stickers to print on, in a fair selection of shapes, plus full transparent or white **glossy sticker paper** pages to cut out and stick to your scrapbook pages.

If your printer only prints black-and-white images, and you aren't ready to consider purchasing a color one, you can still create interesting scrapbook pages in black and white and add color accents with paints, markers, or stamps after they are printed. And you can, of course, load your pictures or finished pages on a CD and have them printed at a local copy or print shop such as Kinko's.

CD or DVD Writer

Do you really need one of these? It's a matter of opinion and mine is "yes, absolutely." There are a couple of good reasons. First of all, most software these days comes on CD-ROM. And most reasonably new computers already have a **CD-ROM** drive built-in. But you need a CD drive that writes disks as well as reads them. It's called a **CD-RW**. CDs are the preferred storage method for archival copies of electronic files. CDs are easy to store and, unlike the floppy disk, are unlikely to become obsolete any time soon. If you have commercially processed pictures returned to you on CD, you need to be able to view and retrieve them to the computer to edit. If you're planning to share your scrapbooks with friends or relatives, sending a CD-ROM through the mail is a lot easier and cheaper than sending a bulky book.

The difference between a CD and a DVD is a matter of size: how many bits of information a single disc holds. **DVDs** are frequently used for feature films because they can hold about three to four times more data than an ordinary CD-ROM. The data itself can be any kind: movies, scrapbooks, music, programs, and games. After all, no matter what you're seeing on the screen or hearing from the speakers, it's all just ones and zeros.

For protection of your precious photos, consider putting them on a CD-ROM and putting it is a safe, disaster-proof place like a safe deposit box at the bank, or a fireproof home safe. Office stores and warehouse stores like Costco or Sam's Club sell them. You can even send a copy to a friend or relative in another town. Then, if there's a fire or natural disaster that floods or otherwise trashes your house, your photos are still safe.

You can also safely store photos online at such places as Snapfish or Hotmail. Go to their sites to register and then follow the directions for uploading your files.

But I Don't Have a Computer!

No computer? I might wonder why you chose this book, but here you are and let's review some options. First of all, look around your neighborhood. Schools might offer adult computing classes, which help you learn the basics of using one. Then, you can go to the local library, or to one of the cyber-cafes that seem to be springing up like mushrooms all over the place. These computers generally have a word processor and some kind of graphics program. Use them to crop and edit your photos or to print out your titles and journaling entries, or buy a half dozen CDs and save each session to a CD-ROM until you're ready to go to someplace like Kinko's to get the final prints.

Kinko's and many similar shops let you rent a computer fully equipped with a scanner and printer and the basic text and graphics programs you need for only few dollars an hour. Be careful if you work on a public machine, though. Some might be infected with computer viruses, and if you save an infected file and then upload it to another computer, you will spread the virus. There's a good discussion of computer viruses and how to avoid them at www.howstuffworks.com/virus.

Finally, as you saw previously, there are printers that work directly with a camera, using a docking interface, whereby you put the camera on the printer and pictures are transferred and printed, using a cable, or removing the little memory cards and simply inserting the cards into the printer and printing the pictures you want. This is never going to be the most satisfactory way to do it, but you have digital pictures, printed, for your pages.

Summary—What You Need to Remember

Computer hardware includes the computer itself and all the things that can plug into it, such as the scanner, printer, and CD-ROM drive. Most computers are sold with one CD-ROM drive built-in, but if you want, you can add a second one or opt for a CD-ROM burner to make your own CDs. Digital cameras come in many sizes, quality and price ranges, and feature a wide range of capabilities. For digital scrapbooking, a point-and-shoot type of camera is usually fine. You don't generally need incredibly high-resolution photos for scrapbook size pictures. Look for a digital camera with macro and zoom capability, though. That way, you can use it as a scanner if you need to copy some pictures or 3D objects to include in your scrapbook. Scanners are like copy machines except that they send the image to your computer instead of printing it directly on paper. If you have a lot of paper photos that you want to put into your scrapbook using your computer, buying a scanner is very worthwhile. Commercial services print your photos for you and put them on a CD-ROM or DVD so you can use them with your computer scrapbook software. You can also download pictures from the Web, as long as you're careful not to use copyrighted material for profit. Anything you find at a Federal government site is up for grabs.

Printers come in different widths. Some can't handle more than an ordinary letter-sized page, whereas others can print up to 13×19". These "wide-body" printers are ideal for 12×12"-size scrapbook pages. You can print digital pictures directly from your camera to paper with specially equipped photo printers. Or you can get them printed at almost any camera store, and then just use them like regular photos on your paper pages.

Digital Tools: Software

Computers need programs, also called applications or software, to tell them what to do. With the help of programs such as Photoshop Elements and Paint Shop Pro, you can incorporate your photographs into any kind of document you want to create, such as a scrapbook page, a printed catalog or report, a multimedia presentation, or a lavishly illustrated Web page. Adobe Acrobat creates files called PDFs that are well suited to cross-platform distribution, meaning that you can share them with Mac or PC users without any trouble. One overwhelming advantage that a digital camera has over a conventional camera relates to software. Within a matter of a minute or two after you've shot a picture, you can open it in a **photo-editing program** like Photoshop and crop, color correct, and place it where you want it. You can handle the entire process yourself. You don't need to send the pictures out to be processed, and then off to a service bureau for color scanning. Just plug the camera into the computer, save the pictures, and carry on.

Because programs such as Photoshop Elements and Paint Shop Pro are actually bit-mapped **paint programs**, they are capable of extremely subtle, pixel-by-pixel corrections as well as quick, all-over changes. You can achieve effects with these programs that you can't possibly manage any other way, certainly not with traditional film-developed photo techniques. **Digital retouching** is much easier.

Standard **color correction** can be done automatically, or if you're looking for something out of the ordinary, you can try as many variations as you like. "Undo" is just a keystroke away, and you're not wasting expensive photo paper and chemicals experimenting. And that's the second major difference. Because you're not constrained by the technical limits of the photographic process or the need to economize, you're free to try as many versions of the picture as you can invent. Save them, print them, or dump them in the trash and start over. All you've spent is time.

Making Versus Taking a Picture

When you use a conventional camera, you "take" a picture. You shoot what's there. If the image is not quite right, you'll have to shoot another photograph and develop it before you know for sure what you have. However, with the combination of a digital camera and software to manipulate images, you're not taking a picture, you're making a picture. Sometimes you know ahead of time exactly what elements you need to make a good picture. Other times, you start with no particular concept and experiment with images until you reach a satisfactory picture. It works either way.

When you look at images in ads, on magazine covers, on software packaging, and practically everywhere else, most of the photos you see are made, rather than shot. It's not always convenient, or even possible, to set up some of the shots art directors ask for. A current fashion magazine has a model dressed in some sort of windblown chiffon dress, standing on an iron girder right at the edge of a new building under construction. No guard rail, no obvious safety belt, and she doesn't look the least bit scared, perched there in her four-inch high heels. The photographer probably took the building shot from the building across the street, and placed the model on a plain white backdrop with a fan blowing on her dress. From there, it's just a few minutes work with the computer and graphics editing software to assemble the desired picture.

Choosing Your Program

There are a number of specific scrapbook programs on the market, and you'll look first at those, and then discuss some other, possibly more versatile, programs that can be used for photo editing, graphic enhancement, and all kinds of similar tasks, including but not limited to basic scrapbooking. Then you'll see what's out there for page layout and look at word processors that you can use to produce parts, if not all, of a page. Finally, you'll consider Web page software as a scrapbooking tool.

Scrapbook-Specific Programs

There are several good ones. This section looks at some of the better known programs. By the time you read this book, there might be newer and better software available. Use these descriptions simply as a rough guide as to what you might expect from each kind of program.

HP Creative Scrapbook Assistant

Because HP Creative Scrapbook Assistant is not only one of the easiest to learn, but also has the added benefit of being compatible with both Mac and PC platforms, let's start there. All scrapbook-specific programs have similar basic features. Some come with more clip art, and others with extra lettering fonts or better selection of shapes to decorate pages and frame your photos. But HP Creative Scrapbook Assistant is very typical.

Should You Buy This Software?

+   For both Macs and PCs

+   Less than $30

+   Easy to use

−   No drawing or painting tools

−   No photo repair tools

Figure 4.1 shows the Mac version of the program in operation. (The Windows version is very similar.) I set up a very simple colored background, imported a photo, and added a title for the page and an additional phrase from their prewritten comments, which are listed under the Phrases tab.

Figure 4.1
HP Creative
Scrapbook Assistant's
interface is clean and
understandable.

As you can see, each element on the page is represented by a tab at the top of the window. The Theme menu, which is shown in Figure 4.2, lets you switch between the 10 or so supplied themes, and also customize and add your own personal themes. You can keep all your scraps organized together in themes and project folders that you create with a mouse click. Everything here is icon-based and intuitive.

Theme

Create New Theme...
Rename Theme...
Delete Theme...

+CK 2003 Hall of Fame
+Hot Off The Press
+the Vintage Workshop
✓ Animals
Babies
Celebrations
Family Milestones
Holidays
Kids
Nature
Sports
Tools And Textures
Travel

To start a new project, you simply click the New Page button or select New Page from the File menu, and then start adding images, shapes, and whatever else you have, just as you do when you are working with paper and glue. Add your own text to the page by clicking the Add Text button and typing your words into the box that appears. Choose a font from all the ones you have installed. Creative Scrapbook Assistant gives you the option of displaying the font list in the actual typefaces so you can quickly and easily choose one that works, just by appearance without having to remember the font's name. You can place text over a picture or shape either by putting the background down first, or by adding a background shape or object on top of the lettering. Then use the Move Forward and Move Backward keyboard combinations or select them from the Edit menu shown in Figure 4.3. On the Edit menu, you'll also find Duplicate, which makes and places a copy of whatever's selected, and Rotate, which lets you paste things at an angle, as I did. As you can see, the Edit menu also has a command that allows you to automatically convert a photo to black and white or sepia. (You'll learn all about sepia toning in Chapter 7, "Working with Old Photos.")

The eyedroppers next to the Text and Background color blocks let you "borrow" a color from anything in your layout. If you look at the Nigel page in the color section of this book (this page also appeared in Figure 4.1), you'll notice that the color block behind "Pets Allowed" is exactly the same copper shade as the cat's eyes. To use the eyedropper, make sure that no items in your layout are selected, and then just click on the color you want to use from the photo or scanned object. The color swatch changes to the closest color to the one you have chosen. Use the Transparency slider to adjust the amount of background that shows through a selected object or photo. If you want to change an item's color to match a color elsewhere on the page, click on the item to select it, click on the Background (or Text) eyedropper, and then click on the color you want.

Figure 4.3

The Edit menu also contains the usual Cut, Paste, and other expected editing commands.

Edit	
Undo Delete	⌘Z
Can't Redo	⇧⌘Z
Cut	⌘X
Copy	⌘C
Paste	⌘V
Clear	
Select All	⌘A
Duplicate	⌘D
Rotate	⌘R
Convert to Black & White	
Convert to Sepia	
Move Forward	⌘F
Move To Front	
Move Backward	⌘B
Move To Back	
Add Text	
Remove All Guides	

This is a good, basic scrapbooking program. It has literally hundreds of themed artwork pieces and backgrounds designed so you can simply drag and drop your own photos and titles in place. What's missing are any kind of drawing, painting, or photo repair tools. You can scan a picture into the program, but you can't correct red eye or do much else except resize it. If you get Creative Scrapbook Assistant, I strongly urge you to pick up additional software such as Photoshop Elements or check out the photo-editing software that came with your scanner or digital camera. You'll need it.

Art Explosion Scrapbook Factory Deluxe

Art Explosion Scrapbook Factory Deluxe (by Nova Development) is a two-CD set with bunches of prepared page layouts, fonts, and clip art for your scrapping pleasure. Unfortunately for Mac folks, it only runs on the Windows platform. If you like "cute," this program is going to make you very happy. The art is of decent quality, but it's slanted toward the cartoonish, or sometimes overly saccharine styles. Figure 4.4 shows the interface, with a premade page from their project series.

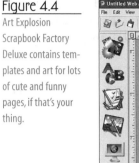

Figure 4.4

Art Explosion Scrapbook Factory Deluxe contains templates and art for lots of cute and funny pages, if that's your thing.

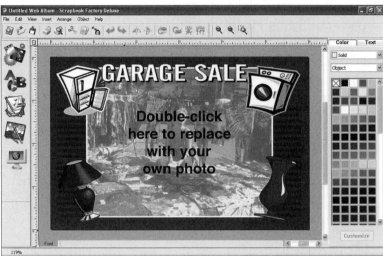

If you prefer elegance and simplicity, you *can* get there from here, but it requires a little more work. In Figure 4.5, I've started with a plain page and added a background called "Marbled Lavender." From there, I can add my photos and captions, on blocks of other colors if I want, or in colored type.

Figure 4.5

This one's on the way to being elegant.

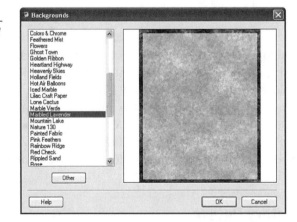

Art Explosion Scrapbook Factory Deluxe has some drawing tools but they are crude and hard to use. You must reselect the tool for each line or shape you want to place, which really slows you down. On the other hand, you might enjoy some of the tricks it can do with type, including checking your spelling and adding a simple shadow to text. Figure 4.6 shows the drop shadow interface. Unfortunately, it's only for type. I inserted a mock drop shadow by copying the cut corner box in black and placing it behind and a bit offset from the original purple box. I cover more about some of these tricks in upcoming chapters.

Figure 4.6

Drop shadows, properly placed, add depth to type. This program is not very flexible.

Art Explosion Scrapbook Factory Deluxe is obviously more complicated, and more capable than Creative Scrapbook Assistant. It has something like 4,000 templates for projects including paper folding and several other paper crafts as well as scrapbooking. (These are contained on a second CD that you must insert each time you want to add something to your pages.) There are 20,000 graphic elements, about 500 fonts, and a very long list of "inspirational quotes" that you might

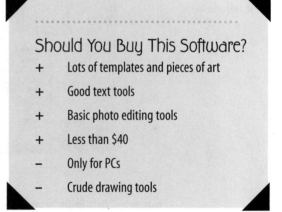

Should You Buy This Software?

+   Lots of templates and pieces of art

+   Good text tools

+   Basic photo editing tools

+   Less than $40

–   Only for PCs

–   Crude drawing tools

want to add to your pages. Personally, I'd rather write my own, or sit with a copy of *Bartlett's Familiar Quotations* until I find the right words.

Nevertheless, this is a good comprehensive program. It includes basic photo-editing tools, including cropping, straightening, and resizing, as well as red eye and some color correction. Art Explosion Scrapbook Factory Deluxe also includes the elementary drawing tools I found missing from Creative Scrapbook Assistant. If you're really not too fussy about fixing your photos, or just want to set titles and use the page layouts and clip art, it's an excellent program for beginning scrapbookers.

Print Explosion Deluxe

Nova Development has also released a program similar to Art Explosion Scrapbook Factory Deluxe for the Mac, but it's not really scrapbook-specific. However, it does have all the clip art that was available in Art Explosion Scrapbook Factory Deluxe, plus 70,000 more pieces. Yep, that's right. 90,000 premium quality graphics, on three CDs. It's called Print Explosion Deluxe, currently available only for the Mac platform. As you can see in Figure 4.7, it's possible to use it for scrapbooking, if you choose elements wisely and do your own layout. I started with a predesigned stationery template to get the scroll. I removed the type that said "From the Desk of…" and so on, and added my own, plus a pirate map and a box into which I'll place a photo of the kids in their pirate costumes. Further pages in the set will probably keep the scroll and have different shapes or frames.

Figure 4.7

Use your imagination to make something original from the canned pages provided. It's like making a gourmet meal from yesterday's leftovers.

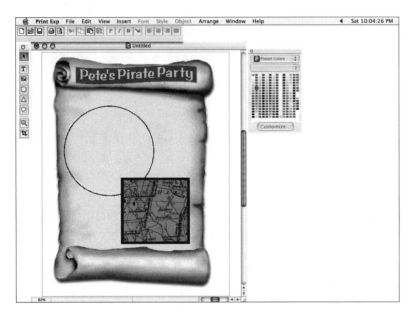

What sets Print Explosion Deluxe apart from other graphics programs is the tremendous selection of clip art, fonts, stock photos, quotations, and premade greeting cards and other templates it comes with. Figure 4.8 shows the interface for finding graphics. When you actually select one to download, you'll have to insert one of the CDs because only the index is stored with the program. There's also a printed catalog containing pictures of the graphics and other goodies on the disks. It's included with the software, and is about the size of a medium-sized phone book.

Should You Buy This Software?

+   Lots of clip art and fonts

+   Printed catalog of graphics

+   Less than $60

–   Only for Macs

–   No photo editing tools

–   No drawing or painting tools

Figure 4.8

These are typical of the less cute designs.

If you like to do your own designing, but also like to have lots of cartoon images, art scraps, and what-nots to decorate your pages (and you use a Macintosh), this is certainly a collection worthy of your consideration. It doesn't have drawing tools or any kind of photo-correction tools, but it sure has lots of "stuff" for your pages, greeting cards, and other projects.

Photo Express My Scrapbook

ULead Systems has a long-standing reputation for good photo-editing software, so I expected Photo Express My Scrapbook to be pretty good. I am pleased to say that I wasn't disappointed, except by the fact that this program is only available for the Windows platform. Photo Express My Scrapbook has basic photo-correction tools, and it makes the corrections automatically, which is a big help for beginners. But, if you know the effect you want or how much color correction the photo needs and what the program wants to give it, you might be disappointed. It seems to over-brighten colors, and overcorrect in general (but that might be because the pictures I was trying it on really didn't need much help.) Figure 4.9 shows the program in use, color-correcting a picture from my son's wedding.

Either fix your pictures first, or find a scrapbook layout you like by clicking the Mode menu and selecting Project, and then work on the photos as you bring them in. Over 100 templates are available, most tending toward "cute" as in the Art Explosion Scrapbook Factory and Print Explosion Deluxe collections. Figure 4.10 shows a few of the many pages. Photo Express My Scrapbook provides a good selection of both 12×12" and 8 1/2×11" page layouts. Be sure you keep the CD handy, as virtually anything you try to open from the collection requires it.

Figure 4.9

You can sharpen, correct colors, and straighten a crooked photo with a few simple mouse clicks.

Figure 4.10

This program also includes templates for other kinds of projects including paper folding.

All Photo Express My Scrapbook's editable files are saved in a proprietary file format called .tpx, so you can't open them in another program and work on them with other software. This is generally true of scrapbooking programs, as opposed to a more generalized graphics program such as Photoshop Elements, which saves and opens files in a lot of different graphics formats, compatible with most other software and hardware platforms. However, Photo Express My Scrapbook can also save your work in a good selection of uneditable graphics and Web formats. Print Explosion Deluxe offers you only .jpeg and .pict (primarily a Mac graphics format) or .html for the Web, along with its own format. Is this really a drawback? It might be, if you intend to put all your work on digital pages for a CD or a Web site. This can become a big issue, especially if some of the friends and relatives you'll be sending the CDs to are Mac folks, and others use only PCs. Cross-platform compatibility is covered in greater detail in the chapter on sharing your pages.

Should You Buy This Software?

+   Basic and automatic photo editing tools

+   Templates in variety of page sizes

+   Can save files for viewing in other programs

+   Less than $30

−   Only for PCs

Hallmark Scrapbook Studio Deluxe

I've heard both good and bad opinions about Hallmark Scrapbook Studio Deluxe by Sierra Home, shown in Figure 4.11. It's a good program for beginners, but it's limited in what it can do. You might be able to find it at one of the larger computer stores, but it's probably easier to buy it online from Amazon or any of the other usual suspects. You can also buy it from sierrahome.com and from some of the larger discount retail stores.

Figure 4.11

Lots of stuff to play with, but the results might not be great.

The quality of the art in this program is a little bit better than some other scrapbooking programs. There are more than 500 scrapbook page templates, and somewhere around 4000 pieces of art you can apply to them. It also includes 300 or so fonts, and a basic digital photo editor that can zap red eye and do some color correction.

The biggest problem people have reported with Hallmark Scrapbook Studio Deluxe is that when you import a photo into a layout, the program resizes it for you to make it fit the box you're putting it into. This often leads to unwanted distortion, because it flattens and widens a rectangular picture into a square, or stretches an already cropped square photo into a rectangle.

Should You Buy This Software?

+   High quality clip art and templates

+   Basic photo editing tools

+   Less than $20

−   Only for PCs

−   Auto photo resizing results in distortion

−   Often adds unwanted white space around photos

Also, you might have difficulties with unwanted whitespace around the photos. Sierra Home, the publisher of this program, says that there's no easy fix for this, except checking the size of the box and resizing your photo in some other program before importing it.

American Greetings Scrapbooks & More

The best thing about American Greetings Scrapbooks & More by Broderbund is the price. For less than 10 dollars, you get a shrink-wrapped set of three CD-ROMs with no fancy packaging. One CD contains Scrapbooks and More; there's also a two-disk set called American Greetings Crafts, which has greeting cards, paper folding projects, and a whole lot more. The second best thing is what you get for your money. There's a very robust photo editor, capable of immediate and intuitive color editing, special photo effects that aren't quite as good as Photoshop—but still surprisingly good and easy to apply—and even customized cropping. Want a jagged edge on your picture? Draw it in and accept the crop. In Figure 4.12, I've applied a heart-shaped crop to a wedding picture. Adjust the size of the cropping frame by dragging on the corners or sides. You can make it as big or small as you want.

Figure 4.12

This is incredibly cool for the price.

Then you can add borders, text, other graphics, or whatever you like from the included collection of art and photos. Oddly enough, the premade scrapbooks are actually on the crafts discs rather than the Scrapbook one. If you're going to design mostly from scratch, work with the Scrapbook program. If you just want to paste pictures into a layout, open the Crafts program. Both have the photo-editing tools and text-entry tools, but they have different art elements. You can also save a project from one and open it in the other, if necessary.

Should You Buy This Software?

+ High quality clip art and templates
+ Customizable patterned cropping
+ Strong photo editing tools
+ Less than $10
− Only for PCs
− American Greetings is taking the software to the Web

But if you want this program, don't delay. American Greetings admits that it is phasing out this software in favor of a Web-based system where you can download page templates, plus matching keepsake holders, page corners, and cut-outs. Figures 4.13 and 4.14 show a couple of examples. Here, too, as befits a greeting card company, the art is a little better quality.

You can try this service for free for a month. Go to http://www.americangreetings.com and register. You'll have to give them a credit card number, so be sure to cancel when you're done trying it if you don't like it, lest you be charged every month.

Figure 4.13

The instructions for the projects are very clear, so it's hard to make mistakes.

Figure 4.14

This is one of the themed packages. You get a basic page template, plus corners, scraps to copy and paste, and even a keepsake pocket.

Pages
Celestial Moments

Photo Page
Celestial Moments

Photo Corners
Celestial Moments

Keepsake Pocket
Celestial Moments

Cut-out Designs
Celestial Moments

YM Diary

The last of the current crop of digital scrapbooking software is called YM Diary, published by JournalTEK (journaltek.com). It's aimed at the preteen to teenage girl, specifically those who also read *Young Miss* magazine (ym.com). The cutest part of this program is that it's password protected to keep snooping moms or little brothers out of your personal stuff. That said, although it does copy photos into a "scrapbook," it really can't be considered a scrapbooking program. It's more like a journal.

Please forgive me if I've neglected to mention anyone's favorite scrapbooking software. This happens to be what was available in November 2003 when I began this project. There will probably be more coming out even before this book is on the shelves. But the bottom line seems to be that they all have some art, some templates, and some way of entering and editing text. Some are simpler than others. Some are capable of beautiful pages, but what you produce with any of these programs is really up to you. If you're satisfied just to use the premade templates and paste your own pictures on them, that's fine.

Photo-Editing Software

As my grandfather liked to say, "there's more than one way to skin a mouse." (He was fond of cats.) Photo-editing programs can also make up wonderful scrapbook pages. In fact, most of the examples you'll see in upcoming chapters are pages I created with Photoshop Elements. Fact is, I prefer it to any of the scrapbook-specific software. There are several good reasons why. First, it's more versatile. I can use it for page layouts, for setting text, and for photo clean-up. Second, it has all the wonderful Photoshop filters, and accepts all the equally wonderful third-party Photoshop plug-ins that let me turn ordinary photos into works of art. Third, it's cross-platform, so I can swap files back and forth between my Mac and my Windows XP machine without even thinking about it. And everything's in the same place on both platforms, so I don't have to unlearn any of my shortcuts or tricks. So, I'll start this section with Photoshop Elements, and then compare how the others match up.

Adobe Photoshop Elements

Actually, the current version is Photoshop Elements 2, but if you have a copy of an older Photoshop Elements bundled with a camera or scanner, by all means use it. Adobe used to have other, simplified versions of their professional Adobe Photoshop software. I remember Adobe Photoshop LE, and before that Adobe PhotoDeluxe. Each new version has more power and is easier to use than the previous one. Now, you can accomplish nearly everything you can do in the latest "professional" release, Adobe Photoshop CS. Those few tools that aren't included in Photoshop Elements aren't anything you are likely to need anyway. Scrapbookers rarely have to deal with channels and paths, for example.

Figure 4.15

The Photoshop Elements screen puts all your tools where you can easily find them.

Figure 14.15 shows the basic Photoshop Elements screen. It has a toolbox on the left and a Tool Options bar across the top. On the right are a couple of *palettes* (helpful little windows that let you work with some of the program's features such as layers and colors), and on the main work surface is a page I just threw together in about two minutes. The accent on the left side of my page is a combination of a colored stripe I drew by drawing a rectangle, filling it with tan paint, and then applying a filter to add noise (little colored speckles), giving it some texture. I then drew a narrower box on

top and filled it with a gradient colored to look like copper. The lettering is simply placed on a colored rectangle. The photo is the real thing, shot in Valley of Fire State Park, and the dancing Kokopelli is a piece of clip art that I copied and flipped so he'd have someone to dance with. Easy, yes.

Where Photoshop Elements really excels, however, is not so much in scrapbooking, but in photo repair and editing. Figure 4.16 shows a photo, before and after I did some badly needed repairs.

Figure 4.16

The original photo, on the left, was in bad shape.

I could also have hand-colored this picture or turned it into a charcoal drawing or an etching or any of a dozen or so other art styles with a couple of clicks. You learn how to do these repairs and turn pictures to art in the next few chapters. Admittedly, Photoshop Elements costs a bit more than the scrapbook programs (suggested retail is about 100 dollars), but it does a great deal more. If I owned only one graphics program, it would be this one.

Should You Buy This Software?

+   Amazing photo repair and editing tools

+   Lots of filters to turn your photos into art

+   For both Macs and PCs

+   Less than $100

–   Not specifically for scrapbooking

Jasc Paint Shop Pro

Paint Shop Pro comes highly recommended by my PC-using friends. There's no Mac version, and according to company sources, no plan for one. As you can see in Figure 4.17, it's somewhat similar to Photoshop Elements. It has many of the same features. You can use it to build pages as well as to repair photos and apply special effects. In fact, I'll be using it in the next few chapters to demonstrate some photo-repair techniques and some tricks you can do with your pictures.

Figure 4.17

Tools aren't in quite
the same places as in
Photoshop Elements,
but everything is
there.

One of the nice things about Paint Shop Pro is that you can try it, fully featured, for 60 days. Go to www.jasc.com and look for downloads. If you decide you like it, you log onto Jasc's Web site and pay for it. If not, the program quietly expires when your time is up, and no, you can't keep re-installing it. It leaves behind a memo somewhere in your system that you've already installed it once, and you can't re-install without a key. Frankly, I wish more software companies used this approach. There have been a good many programs I've installed and ripped out again after a few days of frustration, whereas others I knew after trying them once that I had to have, immediately paid for online, and got my key to unlock them via email five minutes later.

Should You Buy This Software?

+   Good photo repair and editing tools

+   Lots of effects to turn your photos into art

+   Free trial version available

−   Only for PCs

−   More than $100

−   Not specifically for scrapbooking

Jasc Paint Shop Photo Album

Jasc also offers a program called Paint Shop Photo Album. Be careful. It's not exactly an album-making program. What it does, and this might be very useful for you, is organize all the pictures in your computer. You can assign them to different folders, identify them with keywords, and then perform very simple searches to find the picture you need. Jasc Paint Shop Photo Album's familiar, Windows Explorer-like interface is easy to understand. The task-based icons that line the top of the main screen make it simple to install pictures and to search for them. Once you import your pictures into the program, it's easy to add titles, comments, and keywords to help you track them down later. If you haven't entered descriptions, you can also search on a range of standard information, such as date, file size, file type, and even the type of media on which the picture was originally saved.

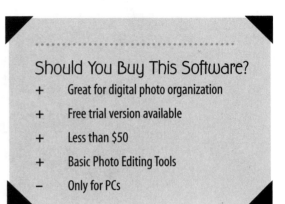

Should You Buy This Software?

\+   Great for digital photo organization

\+   Free trial version available

\+   Less than $50

\+   Basic Photo Editing Tools

−   Only for PCs

Adobe Photoshop Album

Adobe also has a photo album program called, not surprisingly, Adobe Photoshop Album. It's only been released for Windows, however. Installing this software takes a while, and requires restarting the machine, something none of the other programs require. But once you get it going, what have you got?

Figure 4.18

The Photoshop Album interface is clean and understandable.

Pictures can be exported to Web pages, or used in projects. One interesting project, although not really for scrapbookers, is to assemble a photo album with multiple pictures per page, and email the finished creation to Adobe's binding service. You have a choice of full page-size prints or mock album pages holding one or several photos with faked corner pockets. When you're done assembling the album, you simply email it to the address provided, where it's printed and bound in your choice of colors. The entire process takes about two weeks, and the prices of bound photo books start at about 30 dollars.

Photoshop Album has a few photo-editing tools, but for cropping, straightening, and other fairly basic fixes, you have to import the photo into some other application. Photoshop Elements is probably your best choice for that, and many Web sites sell the two programs as a bundle.

Like Paint Shop Photo Album, the real purpose of Photoshop Album is simply to catalog your photos, and let you search them by keyword or date, or whatever information most helps you find the picture you are looking for. It's also pretty good at putting your photos on the Web. It even has a little application embedded into it that lets you assemble your pictures on the walls of a three-dimensional gallery and then wander through with your mouse, stopping to admire the photos as you find them. This is really very cute for a Web page or CD-ROM. Figure 4.19 shows a view of the gallery.

Should You Buy This Software?

+   Great for digital photo organization

+   Basic photo editing tools

+   Less than $50

–   Only for PCs

Figure 4.19

Use your mouse or arrow keys to navigate, or take the guided tour, complete with music.

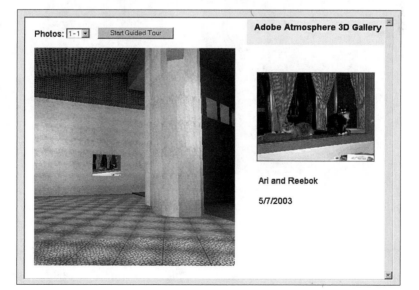

Photos: 1 - 1   Start Guided Tour

Adobe Atmosphere 3D Gallery

Ari and Reebok

5/7/2003

I'm not sure I'd ever think of either of these programs as a "must-have" for scrap-bookers, but they are handy for keeping track of large numbers of digital photos, once you have indexed them. If you can't remember what you shot, or when or where, this software helps.

Microsoft Picture It!

If ease-of-use is what you want in a program, you don't really have to look any further than Microsoft Picture It! or Picture It! Photo Premium. It's strictly for Windows, of course, but has what I call a more Mac-like working environment than Paint Shop Pro. See it in Figure 4.20. It has a well-designed interface, and the task-oriented menus are very helpful.

Should You Buy This Software?

+ Incredibly easy to use

+ Good photo editing tools

+ High quality art and templates

+ Less than $50

− Only for PCs

Figure 4.20

The icons help you find the tools you need.

Microsoft Picture It! is very easy to learn, probably a lot easier than Paint Shop Pro. It's not quite as versatile, in that it doesn't have all the filters and other goodies that make both Paint Shop Pro and Photoshop Elements so much fun to play with. But for a basic program it has some very nifty toys. It comes with a few scrapbook pages and other projects. In Figure 4.21, I've placed a couple of wedding pictures into one of the wedding album pages, and I'm about to add some text.

Figure 4.21

Figure 4.21

You can choose to use either plain text or text set on a wavy line or shape.

One thing I really like about Microsoft Picture It! is the quality of the art supplied with its projects. It even has templates for CD-ROM labels and jewel box cases, so you can create a professional looking presentation for the scrapbooks you send out on CD/DVD. The label and sticker templates are designed to work with standard Avery printable labels, available at any office supply store.

ACDSee PowerPack

Last in this category, but hardly least, ACDSee PowerPack by ACD Systems combines three programs, one for acquiring, finding, and organizing your photos, one for fixing them, and one for designing pages for all sorts of purposes including, but not limited to, scrapbooking. Figure 4.22 shows the basic photo editor setup in ACDSee FotoCanvas. The tools are easy to use and fairly comprehensive. You can fix red eye with a click, remove color casts automatically, or even add them, if you want.

The page layout program included in ACDSee PowerPack is called ACD FotoSlate. Unlike the others, it doesn't come with predesigned page templates, only with blank ones, to which you can add your own pictures and art. There are a half dozen or so photo frames included, and you can choose a

Should You Buy This Software?

+ 3 packages in 1: photo organizing, editing, and page design

+ Automatic and manual photo editing tools

+ Free trial version available

+ Less than $100

− Only for PCs

background color for the page by clicking on Page Properties. Adding type to your page requires that you first place a box on the page, and then select Object Properties from the menu to choose a font and size, and to enter the type.

This is a good all-around package, if you're comfortable with more advanced page design and like doing your own. It's also good for people who just want to get their pictures sorted out, cleaned up, and printed for later scrapbooking use. You can download a free trial at acdsystems.com.

Figure 4.22

The ACDSee FotoCanvas interface is clean and intuitive.

Page Layout Programs

Acting on the theory that a page is a page is a page, there's no real reason why you can't use any page layout software you happen to have as a way to assemble scrapbook pages. Some, like Adobe InDesign, makes the job a snap, letting you place grids for your layouts and duplicate pages until you're bleary-eyed. Of course, for the price, which is about $700, it should also make coffee and massage your back while you work. Quark Xpress and Adobe PageMaker are also high-priced applications that are intended for professional use in page, newsletter, newspaper, and book design. If you have access to one, and have a fairly good idea of how it works, go ahead and play. Placing and resizing photos is a cinch with any of these, and you can certainly add all the backgrounds and embellishments you can design.

An all-purpose office suite, such as AppleWorks or even Microsoft Office or Corel WordPerfect Office, has enough basic tools to turn out scrapbook pages, too. I prefer to use Microsoft Word for page design, but PowerPoint is good, too, and very easy to use. Corel's WordPerfect Office has a program called Presentations that's very much like PowerPoint. As long as you can place art and type on the same page, you can print the results as a scrapbook page. If you like, just print the pieces you need, and assemble them with traditional scrapbook papers and tools. There's no good reason not to mix your media, so to speak. Computer type and computer-printed photos can be awesome on a page with some "real" elements as well. Remember, the only limit to what you can do with computer art is your own sense of creativity and fun.

Programs for "Sharing" Pages Electronically

This final category of software to consider for your scrapbooking pages includes the programs you use for Web page design or cross-platform page distribution. The following is an overview, but in Chapter 11, "For Web/CD-Based Scrapbooks," you'll learn much more about putting your pages on the Web or on a CD.

Portable Document Format (.pdf)

The best known program for creating portable, cross-platform documents is Adobe Acrobat. Because a great many other programs rely on Adobe Acrobat to create universally compatible manuals or Read Me documents, you might already have several copies of Acrobat Reader installed on your hard drive. Adobe Acrobat Reader, of course, is not for program creation, but if you have a Mac running OS X, virtually any program you can print from can save your pages as a .pdf file. (Unfortunately, this doesn't work in Windows. It's a function built into the Macintosh printer drivers.) Figure 4.23 shows the Mac's Print window. To make a .pdf, simply click on the Save As PDF button.

Figure 4.23

Making a PDF is simple for Mac users.

Those using PCs have to invest in Adobe Acrobat to create .pdf files, but if you're going to be sending your work out on a CD-ROM, it's a smart investment. Otherwise, your family and friends might not be able to see your work unless they have the same software that you used to create your digital scrapbook.

Web Pages

There are a lot of good Web page creation programs. Even if you end up printing your pages, you can still lay them out in the .html file format with your favorite Web design software. If you're planning to put your scrapbook up on your Web site, this is the most obvious way to do it, but even if you're not, you can load your .html pages onto a CD or DVD and be fairly certain your friends and relatives will have some kind of Web software that can open the pages you send. I use Netscape Composer for my own Web page work. It's easy and free, as is the rest of the Netscape package. I've been told, however, that Netscape might not be around forever. So I might have to look at Microsoft FrontPage or some other good and easy Web package. They all work pretty much alike. You can also design and save Web pages with the word processor or works programs I mentioned earlier.

My husband enjoys coding Web pages by hand, and can put together a full page in .html with nothing more than a text editor, while I'm still entering a title for mine. Fortunately, design is not his strong point. Otherwise, I'd be out of a job. He uses a program called BBEdit for the Mac, but the fact is that almost any word processor can save your text as .html, even Microsoft Word.

Summary—What You Need to Remember

All you need to remember about software is that you need some, either a dedicated scrapbooking program, or a more versatile photo-editing and retouching program, or both. I strongly recommend Photoshop Elements as a page-creation program as well as for photo retouching and editing. It requires that you use your own creativity, rather than simply relying on predrawn templates and page themes, and isn't that the whole point of doing it?

Better Pages with Your Computer

The rest of this book takes you through some of the many ways to use your computer to make your scrapbook pages more attractive, more interesting, and more fun. You start with some basic **layout** and **design** ideas, and go on to make **interesting backgrounds**. Then you learn how to **rescue old pictures** that are cracked and stained or faded. You discover how to use a scanner to bring your old photos into the computer and how to repair the damage they inevitably have. Then you learn about using a digital camera and **editing digital photos**. I cover **cropping** and **resizing**, **fixing red eye**, and how to remove anything you don't want in the picture, including wild hair, extra inches on the hips, and even your ex-spouse. After that, the next chapter deals with making good pictures out of bad ones by turning them into "art." For instance, when a photo is out of focus, you can turn it into a **pastel drawing**, a **watercolor**, or even **neon tubing**. Not only will it look fine, it can also add something unique to your scrapbook page. Then you learn about working with **type**, including some tricks to make your words stand out on the page. You learn how to use **shadows** and **special effects**, and I talk about journaling—both how to put your words on the page, and how to write something meaningful. Finally, I cover **"paperless" scrapbooks**—putting your pages on the **Web** and on a **CD** or **DVD**. **Web** and **video scrapbooks** can include sounds and movies as well as still pictures. You learn how to add them. You also learn where you can get a free **Web site**, and how to set one up.

Finally, in the back of the book are some suggestions for other uses for your pictures, as well as a **glossary** of computer and scrapbooking terms, and a **list of suppliers** and **Web resources**.

Happy scrapping!

Page Layout and Design

Just the thought of designing a page from scratch sends many a novice scrapbooker running and screaming. There's no need for panic, though. Simply understanding a few basic concepts makes the whole job easy and fun. In this chapter, you learn about layout and page design. You learn about using layers and templates, and how to add design elements without making clutter. Let's start with layers.

Working in Layers

If you want your pages to have a sense of depth or texture, you probably realize that it comes from working in **layers**, adding one piece on top of another. The old-fashioned way is to literally pile up layers of paper on the background sheet. You might, for example, use torn tissue to make an edge around a photo or mount a photo on a piece of double-stick foam tape, so it stands out slightly from the rest of the page. Digitally, layering is even easier.

To really understand layers, think about a cartoon. When Disney Studios turned out its first Mickey Mouse cartoon, *Steamboat Willie*, back in 1928, Mickey was actually created out of about five layers of celluloid, or *cels*, laid over a background, and filmed two or three single frames at a time. Because film runs at 24 frames per second, it took a lot of pieces of celluloid to make Mickey do that happy little dance. But the animators were able to save a lot of time and paint by using one set of cels for his arms, another set for his legs, and one that didn't move as much for his body. That's basically how layers work in photo programs, too. Each thing you add to a page is on a separate transparent layer, so you can slide the photos, text, and frames around until they're in the perfect place. Then, when you save the page, you merge everything so it's all "stuck down" as if you glued it there. Why not leave it in layers? Well, you can, and should, as long as you continue to work on that page. But, just as a lot of pieces of paper and plastic flowers and studs and charms add bulk to a paper page, piling up a lot of layers adds extra bulk to the digital file. If you have plenty of storage space on your hard drive, that's not such a problem, but working with huge files also slows down the computer, and some computers quit in disgust if you ask them to do more than they want to.

The good news about going digital is that with many photo programs, layers are easy to create and can be moved around with a lot less trouble than if you have to glue them in place. Here's how Microsoft Picture It! handles layering. One little quirk is that they call their layers **stacks**. See Figure 5.1.

Figure 5.1

Using the Format menu, you can move an object forward, backward, or to the front or back of the page.

In Picture It! you can select objects and move them up or down, but you can't actually see your layers unless you choose **Show Stack** in the View menu. Then they appear as a strip of frames down the right side of the screen. In any graphics program that uses the layering concept, there's going to be a way to rearrange them, sending one layer backward or forward as needed, but simple programs like Picture

It! don't offer as much control over layers as a more complex graphics program. Both Paint Shop Pro and Photoshop Elements, shown in Figure 5.2, have an actual **layers palette**, so you can see what's where, and move it up or down and even apply special effects accordingly.

Figure 5.2

Photoshop Elements has a more convenient approach to layering.

The **Layers palette** in Photoshop Elements allows you to add or remove layers or rearrange them just by dragging them. As you can see by the Layers palette in Figure 5.2, I have a lot of different layers. Some hold the photos and others the shapes that are behind or in front of them. When I'm done with this page, I'll have added at least two or three more, including the text layer to identify the pictures and an "effects" layer to add drop shadows behind the frames. Then I'll flatten the image by merging all the layers and watch my file become much smaller. That's especially important if I'm going to put the page up on my Web site. Ever waited for a big file to load from a Web page? The page in the figure, even only partially finished, is 24 megabytes. That's a lot of disk space and a lot of download time. If I flatten the image and save it as a .jpg, which is a very Web-efficient format, it'll reduce to 46 kilobytes, which downloads in two seconds or less. Better? You better believe it.

Figure 5.3 shows a closer look at the Layers palette. I've created a document with three layers. There's a **Background layer**, a layer I've painted on, called Layer 1, and a **Type layer**, which is recognizable by the T on the palette. It also has the text I typed as the name of the layer. The **open-eye icons** to the left of the palette indicate that these layers are all visible. If you want to hide a layer, you simply click the icon to remove the eye. The **paintbrush icon** tells you which of the three layers is currently active. That's important because you can work on only one layer at a time. Anything you do to the **active layer** doesn't affect the others. The tiny circular icon at the bottom of the palette lets you add **fill** or **adjustment layers**, which affect only the layer that's active at the time you click on the icon. The **dog-eared page icon** adds a new layer to the stack. Drag layers you don't want to use to the **trash can icon**. The More button at the top of the Layers palette opens a menu that lets you rename layers and merge them, among other useful tasks.

note A fill layer is a layer that holds a color or pattern. An adjustment layer applies an adjustment—such as a change in brightness or contrast—either to the contents of the previous layer only or to the entire document.

Figure 5.3

Whenever you see a button—like the More button shown here—or an arrow on a palette, click it. It will lead you to more menus or tools.

The Layer palette in Paint Shop Pro, seen in Figure 5.4, looks a bit different, but works in much the same way. One obvious difference is that layers are designated **raster** or **vector** (see the "Bitmaps? Vectors? Rasters? Wha'?" sidebar).

The icons above the Layer palette create different types of layers and allow you to move them up or down in the stack. You can also change the transparency of layers so that an upper layer appears to be more or less transparent, letting what's below it show through or not, and make them blend together in different ways. **Layer blending** is best learned by observation and experimentation. To get you started, **Dissolve** gives a speckled effect, and **Normal** is an even mix.

Figure 5.4

Paint Shop Pro also uses the eye symbol to indicate visible layers.

Bitmaps? Vectors? Rasters? Wha'?

All image files can include both raster, or bitmap, images and vector images. (Raster and bitmap are terms used interchangeably.) Let's start at the very beginning, with the bitmap. A *bitmap* is simply a way of describing all the pixels or dots that make up an image on your screen. Think of a map printed on a piece of graph paper. Each little box represents a pixel. Each pixel is identified in a code that tells the computer its precise location and color. When you send a picture to the printer, each bitmap pixel asks for, and gets, the right mix of inks to reproduce the color. Cool, huh? It's what makes computer graphics possible.

Vector images, instead of being described dot by dot, as bitmap images are, are geometric codes. The computer draws a box, for instance, by being told: Start at this location. Draw a line one pixel thick at 90 degrees for a distance of one inch. Draw a line from that point 180 degrees south for a distance of one inch. And so on, until the whole box is described. This system can describe intricate curves and shapes, too, which is why it's used for type.

In Paint Shop Pro, Vector layers are transparent layers added on top of the basic bitmap. They hold type and shapes, just as they do in Photoshop Elements, although Adobe doesn't call them "vector layers." In Photoshop Elements you have separate type and shape layers, which are actually vector layers. When you're finished making changes to the vector layer, you can rasterize it to make it a bitmap by choosing Simplify Layer from the Layer menu. It's as if the lines on a vector page were just made of some kind of imaginary string, and until you paste them down, they aren't really there. *Rasterizing* transforms them from lines back to bitmaps, which is what all computer pictures are.

After type has been **"rasterized"** in Paint Shop Pro, or **"simplified"** in Photoshop Elements, you can't go back and edit it, so you need to check your spelling before you take that final step. If you want to change the typeface or the size again, you *must* do that before you convert it. You can still drag the rasterized type around on the page, independent of the other layers in your document, until you flatten the image, which places everything on the same layer. Another option is to duplicate a type layer and rasterize the duplicate, preserving one type layer in case you want to make changes or use that type in another form within the same document. You can make the duplicate layer invisible, and still know that it's there if you need it.

Working with Templates and Grids

The programs that are specifically dedicated to scrapbooking, such as American Greetings Scrapbooks & More or Art Explosion Scrapbook Factory Deluxe, come with dozens of premade templates, complete with backgrounds, and some designer's ideas as to which decorations are appropriate and where the pictures are to be placed. You can use these to get started, but sooner or later you will stop being satisfied with somebody else's ideas and want to make your own.

If you have a more robust graphics program, such as Paint Shop Pro or Photoshop Elements, making your own templates is very easy. In Paint Shop Pro, for example, you can simply drag **Guides** from the rulers onto the page, and then use those guidelines as a basis for your layouts. If you are consistent with regard to color, type styles, and picture placement, your pages are pretty much guaranteed to work well together. This absolutely does *not* mean that you must use exactly the same layout template for each page in your scrapbook. Just make sure that some element of the page design—be it colors, type, or photo placement—is consistent from one page to the next.

The easy way for Paint Shop Pro users to achieve consistency is to draw a **layout template** using **guidelines**. Guides or guidelines are lines that you place by dragging them from the rulers onto the page. To draw a page template in Paint Shop Pro, you need to make the rulers visible, and then drag the lines from the top down, and from the left side across the page. This also works in Photoshop, but not in Photoshop Elements. If you are using Photoshop Elements, the easiest way to create a template is to add a layer and draw lines on it.

You can also use a **grid**, which is a pattern of crossed lines, like graph paper, that you turn on and off from a menu. In Photoshop Elements, you can show or hide the grid by choosing View→Grid. You can customize the size of the grid by clicking on Edit, clicking on Preferences and selecting Grid, and then entering the measurements you prefer. Grids can be single or double page, and they don't print with the rest of the page, so you can place them wherever you think they'll help you keep things aligned, and not have to worry that they'll show up in the final page. Figure 5.5 shows an example of a basic layout template, drawn in Paint Shop Pro.

Figure 5.5

I've placed this grid to divide the page into thirds both horizontally and vertically.

After you open the Preferences dialog box in Photoshop Elements, choose Grid. You'll see a window something like the one shown in Figure 5.6. I suggest that you set the Grid lines to inches and the division to quarter inches, unless the metric system is used where you live.

You can even adjust the color of the gridlines so they show up against a colored background. If they get in the way, turn them on and off in the View menu.

tip The Photoshop Elements Preferences dialog box lives on the Edit menu in Windows and Mac OS 9. If you use Mac OS X, it's under the Photoshop Elements menu.

Figure 5.6

The pop-up menus open when you click the arrows.

If you like placing pictures at an angle, use the grid anyway, to help you keep the photos from bumping into each other or running off the page.

Composing a Page

When you are laying out a page, keep in mind that you have several elements to work with. First of all, you have the **pictures** that you're putting on it. Secondly, you have the **background** you're putting them on. Third, you have **type** that tells you, at the least, who or what's in the picture and possibly when and why it was taken. Fourth, you have any other **design elements** you want to use, such as blocks of color, lines, frames, and embellishments of all kinds from rubber stamps to charms to ribbons and more. These can be overwhelming, if they're not carefully placed. One of the main design points to remember is *don't crowd*. A cluttered page is unattractive and hard to read.

The Importance of Whitespace

Well, first of all, **whitespace** doesn't have to be white. Colored backgrounds are nice, too. But you do need to leave some space on your page. When you fill up a page with text and pictures, it's hard to look at because there are so many elements competing for your attention. Whitespace, sometimes called **negative space**, describes the open space between design elements. It can be between words or paragraphs of text. It can be space inside or around a picture, or between the elements of the page. It's easy to concentrate on what you're putting into a page, to the point that you ignore what you ought to leave out.

If the viewer's eye is to flow from one photo or paragraph to another, you need to give it a reason to do so. The reason can be whitespace. Whitespace is essential for providing **spatial relationships** between visual items, and actually guides your eye from one point to another. Whitespace doesn't have to be large. Just a generous **"gutter"** between text and pictures can make a big difference, as you can see in Figure 5.7. (*Gutter* is a typesetter's term for the space between columns of text.) The page on the left in Figure 5.7 is jammed full of stuff. The same elements, on the right page, have added just a bit of space and there's a noticeable difference in the "viewer-friendliness" of the page.

Figure 5.7

This is a journal-style scrapbook page. It's important that the text be readable.

Eye Leading

The way you place your elements on the page can determine whether they're seen. The reader's natural tendency is to look from top left to bottom right, at least in English-speaking countries and in most of Europe. Therefore, you want to arrange your pictures and text so there's a natural flow from the upper-left side of the page to the bottom right. This is especially important if, as in the example shown in Figure 5.7, there's a lot of text to read. Use the photos to balance the page.

Wide **margins** also direct the reader's attention to the center of the page. Remember that the wider the columns of type, the more space needed between them. If you have three narrow columns of type, the gutter can be narrower than if there are only two. Also allow ample vertical space between the lines (called *leading*, it rhymes with sledding, as opposed to eye "leading," which rhymes with pleading) for the sake of legibility. Tightly spaced text "darkens" the page and makes it less attractive.

When you use a photo, try not to place it so the subject is looking away from the page. If you have a right-facing subject, place it on the left side of the page. This way he, she, or it appears to be looking at the text, not away from it. If there are no characteristics like type in the photo that will give away the secret, you can flip a picture horizontally to give you more flexibility in the layout. Your reader tends to look in the same direction as the photo subject, and you want to keep the reader's eyes on the page.

tip Flipping pictures is okay, unless there's somebody wearing a T-shirt with words, or a guy with one earring, or an obvious wedding ring, or a sign or anything similar that readers might notice.

The Rule of Thirds

Much to my surprise, when I started laying out scrapbook pages, I discovered that the same principles apply to a page as to a single photo. Make shapes work together within the context of the whole design, be it page or picture. Avoid crowding. Decide on a center of interest, and make it the focal point of the page.

Good photos and good pages have what's called a *center of interest*. In a portrait of a single person, it's the face. In a group of people, there's ideally one who dominates, whereas the rest are subordinate. The dominant one, because of position, size, or placement, is the center of interest. In a landscape or still life, it's the part of the picture to which the viewer's eye is attracted first. Your first step in composing a picture—or a page—is to find the center of interest. Most of the time, it's obvious. It's the dominant feature of the landscape. It's the one yellow flower in the field of red ones. In the world of advertising, it's the widget that goes next to the catalog description, or the house that's for sale. It's the reason why you're taking the picture or making the page. On a page about your child's birthday, it's the child blowing out the candles on the cake.

After you locate, or decide upon, the center of interest, look for anything that might detract from it. Is there something behind the portrait subject that interferes with him? Does he have a lamp, or a window, or some other object in the room that appears to be growing out of his head? If so, change your camera position, or else move him to a more neutral background.

Deer Me!

I once saw a remarkable portrait of the CEO of a large corporation. He apparently liked hunting, and had a trophy deer head mounted and hung on a wall in his office. The photographer who was sent to shoot a portrait for a business magazine was an animal lover, and managed to position the CEO so that he appeared to be wearing the deer's antlers. He looked idiotic. (What was *most* remarkable about the picture was that the magazine editor allowed it to run.)

The center of interest generally shouldn't be right in the middle of the page, unless it's the only thing of importance on the page. The center of interest also shouldn't be right at the edge of the page, because this tends to draw the viewer's eye away from everything else, and usually right off the page. It knocks the viewer off balance.

If you analyze a number of successful pages, you'll probably find that in more cases than not, the center of interest falls in one of only four spots. These spots can be defined, and even turned into a rule that artists and designers know as the **rule of thirds**. Quite simply, you divide the frame into thirds, vertically and horizontally, as in Figure 5.8. The four points where the lines intersect are the approximate "best" locations for the center of interest. The ancient Greeks had discovered this, along with many other geometric "rules" for artists and sculptors. They were used in everything from the design of the pyramids in Egypt to the Parthenon, to DaVinci's painting of the Last Supper, and are found with astonishing frequency in nature. If you want to learn more, visit http://www.goldennumber.net/.

Like all good rules, it's meant to be broken occasionally. (Think how much better the chocolate cake tastes after a week of dieting.) But if you follow it more often than not, your pages have a greater impact.

Figure 5.8
The rule of thirds applies to any size or shaped page.

Coherent Pages

The main goal for your scrapbook pages is to be enjoyed and understood. Although it's lots of fun to use exotic fonts and quirky layouts, don't lose sight of the goal. When you have too many gimmicks on a page, your viewers don't bother with it. Limit yourself to a few interesting but legible fonts per document. Make your titles stand out by leaving whitespace around them—it's better than big black type for attracting attention.

When you are working with facing pages, try to do the two at once, or at least consider how the right-side page will relate to the left one as you put it together. Remember to put a "strong" element like a large title or contrasting color block and/or a large photo in the upper-left corner of the right page, so the viewer's eye is attracted back up, instead of continuing across the bottom of the right page, and out of the book. Figure 5.9 shows how this might look.

Figure 5.9

Figure 5.9
Facing pages need to
work together.

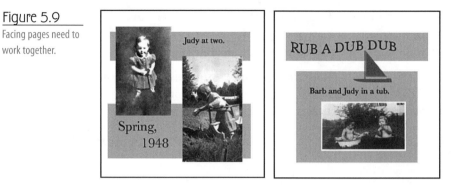

Design Elements

You might find that, despite your best efforts to follow the rules, your pages still don't quite "work" the way you want them to. Perhaps they are too formal, or too plain. That's when it's time to think about adding more elements to the total design. You can use **lines** or **blocks of color** or **texture** to help with eye leading. A line next to or under a picture really helps to draw your attention to it. In Figure 5.10, I've experimented with a couple of ways to make the square page from Figure 5.8 more interesting.

Figure 5.10
Adding another ele-
ment makes the
page layout more
effective.

If there's only one photo on the page, you can put it in the center and maybe add a frame around it, or a block of color behind it, so it's obviously the center of attention. Better yet, try it off-center with a color block, or put some embellishments behind it. Figures 5.11 and 5.12 show a couple of examples.

Figure 5.11

The schoolmarm gets a background of old report cards.

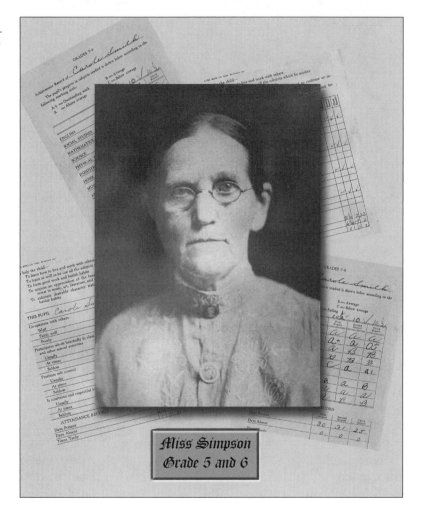

Figure 5.12

The dog looks better a bit off-center. Notice how the color block helps balance the page.

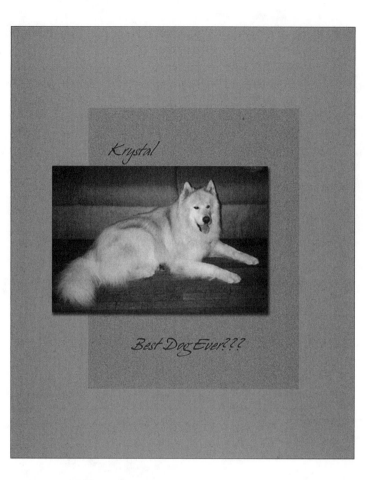

Adding Textures in the Computer

If you look closely at the color version of Figure 5.12, you can see that I added some texture to the colored block. It's very easy to do this in any reasonably versatile graphics application such as Paint Shop Pro, Photoshop Elements, or even ACD FotoCanvas, which is shown in Figure 5.13. There's a filter called **Noise** in the filter list. You can remove noise or add it.

Noise, by the way, is not a soundtrack for your pictures, or even a comment on them. Noise is a random pattern of single dots or pixels kind of like we used to see on TV back in the days before cable and satellite when trying to tune in a distant station. Really bad noise looked like dirty snow. You will probably need to remove noise from scans of old or dusty pictures. In this case, to make a textured background, you want to add some noise. You can choose colored or monochromatic (black) dots, and decide just how random the placement is. Photoshop Elements offers you a choice of uniform or Gaussian noise. Gaussian noise is supposedly more random.

Figure 5.13

The ACD FotoCanvas has its own palette, so you can select the color of the noise as well as the amount.

There are lots of other ways to add texture to a block of color. Assuming that you are doing the whole page on the computer, you can scan pieces of cloth or lace, or even things as common as a paper towel or a piece of interesting textured paper, and apply those, just as you might paste the real item on a page. Photoshop Elements has a filter called **Texturizer**, which adds texture to a selected object or a page. It's shown in use in Figure 5.14. I've created one texture from its basic Sandstone preset, and another from a texture I loaded from the textures folder called Feathers. You can vary the size and depth of the textures you create, as well as experiment with which way the light strikes them.

Figure 5.14

In Photoshop Elements, the path to the Texturizer is Filter→Texture→ Texturizer.

I strongly urge you to experiment with your **filters** and **plug-ins** in whatever graphics program(s) you have. You can learn a lot just by poking around with them and trying different combinations of filters. Remember, you really can't break the computer by trying new things. If there's not enough memory to do what you want to do, the application might crash. There are at least a dozen other reasons why the computer might crash, and it's almost inevitable that one day, it will. The worst that will happen is that you'll need to restart the computer and start over. For that reason alone, it's important to **save your work frequently** as you go along. If a program crashes with unsaved work, you *cannot* recover it. Save every time you add something. If you can save in a format that allows you to keep layers active, such as TIFF (.tif), Photoshop (.psd), or Paint Shop Pro (.psp), do so. It makes recovering from a crash that much easier. That way, you can resume at least close to where you were, as opposed to having to start from scratch again.

Textural Objects: Ribbons, Fiber, and Fabrics

Don't forget that it's okay to mix "real" stuff with computer-generated pages. A piece of glued-on ribbon or fabric or lace might be just what your page needs to bring it up from good to great. I sometimes outline nature photos in twisted grasses or sisal twine. They work fine, as long as they are stuck down well and the page goes into a page protector sleeve when it's done.

Clip Art for Scrapbookers

Clip art is another element that you can, and should, consider when you are designing pages. The term *clip art* comes from the precomputer, even pre-office copier days. Artists, mainly those who worked for newspapers and advertising agencies, subscribed to clip art services, which supplied a book of art every month. The individual pictures included anything from a platter of roast chicken for a grocery ad to a young man on one knee gazing fondly at his girlfriend as he slipped a diamond ring on her finger. These were cut out with scissors and pasted right into the ads, or enlarged or shrunk with a Photostat camera, which made a copy on photo paper.

There are lots of sources for clip art. You can find it for sale in the back pages of computer magazines such as *MacAddict* or *PCWorld*, or on many CDs, including those that accompany certain scrapbooking software. Figure 5.15 shows a single page from the Print Explosion Deluxe catalog.

Figure 5.15

The Print Explosion Deluxe clip art catalog shows everything in very small black-and-white illustrations, but the actual art is in color and can easily be resized as necessary.

In this Macintosh-only program from Nova Development, there are 90,000 pieces of clip art, which you can use for any non-commercial purpose. (You're not allowed to resell them or to use them on commercial Web sites.) There are also a bunch of fonts that work with any Mac graphics or word processing program. There's a very similar collection for Windows users called Art Explosion Scrapbook Factory Deluxe. It has the same font collection and a lot of clip art from the same sources, but selected to be more useful specifically for scrapbooking.

Online Sources

Just for fun, I did a Google search on clip art for scrapbooks. The Google search engine (www.google.com) returned 16,500 sources. I didn't investigate more than a few, but here are some to get you started. These also have links to even more art sources. There's tons of stuff out there, if you know where to look.

- http://scrapbooking.about.com/cs/clipart/
- http://www.gatherings.info/capture/clipart.asp
- http://www.countryclipart.com
- http://www.leavesoftime.com/tfree.html

These places have free downloadable clip art and some that you have to pay for. If you really like the art and the style of the artist(s), it's worth buying a CD. The typical price is around $10–20 for a full collection, and having a bunch of clips in the same style helps you keep the theme and flow from page to page in your books.

Summary—What You Need to Remember

Pages, whether designed on the computer or with pieces of paper and other scraps, are composed of layers of different elements. Most computer graphics programs allow you to work in layers as you assemble your photos, type, and other page elements.

Using templates and grids helps you keep things in line, or consistently out of line, if that's what you want. You can use predrawn templates that someone else designed or you can invent your own.

Remember to consider the natural tendency of viewers to read a page from upper-left to lower-right, just as they do a page of type. You can make this eye leading work for you by placing important objects in specific places on the page and leaving whitespace in between them. The best places to put the pictures are at the junction of imaginary lines that divide the page into thirds vertically and horizontally. Don't crowd the page, but remember that a block of a contrasting color can help balance a photo. Color blocks, texture blocks, and lines, properly used, help your page design. Don't be afraid to experiment with the features in your program—you can't really break the computer.

Clip art is readily available and can also be used to maintain a style over the course of many pages. Some clip art comes with most commercial scrapbooking programs, and more is available for sale, or free, on the Internet.

Creating and Using Backgrounds

There's one question that scrapbookers have to resolve when going digital for the first time. How far should you go? Should you print the background on the page or assemble the page from computer printed titles and photos on a preprinted background? Really, you can do it either way. Many printers can print on card stock, either by adjusting the rollers for paper thickness, or because the printer has a slot in the back of the printer, through which you can feed a single sheet of heavy paper or card stock. If your printer can't handle the heavy card stock you'd otherwise use, print on regular paper, and slide a piece of plain white card into the plastic sleeve behind the printed page. If you're not using sleeves, you can, if necessary, mount the page on card stock as a last resort.

Using Premade Backgrounds

The craft stores have stacks and stacks of different **preprinted background pages**. Figure 6.1 shows a handful I bought this afternoon at the local Michaels. These cost about 25 cents per sheet, and come in a wide selection of styles and colors. Backgrounds come in sets with elaborate backgrounds as well as plainer, harmonizing ones, so you can use a fancy first page and follow up with related but simpler sheets for the following pages. That way, the project hangs together a little better than it would if every page were the same, and if they all screamed Christmas, or wedding, or whatever.

Figure 6.1

A modest collection of preprinted background papers.

No matter what else you do with the backgrounds, make sure they relate in some way to the photos. Figure 6.2 is a good example of a background that doesn't quite work. This comes from Photo Express My Scrapbook by ULead Systems. The baby toys and pastel colors are fine with the baby picture and the title "our first baby," but in two of the three shots the kid looks to be about five. Something about "then and now" or "growing up" would be better.

Figure 6.2

This kid might be embarrassed by the baby blocks and toys.

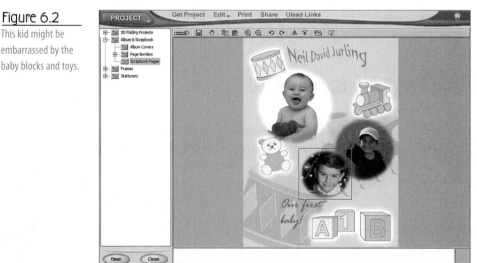

Another—and in my opinion better—set of backgrounds is provided in American Greetings's Scrapbooks & More software package. Each set has a title page, a preprinted page with a central color and border as in Figure 6.3, and several pages of embellishments, frames, and borders all related to the same theme. Using these, it's hard for a beginner to go very far wrong. Just remember that the pages of frames and borders are to be copied and placed on different pages, not used all together as they're displayed on your screen.

Figure 6.3

There's a wide range of formats for special occasions and holidays as well as "everyday" pages.

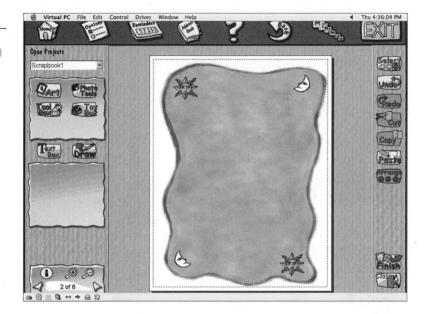

Remember that you can always copy elements from a predesigned layout and add them to a blank page you have started "from scratch." If you can't draw, this is a good way to pick up some useful art, without being stuck with somebody else's page. Isn't it better to personalize your pages? When you go to cropping parties, you're probably going to see other people's pages using the same backgrounds. The first time that happened to me, I felt as if I'd gone to a party wearing the same dress as the hostess. And I decided that it would never happen again.

Here's an example of a **customized page**, based on a purchased one. Working in Photoshop Elements, I copied the little bear and flipped him horizontally so he faced the other way. I filled in the moon with a small brush and the same shade of yellow. Then I used a large, soft-edged brush to fill in the clouds, and added a background layer in the same shade of sky blue as the original. Because they were beneath the cloud and bear layer, the soft edges blended nicely. Finally, I took a star-shaped brush and placed stars where they seemed to want to be, changing the brush sizes occasionally so the stars wouldn't all look the same. The original page is shown in Figure 6.4 and my version is in Figure 6.5. They'll be great as a double page spread for sleeping baby pictures.

Figure 6.4
This is the page I bought…

Figure 6.5
…and this is the page I made.

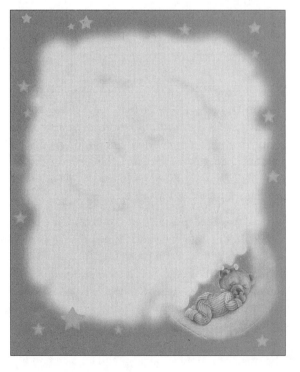

When you use a better equipped graphics program like Photoshop Elements or Paint Shop Pro, rather than the limited tools in the typical scrapbooking program, you can do things like **color matching** very easily. These programs include an **Eyedropper tool** that you use to click on the bit of color you want to copy. The **active color** (also called the foreground color) becomes whatever you have selected.

Backgrounds from the Scanner

Your scanner can be a good source of **textured backgrounds**, too. Try scanning things like paper towels, wrapping paper, and even torn pieces of Japanese mulberry paper, or cardboard. You can scan any kind of reasonably flat material including flowers, rice, beans, jelly beans, or any kind of colorful candies. Making a frame of (unwrapped) candy canes would be fun for a Christmas page, and you've then got a treat to enjoy while you're working. Just be sure to clean the scanner glass afterward.

If you don't happen to have a scanner, or don't want to risk putting food in it, you can also lay the stuff out on a sheet of paper or cardstock and photograph it. Try to shoot straight down, as much as possible, so you're not dealing with perspective. When you're out walking around, keep an eye open for natural objects that might make an interesting page. In the fall, especially in New England where I live, the leaves turn wonderful colors, and can make a great background. In the spring, we get asparagus and fiddlehead ferns, which also make a nice accent for a page, especially if you scan them along with a piece of handmade paper or mulberry textured tissue.

When you go to fabric shops or even rummage sales or yard/garage/tag sales, be on the lookout for interesting pieces of fabric to scan. I bought one hand-woven placemat at a church fair, and scanned it as a background for a recipe collection. It tied everything together nicely. I was also able to change the color in Photoshop Elements and tint the texture yellow for breakfast foods, light red for meats, blue for chicken or fish dishes, and other colors for cookies, desserts, and salads and veggies.

The only rule to remember when using textured backgrounds is that the texture shouldn't overpower the pictures. If you have a "busy" photo, with lots of colors and lots going on, the background needs to be fairly simple. On the other hand, when you are dealing with a page of head and shoulders portraits or a bunch of old black and white photos as in Figure 6.6, a textured page or a texture block behind the pictures really does help to make the page more interesting and appealing.

Figure 6.6

These textures are supposedly stucco and rust flakes.

Bar Harbor
Summer, 1948

Papers: What's Available

Take a walk down the paper aisle at your favorite scrapbooking store. You will find all of those preprinted pages we've talked about, plus a whole lot more stuff that you really need to try. There are lots of textured papers in white and colors. Some are even suitable for running through a printer. You'll also find **Japanese mulberry paper** (which is semi-transparent and has textured bits pressed into it), **tissue**, **vellum**, and more. Vellum is also a semi-transparent paper, intended to mimic the look of old parchment scrolls.

What you shouldn't use for scrapbooking, or for any kind of inkjet printing, is **office copier paper** (with one exception that you'll learn about shortly). Why not? The main reason is print quality. Copier

tip

If you have an inkjet printer, read the manual before you go paper shopping. Find out if there are any kinds of paper that are *not* recommended, and if so, avoid printing on them. Also, avoid the handmade papers with twigs, leaves and flower petals embedded in them. They'll shed little bits of stuff into your printer, and that's not good for it. If you want to use these, scan them or photograph them instead.

paper is intended for quick cheap copying of documents that are most likely going to be read and thrown away. It's not pure white, so it won't give you true colors from your inkjet inks. It might not be acid and lignin-free, so it could affect other parts of your page, such as photos or embellishments. (Refer to Chapter 2, "Basic Scrapbooking Tools," for more information.) It's more likely to jam than paper designed for the inkjet process, and it just doesn't look or feel as good.

Consider the **basis weight** of the paper you buy for scrapbooking. *Basis weight* is the standard measurement of an amount of paper. For example, the basis weight, is determined by the weight of 500 sheets of 17"×22" paper (the parent size). If a ream of 17"×22" paper weighs 20 pounds, this is called 20-lb. bond paper. Good quality office paper is usually 20– to 24-lb. bond. Greeting card paper is more like a 60– to 65-lb. card stock. It's flexible enough to print on easily, but holds a crease well, if you need to fold it. Index card stock is heavier still. It runs from 90- to 150-lb.

Paper whiteness is a measurement of how much light it reflects. Whiter papers reflect more light, and therefore represent bright colors better. What's most important is whether the paper tends toward a bluish-white or a warmer yellowish-white. Bluish-white papers are perceived as cleaner and cooler. The yellowish-white gives an impression of warmth and humanity. For the best overall color, choose a neutral white.

Photo papers are classified differently, of course. Nothing's ever consistent in the world of printing. Instead of pound weights, they are measured by thickness in millimeters or *mils*. A typical glossy photo paper is somewhere between 8.5 and 10 mils thick.

It's equally important to consider the surface of the paper, along with the way you intend to use it. Epson and Hewlett-Packard (HP) both make a wide variety of papers for inkjet printing. For pages with crisp lines and intense, high-quality color, look for a **matte** surface like HP or Epson Bright White or Premium Inkjet paper. Epson Archival Matte is also excellent for scrapbooking. Kodak and Canon also have a wide selection of papers, but I haven't really experimented with them enough to say that they are necessarily better than the other brands.

Glossy paper gives more of a "photographic look" and produces vibrant color, but is susceptible to fingerprints. That's why a heavier weight matte paper might be a better choice for prints that will be handled often. If the prints are going on a page with a page protector, photo glossy paper is great. You can even get fancy edging scissors and give it that "drugstore processing" look. It makes sense to pick up a sample pack of assorted papers, so you can see for yourself what looks and feels right.

tip
You can buy small sample packs of various kinds of photo-realistic art papers and even printable canvases at http://www.inkjetart.com.

You might also discover some other interesting papers. My Epson sample book, shown in Figure 6.7, includes **backlight film**, **canvas**, four kinds of **artist paper**, and even **synthetic paper** with and without an adhesive backing for outdoor use. Because it's waterproof, synthetic paper also makes a great scrapbook cover, stuck carefully over book-binding boards.

Figure 6.7

This is just one of Epson's sample books.

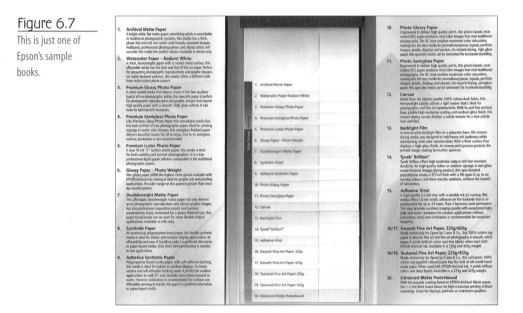

Art papers should be considered when you're printing photos that have had filters applied to make them mimic some other medium. There's something about the texture of **watercolor papers** and the way they absorb ink that makes your filtered photo art look more like the real thing. I've done photographic "watercolors" that, from a reasonable distance, would fool an expert. The Photoshop filters include some that turn your photos into charcoal or chalk drawings; they look much more real on an appropriate art paper. The Arches, Legion, and Somerset brands are all very good for printing. These papers come in several surfaces. **Smooth** is nearly so, having only a little bit of "tooth" to help hold onto the inks. **Velvet** is, as you might expect, rougher than smooth. It's about halfway between smooth and textured, which is the somewhat bumpy surface preferred by many painters. Both photos and digital art look really good on these papers.

There are, of course, other specialty papers, such as **iron-on transfers** and **transparency films**. Your computer store or art supply store will probably have these too, and they might lead you to think up some interesting uses for them. How about setting a scrapbook title and a photo or some clip art and ironing them onto a piece of fabric for a scrapbook cover? Or turning your favorite pages into t-shirts for your family? Transparencies give you the opportunity to layer type over a photo without damaging the photo itself. You can print frames on them, and cut and stick them over photos for protection. Just be careful to use archival-quality plastics.

HP even has a **temporary tattoo paper**! You can simply print some clip art on the transfer paper to make a temporary tattoo, paste it on the kids, and then pose them for a photo to go on a page with the same piece of clip art.

When you have small pieces of paper that you want to print on, use a temporary adhesive to stick them to a **carrier sheet**, which can be any kind of paper that glides happily through the printer. I admit I keep some cheap copier paper on hand for carriers and to print "proofs" before I attempt to print on something fancy. In this case, the proof is used strictly for positioning, and the paper is thin enough that I can put the fancy paper behind it and use the proof to make sure that my type or photo will fall in the right place.

tip

When you work with iron-ons, tattoos, or transparencies, be sure you flip the artwork before you print it. In order to appear correct when ironed or applied, the picture must be backward on the transfer paper. Similarly, if you are printing on transparency film, you want the type and art to read through the film, so the ink is protected from being scratched or rubbed off. Please note, however, that the rules are different for iron-on paper designed for dark fabrics. These are printed on a white page and not flipped before you print.

Other Materials You Can Print On

Let's start with **cloth**. Canon has a white cotton fabric that will work with any wide-body printer. It measures 9 1/2 by 14 inches, so it's too big for the letter-size printer.

Epson has a **canvas** material specifically for wide body printers. The narrowest size available is 24 inches wide on a four-foot roll. Although you probably can't work with it at home, it's worth calling the local copy shop to see whether they have it and can make big prints for you. Imagine a wrap-around cover for a scrapbook, printed on canvas. You could use art and photos from inside pages on the cover, as well as add the title, date, or whatever else you want.

Art supply stores and some computer stores will also have canvas and other printable materials from less well-known makers, and you can find even more on the Internet. I have letter size canvas from both Xerox and Labelon. Xerox has an ivory cast and a heavier texture. The Labelon product is coated with bright white on the printable side, and is much more flexible. Both make decent prints. Figure 6.8, and the color section, show the same picture printed on both on a standard Epson inkjet printer. As you see in the color version, the colors are definitely "off" in the Xerox canvas, and the canvas texture is more obvious.

Figure 6.8

Labelon on the left;
Xerox on the right.

Be sure to read and follow the instructions when you're working with any "unusual" papers, such as canvas or heavy art papers. Usually, they ask you to insert only one sheet at a time into the printer, as opposed to thinner papers that seem to feed into the printer better if there are at least a half dozen sheets in the tray.

There are presently not **metallic inks** for laser or inkjet printers, but if you really need three-dimensional gold lettering, you can make a pretty good imitation. First, print the type in a medium gold color, and then go over it with the adhesive and metallic powder that rubber stampers use (see Chapter 2 for more information). Finally, fuse it to the paper with a heat gun. The resulting type looks and feels as if you used a thick gold paint.

tip

If you think something metallic-looking might be in order, visit www.paperandmore.com to see their line of metallic vellums. They have standard metal colors as well as a collection of shimmering pearl-like colors that are great for wedding or baby pages. They also have card stocks of various kinds and a lot more, and most important, they are scrapbook savvy, so their products are generally safe to use with most printers.

In Chapter 10, "Adding Text," I'll teach you some tricks to make ordinary type look as if it's set in molten metal, chiseled into bronze, or drawn with a squeeze bottle of mustard.

Summary—What You Need to Remember

Backgrounds are the paper on which you put your memories. That's why paper is important, whether you're pasting on it or printing on it. Choose the right paper for the job, but be careful about always using preprinted page backgrounds. They are easy and affordable, but your scrapbook could end up looking just like your best friend's or neighbor's, with the same theme but different faces. Anyway, it's just as easy and a lot more creative to make your own.

Keep an eye out for interesting textures that you can photograph or scan. Fabrics are good, but so are natural objects like leaves and ferns. A tray full of jelly beans or candies makes an interesting background, as does popcorn or pasta or anything else of that nature.

Get to know what kinds of papers are available for your printer. Look for paper sample packs in various kinds. Papers come in matte, glossy, and textured surfaces. Use those that are acid and lignin free and avoid plain office copier paper.

Glossy papers make photos look more like the darkroom kind, but they can be damaged by fingerprints. Matte papers are more durable, and are ideal for printing entire pages or journal entries. Art papers and canvases add an interesting depth and texture to pages, but read the instructions before you use them to make sure they are suitable for your printer.

Above all else, remember that backgrounds are the basis for everything else.

Working with Old Photos

If there's just one thing that scrapbookers can do better with a computer, it's rescuing old photos. Actually, there are a lot of things that computers do better, but I have to admit that taking an old, ripped, cracked, and faded portrait and turning it back into a useable photo is one of my favorite tasks. For one thing, as you get deeply into these old pictures, you begin to get a real sense of who the person was—how he spoke, or how she laughed. And you find family resemblances that you might not otherwise have noticed. One of my sons has his grandfather's nose and eyes, and in turn my dad had *his* grandfather's nose and eyes. So, that nice nose has been handed along through five generations.

The first step in working on an old photo is to find a way to get it into the computer. As I mentioned in an earlier chapter, if you don't have a scanner, you can simply take a nice close picture of the photo. Use the macro setting for close focus, if your camera has one. It won't be quite as clear, but it'll work. Scanning is better if you have that option. You could also contact a professional photographer who could do it for you, for a price.

Getting a Good Scan

To get the best scan you can, first study the photo. Is there **dust** on it that you can wipe off with a soft cloth? Is it in **black and white** or **sepia** (brown)? (If it's a newer, color photo, set it aside until the end of this chapter and find a really old one to work on.)

Make sure your scanner software is properly installed and working. You need a **scanner driver**. This enables the computer to "drive" the scanner, telling it when to make a low-resolution preview of your photo, when to perform the real scan, and where to put it when you are done with it.

Next, look at the scanner. Do you know how to work it? If not, stop and read at least the first few pages of its manual. Is the **glass plate** clean and free of scratches? Any dust or hair on the glass will show up in the scan, and it takes time and practice to remove it all. If you can avoid the problem, do so.

No two scanners work exactly alike. Some scan from top to bottom, others from bottom to top. No two scanner software programs are alike, either. But there are a few basics that you can apply in just about all cases. First of all, if you are scanning a black-and-white photo, scan it in **grayscale**, not in color. If the picture is sepia toned, I usually scan it in color, and then remove the sepia later.

tip *Sepia* is a brown dye, originally made from squid ink, that is sometimes applied to photos to make them "warmer" toned. Otherwise, the grays sometimes tend to look bluish.

If you intend to print the photo, set the **scanner resolution** to 200dpi, or 300dpi if it's a very small photo. This will give you a larger file, but will pick up more detail. Although screen resolution is usually 72 or 96dpi, you should still scan your picture in at a higher quality even if you know for certain that this picture is only going to go on a Web page or CD album. To save file space, you can reduce it to 72 or 96dpi when you're done working on it. Also, remember that the farther the scanning arm has to travel, the longer it takes. If you have a tall, portrait-shaped picture, you can save a minute or so by scanning it sideways and then rotating it in your graphics program.

Before you settle on a resolution, think about the picture. If the photo you have is very small, scan it at a higher resolution, even as much as 600 dpi. You'll pick up more detail that way, and you'll be able to enlarge the picture to a more useful size.

Many scanners include a slide scanning tray, and/or a carrier for larger transparencies. If yours doesn't, your local photo shop can make prints from your slides. But if you are lucky enough to have one of these gadgets, you can do the job yourself.

Scan **slides** at a resolution of 200 dpi or more, to pick up as much detail as possible. Remember, the inch-high picture was intended to be seen on a four to five foot screen, so the detail is there. You can generally expect that color slides will need some color adjustment. Kodachrome film is very contrasty. European-made slide films, like Agfa, seem to favor cooler colors than Kodak. So you might want to consider decreasing the contrast or warming up the color, if necessary.

Basic Photo Corrections

Now that you've got the picture into the computer, you're ready to get to work. Let's start by looking at some of the things you can do to fix an old picture that might have faded, yellowed, or been damaged. First, we'll consider a couple of old family photos that need a little bit of adjusting and touching up. We'll run through the steps involved in fixing them and the tools you'll need to know how to use. Finally, I'll take an extremely damaged picture and work through it step by step, until it looks like new again.

Figure 7.1 shows the example I'm going to be working on first. This is a pretty good scan of a not-so-great photo, from some time in the late 1930s or early 40s.

Figure 7.1
You can see that she's holding something, but you can't tell what. (Photo courtesy of D. Maynard.)

Compared to many of the photos I've worked on, this one's easy. It's in sepia, of course, because that was the style back then, but will probably look just as good or better in grayscale. This picture has mainly dust and focus problems. It can also use a little more contrast, and it needs its corners cropped away. (You'll learn about **digital cropping** in the next chapter, "Working with Digital Photos".) If you look closely you can see that someone trimmed this picture into an oval, and someone else tried to make it a rectangle again. Net result: four missing corners.

I'm going to be working on this picture in Photoshop Elements, but you can do the same things in Paint Shop Pro, or with the photo tools supplied in some—but not all—of the scrapbooking programs. I'll edit the next example image in Paint Shop Pro. I really urge you to invest in a graphics program like Photoshop Elements or Paint Shop Pro if you're going to be using many old photos. It makes the clean-up job so much easier.

To begin fixing this picture, use the **cropping tool** to first crop the borders and remove the edges. Just drag a box around the part of the picture you want to keep, and then click inside the box or use whatever method your program demands to confirm the cropping.

Adjusting Levels and Contrast

Now that the picture has been properly cropped, it's time to correct the damage to the image. Set the mode to **Grayscale** (Image→Mode→Grayscale), which removes any color information that the scan picked up. Doing this immediately eliminates the yellow and brown tones. The next step is to improve the **contrast**. You can do this two ways: with Quick Fix, which is at the top of the Enhance menu; or the way professionals do, by adjusting the levels. The Levels dialog box (Enhance→Adjust Brightness/Contrast→Levels) is shown with the photo in Figure 7.2.

Figure 7.2

The Levels dialog box is actually a histogram that measures all the dark and light pixels in the photo.

If you took statistics in school, or almost any kind of a science class, this graph should be familiar. It's a histogram, and it shows the range of tones in the picture from black to white. If you managed to avoid most math and science classes, as I did, a histogram is simply a display that uses vertical lines to denote the amount of something in a larger something. In this case, it's showing how many pixels in the photo are in each of the 255 shades of gray. With a little experience using histograms, you can easily see what the problem is. There are no real whites or blacks, just a lot of light and middle grays. You need more contrast. To get it, select the empty **eyedropper** (it's the one on the right) and click it on the lightest point you can find in the photo. You'll notice that the white triangle under the histogram will jump over to a spot under where the histogram begins to peak for whiteness. Click the left-hand black eyedropper on the darkest point in the picture. Its triangle in the histogram will also move. Now click on the gray middle triangle under the histogram and slide it back and forth until the picture contrast looks right. Figure 7.3 shows the result. Remember to click OK to make the changes and exit the dialog box.

Figure 7.3

Now you have a better-adjusted photo.

Dodging and Burning

Now it's obvious, as it wasn't before, that she's holding a black kitten. A little **dodging** and **burning** will help bring out the details of her dress, and will separate the cat from the background. Dodging and burning are probably quite familiar to anyone who ever worked in a real (non-digital) darkroom. In the photographer's darkroom, dodging is accomplished by waving a dodge tool, usually a cardboard circle on a wire, between the projected image from the enlarger and the photographic paper. This blocks some of the light and makes the dodged area lighter when the print is developed. It's also called "holding back" because you effectively hold back the light from reaching the paper. Photoshop Elements's **Dodge tool**, shown in Figure 7.4, looks just like the darkroom version.

Figure 7.4

To me, the Dodge tool always looked like a black lollipop.

The **Burn tool** has the opposite effect of dodging—it darkens the area instead of lightening it. In the darkroom, burning in is accomplished either by using a piece of cardboard with a hole punched out (the opposite of the Dodge tool) or by blocking the enlarger light with your hand, so the light only reaches the area on the print surface to be burned. The Photoshop Elements Burn tool icon is a hand shaped to pass a small beam of light. Both the Dodge and Burn tools are considered to be **brushes**, and you need to select a brush size and shape before you apply them. You can do this on the Tool Options bar at the top of the workspace. Like any other brush, you apply it by holding the mouse button down and dragging it over the area you want to affect. I almost always use a soft-edged brush for dodging and burning. The softness helps hide the fact that I've done something to change the picture.

If you are working on a small part of the picture, as we are in this example, it helps to **zoom** in and make the image bigger, so you can see what you are doing. Use the **Zoom tool** (magnifying glass) to click on the area you want to enlarge. To zoom out again, press the Option/Alt key as you click the tool on the image. Each click takes you a step farther in or out. (See Figure 7.5.)

Figure 7.5

Working at twice the normal size makes it easier to see and fix details.

Click the Dodge tool and look at the Range drop-down menu in the Tool Options bar. As you can see, it gives you three choices:

- Shadows
- Midtones
- Highlights

These options indicate the types of pixels that the tool will affect. If you want to adjust the shadows, such as making them lighter and leaving the lighter pixels untouched, choose **Shadows**. The default option for the Dodge tool is **Midtones**. This is a good choice when you want to affect the midtone pixels, or when you are unsure of how to proceed. Select **Highlights** when you want to lighten already light-colored areas, leaving the darker areas untouched. For the moment, I'll set it to shadows and use it to lighten the area behind the kitten. After all, he's the real subject of the photo. To see him, refer to Figure 7.5.

I used the Burn tool to bring out the details in her lace collar, and to darken her hair.

Cleaning Up Dust Spots with the Clone Stamp Tool

There are some **dust spots** you can remove, with the **Clone Stamp tool**, which looks and works like a rubber stamp. It copies pieces of the picture and clones them over other places when you click. To use it, you first select a brush size that's appropriate for what you want to cover. Alt-click (Option-click on a Mac) on the piece of the picture you want to copy, and then click the Clone Stamp tool on the spot you intend to cover. You can use whatever matches.

If **Aligned** is checked in the tool options bar, the source point to be duplicated moves with the tool. Say you Alt-click or Option-click to set the source, then move slightly up and to the right to use the tool. Each time you click, or as you drag the rubber stamp, the source point moves with your mouse to stay exactly the same distance away from the stamp. Conceivably, you can reproduce the entire image if you have enough blank canvas in the working document.

If you don't choose Aligned, the Clone Stamp tool behaves differently. After you select your reference point and start painting, the duplicate portion of the image expands only while you continue to hold down the mouse button. When you release the mouse button and press it again, you start painting another duplicate image from the same reference point.

tip

When you use the Clone Stamp tool to retouch in Photoshop Elements, always choose a soft-edged brush in a size only slightly larger than the scratch or blemish you're hiding. Retouching is generally easier if you zoom in on the image first.

For this job, I am using a small soft-edged brush, and copying the adjacent tone. Then I'll use the **Sharpen filter** (Filter→Sharpen) to put things in better focus. Figure 7.6 shows the finished picture.

Figure 7.6

Now you can see the kitten and her new mommy much better.

Other Touches

I'd call this picture finished, although there are a few more things you can do to it. You can bring back the sepia tone by returning the image to RGB color (choose Image→ Mode→RGB Color). Then you can apply color variations (Enhance→Adjust Color→Color Variations) and add red and subtract blue until you have a believable sepia. You can also apply the Unsharp Mask filter (Filter→ Sharpen→Unsharp Mask) to strengthen the focus. But it looks fine, and it will do very nicely for my friend's genealogy album.

Retouching in Paint Shop Pro

Here's another image in need of minor retouching. This time I'm working in Jasc Paint Shop Pro. Its toolbox icon, the one selected in Figure 7.7, represents a pair of clones. But as soon as you go to apply it, you see your old friend the **Rubber Stamp icon** where you're stamping. It works much like Photoshop Elements's Clone Stamp tool. In Paint Shop Pro, simply right-click on the piece you want to copy, and then click where you want to put it. This tool is extremely useful for removing all kinds of spots and also for filling in

tip Did you ever wonder where those little spots are coming from? Black spots are usually dirt on the photo or on the scanner glass. White spots on the photo were caused by dust or dirt on the negative. The dirt stopped the light from passing through the negative and exposing the print. You can often get rid of black spots by wiping the print and the scanner with a soft cloth and then rescanning. White spots need to be digitally retouched.

backgrounds that you want to change. Use the **Aligned Mode box** in the tool options bar at the top of the window to make aligned copies.

This tool is probably one of the ones you'll use most in restoring old photos. Be sure to spend some time learning how it works and practicing with it.

Figure 7.7

Notice the brush options on the options bar. You can adjust the brush size as large or small as you want it.

Moving Paint: Blurring, Sharpening, and Smudging

Did you ever wonder why artists always have those paint-soaked rags lying around, and why they always have paint on their hands, under their fingernails, and all over their clothes? It's because you don't just paint with a brush; you sometimes paint with your finger, or with a piece of cloth, or with your elbow or some other tool that will help you blend the paint or lighten or darken it just a little bit. You can learn the tricks that painters and darkroom technicians have been using ever since their respective art forms were invented. The early cave people knew the value of "hands-on" art. The famous cave paintings at Lascaux were done, literally "by hand", and there are many hand prints on the walls along with the drawings of the bison, horses, and other animals.

Smudges

Smudge is the artist's term for blending two or more colors. In Photoshop Elements, and most other applications that have a similar tool, the **Smudge tool** looks and works like a finger. It's in the same toolbox compartment as the Blur and Sharpen tools. The Smudge tool picks up color from wherever you start to drag it and moves it in the direction in which you drag. Honestly, nothing is simpler. You do, however, have to use the Tool Options bar to set the pressure of your smudging finger. At

100% pressure, the finger simply wipes away the paint. At 50%, it smears it. At 25%, the smear is smaller. Figure 7.8 shows these **smear pressures**. Photoshop Elements considers the Smudge tool to be a brush, so you can set the width of the finger by choosing an appropriate brush size in the Tool Options bar.

<u>Figure 7.8</u>

The lighter the pressure, the less you smudge.

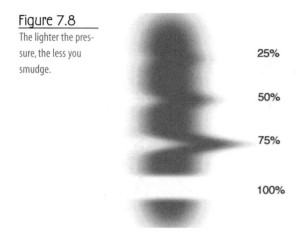

25%

50%

75%

100%

Focus Tools

Now focus your attention on the **Focus tools**. These tools, **Blur** and **Sharpen**, are great for touching up an image, fixing tiny flaws, and bringing items into sharper contrast. They can't save a really bad photo, but they can do wonders for one that's just a little bit off. Sharpen can bring up the contrast to create the illusion of sharper focus, whereas Blur is most useful to rid the background of unwanted clutter and to de-emphasize parts of the picture that you don't want viewers to notice.

Sharpening

Sharpening is definitely a useful tool, especially because many of the photos you work on will be fuzzy. The older the picture, the fuzzier it's likely to be. Back then, lenses and cameras just weren't as good. Early photo plates required a long exposure, and it was sometimes difficult to make people stand still for the five to ten seconds it took to make a photograph on a glass plate.

There are two ways to sharpen a picture. The first is the method you used on the cat lady photo: the **Sharpen filter**. There are actually two Sharpen filters that you'll use most: **Sharpen** and **Sharpen More**. The latter simply applies twice as much sharpening as the first. You can keep on applying these filters until you are satisfied with the result, or until you realize that you have overdone it because the image has a very jagged, pixelated appearance. In Figure 7.9, you can see the result of **over sharpening**.

The way to sharpen just a small part of a photo is to use the Sharpen tool. Select it, and then click and drag it over the area you want to sharpen. If you use it carefully, it can be extremely helpful, but don't overdo it. In Figure 7.10, I have sharpened the woman's face and left the man alone.

Figure 7.9

This kind of sharpening works by increasing the contrast between adjacent pixels.

Figure 7.10

She's been sharpened. He hasn't. It does make a difference.

Blurring

The **Blur filter** and the **Blur tool** (which looks like a drop of water in Photoshop Elements) work similarly to Sharpen, except that rather than increasing the contrast between pixels, they lower it slightly. That produces the blur.

You might be wondering why you'd deliberately want to blur something, but there are times when it's a very valuable tool. The Blur tool, simply put, creates blurs in images. In other words, it softens or evens out pixel values. It's helpful when you need to separate a person from a busy background, or disguise something that there's no other way to get out of the picture. To use it, select the Blur tool from the toolbox. The Tool Options bar will show you the Blur tool's options. When you are working with the Blur tool, you can temporarily select the Sharpen tool (and vice versa) by pressing Option (Mac) or Alt (Windows) on your keyboard. The Use All Layers option only affects the image if your image has more than one layer. In Figure 7.11, I've blurred the background behind the lily, so the photo focuses on the lily and not on the whole bouquet.

Figure 7.11

The first picture is the original, in the second, I've blurred the background.

Removing Dust and Scratches

If you are using Photoshop Elements, cleaning up dust is easy with the **Despeckle** and **Dust** and **Scratches filters**, both found under Filter→Noise. Equally easy are the same tools in Jasc Paint Shop Pro, shown in Figure 7.12. The difference is that they are on the Adjust menu rather than the Filter menu, and the Dust and Scratches filter is named the **Salt and Pepper Filter**.

Figure 7.12

Despeckling removes both black and white dust. You can decide for yourself how much to remove.

Rescuing a Badly Damaged Photo

Now, let's take a look at a picture that really needs some work. In Figure 7.13, and in the color section, you can see this picture of a little girl, taken about 1908. It was printed on a heavy paper which cracked, and suffered some damage in an oval frame. Can we save it? Of course, we can. For this example, I'm working with Photoshop Elements again.

Figure 7.13

The photo has some bad damage, but it's all fixable.

First, convert it to grayscale to get rid of the sepia (choose Image→Mode→Grayscale). Figure 7.14 shows how easily this is done in Photoshop Elements. The other graphics programs can do it too, usually as a menu item.

Figure 7.14

Convert to grayscale because it's much easier to match grays than sepia tones.

Now, you're ready to start repairs. The first step with this picture, and with most of the ones you'll be working with, is to **crop** it. Anything you can remove doesn't have to be retouched. I can't crop too tightly because she fills out the frame pretty well, but I can get rid of some of the edges and one big spot. Figure 7.15 shows the **cropping frame** in Photoshop Elements.

Figure 7.15

Just drag the corners of the cropping frame until you're satisfied with the crop, and double-click inside it to confirm it.

The next step is to improve the **contrast** in the photo. It's good to do this now so that when you start moving pieces of her dress and the background to cover the cracks, you won't have a problem making them blend in. In Photoshop Elements, the quickest way to fix the contrast is to use **Levels**, as you did before. Other programs might have other ways of adjusting contrast, so check the help screen or the manual if you aren't sure how to proceed. Figure 7.16 shows the result of this step.

Figure 7.16

It's looking much better already.

By increasing the contrast, you saved yourself some work. The next step is to work with the **Clone Stamp tool**, to rubber stamp over the cracks. Figure 7.17 shows a closer look at this process. Using a fairly small, soft-edged brush, with Aligned checked in the Tool Options bar, you can stamp the areas next to the bad crack over her face and fill it in. I also filled in the missing corner of the picture.

Figure 7.17
You need lots of patience to do this well.

From here on, it's just a question of more stamping to cover the rest of the cracks and corners. When you have delicate areas to fix, like faces, enlarge the picture as much as you can. Most graphics programs have a **"Zoom" tool**, which lets you to move in and out on the picture as you're working. Usually, the icon looks like a magnifying glass. Click it to zoom in, and Option/Alt-click it to zoom out. In Figure 7.17, I zoomed in to work on the crack on her face. In Figure 7.18, I zoomed out again to look at the whole picture.

Figure 7.18
It's pretty close to done now.

The Clone Stamp tool took care of all the spots and other damage. I used a small brush to complete the toe of her shoe. But I think I'll put back the sepia. In Photoshop Elements the easy way to do this is to reconvert the photo mode to RGB color (choose Image→Mode→RGB Color), and then use the **Color Variations** dialog box to first add red and then decrease blue, which gives you a nice believable sepia tone. Be sure to see this in color in Figures 7.19 and 7.20.

Figure 7.19

You can also use this to turn a photo or line drawing green or purple or whatever color strikes your fancy.

So, here it is, as good as it's ever going to be and pretty good indeed for a picture that's nearly 100 years old. That looks like one of the very early Steiff teddy bears.

By the way, most graphics programs have some way of reapplying sepia. In Picture It! Photo Premium from Microsoft, it's an option called **Antique**, under the Effects menu. Another way to do it in Photoshop Elements or Paint Shop Pro is to use the **Hue/Saturation sliders** to adjust the color to whatever looks right to you.

Figure 7.20

The final photo, restored to probably better than the original.

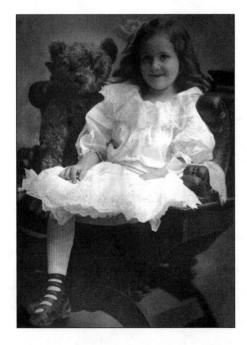

Vignetting a Picture

I can still take this one step further, if I want, by converting it back to the oval format it was in originally. But I don't think I want to do that to this particular photo since I've already cropped it tight. Instead, let's take a different portrait and turn it from a rectangle into an oval. This process is called **vignetting**, and it's a very common format for old pictures. The main reason it was used so often in the early days of photography is that the lenses weren't very good. Only the center part of the lens produced a sharp picture. The edges kind of fuzzed and faded out.

Microsoft Picture It! Photo can't do vignettes, so you'll work on this one in Paint Shop Pro. Figure 7.21 is the original photo. It's pretty awful, but Paint Shop Pro's Enhance Photo→One Step Photo Fix command, located in the Tool Options bar, will bring back the contrast and solve many of the problems.

Figure 7.21

Nice lady, lousy picture.

If you look carefully at Figure 7.22, you can see the improvement in the picture, as well as the selection tool I'm using, which is an ellipse, chosen by clicking Selection Type in the Tool Options bar. I've drawn an oval frame by dragging the tool across her, in the process trimming away the forearms worthy of Popeye the Sailor, and I've also feathered the selection by 20 pixels. The effect of this is to soften the edge of the oval so it looks like it's fading away. The **Selection Tool** and **Feather options** work very differently in Paint Shop Pro than in other graphics programs. In Paint Shop Pro, the amount of feathering is determined by adjusting the Feather option on the tool options bar. (In Photoshop Elements, it's on the Select menu.) The amount of feathering must be determined before placing the selection marquee. Also, in order to adjust or move the selection marquee without affecting the image, the user must select the **Mover Tool**, then right-click inside the marquee and drag it to the desired position. If the user clicks and drags the marquee with the **Selection Tool**, the image will be changed. A right-click with the Selection Tool deselects the marquee.

Figure 7.22

The middle is selected.

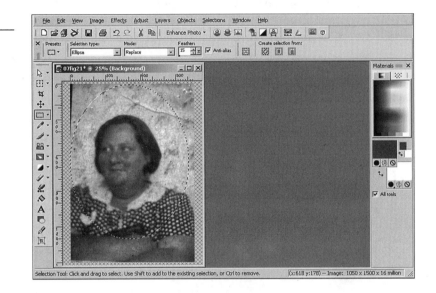

Because what I've selected is the middle of the picture, and what I want to remove is the edge, I need to **invert** the selection (choose Selections→Invert). This simply shifts the "working" part of the selection marquee from the middle to the outer part of the picture. Instead of just the oval, you can now see the corners of the picture selected, too. After that part of the picture is surrounded by the selection marquee, either press the Delete key, or press Control+X to trim it. (Photoshop Elements users: Other than the One Step Fix, you will follow the same process. Select with the oval marquee, making sure to feather the selection. Invert the selection (choose Select→Inverse) and delete the edges.)

This photo still needs some clean up and despotting, but it's much improved. The final version, in Figure 7.24, has also had the contrast adjusted. There's something about vignetted photos that always reminds me of my mother's and grandmother's prized cameo brooches. A good setting for a vignetted portrait might be to simulate a silver or gold frame from a brooch. Of course, if you've done the same thing to a portrait of a man, the delicate look won't do. Instead, perhaps a dark oval frame, looking like wood.

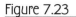

Figure 7.23

After inverting, the edges are selected, and then removed.

Figure 7.24

Even without a frame she looks much better, and thinner too.

If you wanted to put a **frame** around this photo, there are several ways to do it. You can find one in a clip art collection and stretch or shrink it to fit. If you have a frame-generating plug-in like Auto FX Photo/Graphic Edges, you can use that. Otherwise, make a new layer, and drag an oval selection around the photo. If it's not quite where you want it, click the edge and drag it until it's centered around the photo. When the oval is properly placed, select Edit→Stroke or right-click in the selection and choose **Stroke** from the pop-up menu. Enter a number of pixels to create a wide or narrow frame and decide whether it will draw inside, outside, or centered on your oval selection. Before you Stroke the selection, be sure that the **Feather** is set to 0, unless you want a fuzzy frame. You can then go ahead and have some fun with it. Using the **Layer Styles window** (Window→Layer Styles), as shown in Figure 7.25, I chose Wow Chrome Dark from the Wow Chrome effects. Actually, I tried a couple of others first, but liked this one best.

Figure 7.25

The Wow Effects are presets that combine several effects to make a complex one. They definitely add some wow to your pages.

Photo Tinting

Years ago, before color film was readily available, it was common to see **hand-tinted photos**. These had been painstakingly overpainted with thinned-out special paints to add a pale suggestion of color to the picture. The Photoshop Elements brushes are well suited for re-creating the look of a hand-colored photograph. You can even do the whole Ted Turner routine and colorize stills from your favorite Marx Brothers movie or Bogart classic. (You can find lots of movie stills and movie star pictures on the Web to practice on. There may be copyright issues on these, so don't try to sell them. You can use them safely in a personal scrapbook.)

After you have cleaned up the image that you want to hand-tint, change the image mode to RGB color. Make a new layer and set the **layer opacity** to between 10% and 30% in the Layers palette. Select the **Brush tool**, set the Brush opacity to 80% in the Tool Options bar, and paint your tints. Alternatively, leave the layer at 100% opacity, change the blending mode to color in the Tool Options bar, and paint away! Always use a new layer for each color in case you make mistakes.

If you have large, uncomplicated areas to tint, use one of the Selection tools, such as the **Lasso** or the **Magic Wand**, to select the area. Select a foreground color and choose Fill from the Edit menu; a dialog box will appear as shown in Figure 7.26.

Set the Opacity to about 25% and choose Multiply from the Blending Mode menu. Do *not* check **Preserve Transparency**, because your fill effect won't show up if you do. Set **Foreground Color** on the Use pop-up menu. Click OK to fill all the selected areas with your chosen color at that opacity. If it's not enough, either reopen the Fill dialog box and apply it again, or undo it (choose Edit→Undo) and set a higher percentage. If it's too much, undo and set a lower percentage.

Figure 7.26

Use Fill for large areas. It's faster and smoother than painting. (Photo courtesy of D. Maynard.)

Continue selecting areas and coloring them until you're done. **Flesh tones** can be tricky. Caucasians tend to look either too pink or too yellow when you try to guess at a flesh tone. My suggestion is to do your best, and then if you are working with Photoshop Elements, choose Enhance→Adjust Color→Color Variations and tweak the adjustments until the skin color looks right. Remember that you can adjust individual layers, as long as you haven't already flattened them.

Correcting Off-Color Photos

Old color photos are sometimes more difficult to repair than old black-and-white ones. The dyes used in the color printing process can either fade or darken. Along with the other kinds of damage you have already seen, it makes some pictures very difficult to rescue. Relatively recent photos, on the other hand, don't need much correction and usually aren't ripped and stained the way the really old black-and-white ones are. Pictures printed after 1950 or thereabouts just don't get brittle the way the older ones do. First, the pictures aren't as old, so they are somewhat less likely to be physically damaged. The paper tends to be heavier, and being gloss coated, is sturdier and less prone to tearing or folding. So instead of just doing damage control, you can actually improve the pictures.

The single biggest problem I've seen with color photos from the late '40's and '50's is **color cast**, or in its more severe form, **color shift**. When this happens, the entire photo can take on what looks like an overdose of a single color, often pink or purple, but any color can be affected. It's generally blamed on heat or exposure to sunlight, but having seen it happen to pictures that were tucked away in an album or used as a bookmark, I don't think that's necessarily the case. The dyes used back then just weren't stable. Bad processing or letting the film sit in the camera outdoors on a warm day were enough to throw off the color, perhaps not immediately, but as the photos aged.

Of course, bad things can happen to recent pictures, too. The sun ducks behind a cloud just as you shoot, and the colors look washed out. The flash doesn't go off as expected. Nothing is immune to spilled drinks, dog/cat/kid damage, and all the other perils of daily life.

You can't save them all. Some are just too far gone, or the data (color and detail) was never there in the first place. But, with a good graphics program, you can pull off some pretty amazing rescues.

Correcting Color Cast

Several of the available photo-editing programs make color-cast correction pretty nearly automatic. Figure 7.27 shows an old photo that's so badly yellowed, it's almost brown. Be sure to see this example in the color plate section.

Figure 7.27

Figure 7.27

Can this one be
saved?

To correct this kind of color cast in ACD FotoCanvas, there's a simple step-by-step
wizard that does a surprisingly good job. It leads you, one dialog box at a time,
through cropping, rotating, sharpening, correcting contrast, removing color cast,
removing red eye, and finally saving the much improved photo. Be sure to see
Figure 7.28 in the color section to see ACD's version of the picture.

Figure 7.28

ACD FotoCanvas at
work. Color correction
is easy with this
program.

Paint Shop Pro also has an automatic **Enhance Photo** function, shown here in
Figure 7.29. When you select it, the program runs through its repertoire of corrections, without asking for any input. The result is, well, not so good. See it in Figure
7.29 in the color section. You can also make the corrections yourself, using the tools
supplied on the Enhance menu, and you'll probably have much better results.

Figure 7.29

I recommend that you skip this and do it yourself.

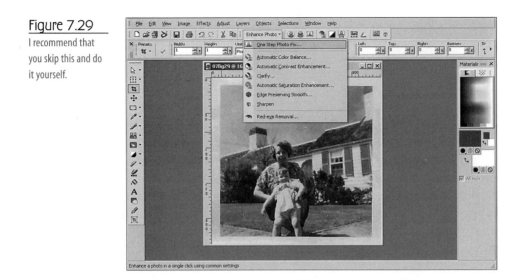

Photoshop Elements also has an Enhance menu, shown in Figure 7.30. As you can see, there's a **Quick Fix** option, which does some of the correction for you, but like Paint Shop Pro, it's not perfect. Figure 7.31 shows the Quick Fix dialog box.

Figure 7.30

Each of the Adjust items has a pop-up menu.

Figure 7.31

Here, too, doing it yourself will give better results.

Using Photoshop Elements, let's work through this photo step by step. First of all it needs to be cropped (choose Image→Crop). Getting rid of unnecessary edge clutter will help. Let's keep a little of the white border, though, until you decide how you want to use it on a scrapbook page. To start improving the color, choose Enhance→Adjust Color→Color Cast. Figure 7.32 shows its very simple dialog box. This tool evaluates the amount of color in what ought to be a black or white pixel. It then applies the same amount of the opposite color (from the color wheel) to cancel out the overdone one. In this case, the color cast is yellow, so Elements adds an equal amount of blue. If the color cast turned the picture red, it adds cyan. If the cast were green, it adds magenta, and so on.

Figure 7.32

Try to find the darkest black or the whitest white.

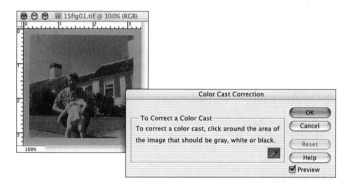

To judge the "correctness" of the correction, find part of the picture that's critical, color-wise. Flesh tones are always a good benchmark. I clicked on several areas that I thought should be white, and most seemed to make things worse instead of better. When I tried the baby's dress, though, the flesh tones looked right, even though the picture still needs a lot of work. Figure 7.33, and the color plate, show this step.

Figure 7.33

Better, but not there yet.

Using Fill Flash

Even though the picture was shot in bright sun, there are **shadows** on both faces. Choose Enhance→Adjust Lighting→Fill Flash to correct this before you finish color correcting. After all, it's the faces that are the most important part of the photo. Choose Enhance→Adjust Lighting→Fill Flash to access the dialog box shown in Figure 7.34. As you can see, I have just moved the sliders up a little, to lighten the picture and increase the overall color saturation a small amount.

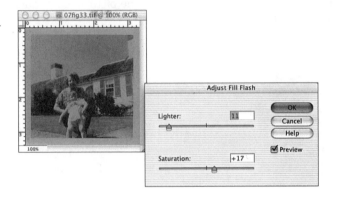

Figure 7.34

If the photographer had used a fill flash, you wouldn't need this step.

Selective Color Adjustments

Nothing you've done so far has had an effect on the sky. It's still brown, and the only way you can turn it blue is to select it and force the change. So that's what you'll do. You can select the sky with either the **Magic Wand** or the **Lasso tool**, or a combination of both. Because this photo has a number of places where the trees or other objects stick into the sky area, these are best selected with the Magic Wand. As long as you hold the Shift key down, you can keep on adding to your selection. If you select a piece that you don't want, immediately undo (just once) and the rest of the selection will remain selected. With the entire sky selected, you can open the **Hue/Saturation** dialog box (see Figure 7.35) and make the sky as blue as you want it. In this case, because the rest of the colors are actually quite subtle, I'll resist the urge to improve the weather and go with a pale blue.

That worked so well, and looks so good, I'll do the same thing with the grass, turning it green instead of blue, of course. Figure 7.36 shows the final image, but you really need to go to the color plate section and compare it to what we started with.

Figure 7.35

"Blue skies, smilin' at me…"

Figure 7.36

Maybe it's not quite perfect, but considering how much better it is, I'm satisfied.

That shows what you can do with a bad picture and good software. On the other hand, some scrapbooking programs either can't do this at all, or don't do it very well. I tried using the tools in Photo Express My Scrapbook from ULead on the same picture, but the results weren't good enough to print. It did, however, convert it to grayscale.

There are very few photos that can't be saved one way or another. If the color is really bad, and the photo is otherwise clear and well focused, you can convert it to black and white and hand-tint it. You can also convert it to sepia, and make the page surrounding it sort of moody and nostalgic, as long as the clothing or other surroundings won't give away your secret. If they do, and you still want to use that trick, enlarge the picture and vignette it so you only see the face.

Summary—What You Need to Remember

First of all, you need the right tools for retouching your pictures. That means a good graphics program. Adobe Photoshop Elements 2, which is the one I prefer, comes in both Macintosh and Windows editions for about $85. Jasc Paint Shop Pro (a $79 download) and ACD FotoCanvas ($50) can also do most kinds of corrections.

The steps in rescuing an old damaged photo are easy. First, make a good, clean scan. If the picture is in sepia, convert it to grayscale. Crop away anything that doesn't need to be there. Then adjust the contrast. Use the Burn tool to darken areas that are too light, and the Dodge tool to lighten dark places. Use the Clone Stamp tool to cover dust spots, cracks, and stains. You might even have to paint in missing parts. Finally, if you want, you can replace the sepia tint.

Vignetting isolates the center of the picture so it seems to fade to white. It can make a recent photo look old, if that's what you want, or hide a bad background. You can also make a grayscale photo more interesting, and give it that 1930's look by hand tinting it. Remember to work in layers.

Color correction is often needed when you work with old color pictures. The more sophisticated graphics programs like Adobe Photoshop Elements and Jasc Paint Shop Pro do it better, manually, than any of the "auto-correct" or "auto-enhance" functions in those, or other programs.

Working with Digital Photos

In the last chapter, you worked with scanned images. In this one, you're primarily using pictures from a digital camera. And anyway, as soon as a picture is in the computer, it's within the digital realm. So even if you don't have a digital camera, there's a lot of helpful information coming. Don't skip ahead. In this chapter, you learn about **retouching** and **color correction**, as well as **cropping** and **resizing** your pictures. You learn how to repair the dreaded **red eye**, and how to remove things—even people—that clutter up the picture.

Shooting for Scrapbook Pages

With today's automatic "point-and-shoot" cameras, there's not that much that can go wrong, technically anyway. If you wait for the camera to find its focus, which it generally indicates with a little green light, and you hold it steady, you're going to have a reasonably sharp picture. If the subject needs more light, the camera indicates that you need to turn on the flash, decides how bright the flash needs to be, and makes it happen. Nevertheless, you really need to sit down with your camera and manual and learn all the buttons and menus. It's not difficult, and you'll take much better pictures when you know what the camera can do. Be sure to keep the manual handy to refer to when you have questions. You can also find help at the camera maker's Web site.

Of course, there are things you just can't do with any average camera, digital or otherwise. Let's say you're sitting in the nosebleed section at a hockey game. You really want a photo of your favorite player, so you pull out your digital camera. It's kind of dark where you're sitting, so you activate the flash. You aim. You shoot. You *don't* score. Well, you might be able to tell which speck on the ice is him—or her—but you won't get much of a shot. Here's why. First of all, you're too far away. A low-end camera (say $400 or less) doesn't have a good enough lens or good enough **resolution** to let you enlarge the photo enough to see your player. Even if you have a more expensive camera, with higher resolution and a **zoom lens**, you're still not going to get much. For a meaningful picture, get close. Talk your way down the aisle to the barrier, but stand a few steps back so you can shoot over the Plexiglas. You want to see people, not scarred plastic. Zoom in as much as you can. Aim the camera a little bit ahead of the skater. Remember, they move fast. With many cameras, there's a short delay between the button press and the actual shot. This way, he or she will skate through the picture, not out of it. Also, don't use the flash. It's effective only with a distance of 10 feet or so. After that, it's useless and throws off the **automatic exposure** settings.

That's kind of a far-fetched example, but the point is, unless you're shooting the **scenery**, come close. Generally, it's the close photos that look better and work better on your scrapbook pages. You want to see **faces**. Of course, variety is good, too. Let's say you have a kid who likes hanging by her knees from the monkey bars. For your scrapbook page, you can take a shot that shows her upside down, full length, and then you need to move in and get one of just her red face and hair hanging upside down. Much more interesting than just the single shot.

Even when you are shooting scenery, as I was last spring in Nevada, look for variety in your shots. Here's a page I put together about the Valley of Fire State Park. (See Figure 8.1.) As you can see, I have a **long "scenery" shot**, a **mid-shot**, and a **close-up**. These three, plus a few words of description, are all I need to convey my own sense of what it was like to be there in this very foreign place. Where I live, the ground is flat and all the rocks are gray.

When there are people in the picture, try to have them doing something other than just standing there. We've all seen the vacation pictures that friends and neighbors bring home, the ones with the narration that goes something like "This is me in front of the Eiffel Tower. This is Fred in front of the Eiffel Tower. This is me in front of the hotel." And so on… until we're looking for excuses to escape. The people in the pictures are usually hot, tired, and cross, and don't seem very happy to be there. When you shoot photos of people, try to catch them at their best, not at their worst. Let them sit when there's something to sit on. Or let them lean against a railing, tree, or whatever. If I had to pose my kids with the Eiffel Tower,

I'd have them turn around and look up at it, rather than at the camera, and then crawl around until I found an angle that shows their faces and as much as possible of the structure.

Figure 8.1

Be sure to see this figure in the color section.

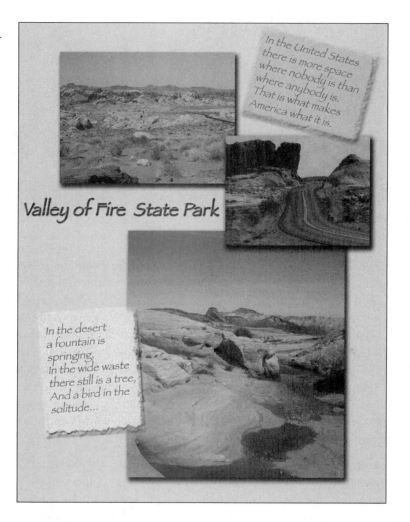

In the United States there is more space where nobody is than where anybody is. That is what makes America what it is.

Valley of Fire State Park

In the desert a fountain is springing, In the wide waste there still is a tree, And a bird in the solitude...

Figure 8.2 shows another piece of scenery. In this one, and you have to either take my word for it or jump over to the color section to look at it, the point of the photo is that the tree branches are exactly the same color as the rocks off in the distance. I shot this in late afternoon, and the low angle of the sun lit up the tree very nicely. What I like about this photo, aside from the color, is that there's something close as well as something far away. This difference adds **perspective** to the picture, and you can get a better sense of how high the rocks are, and how small the tree is.

Figure 8.2

This is Red Rock Canyon, 15 minutes from downtown Las Vegas, and a world away.

Of course, there are exceptions to the "get close" rule. There are exceptions to every rule. Zooming in on the Grand Canyon, for example, misses the point, which is how enormous it is. Suppose you are trying to get a shot of the Grand Canyon that expresses how big it is. You're standing at the railing at one of the many "scenic overlooks," staring downward a mile or so to the canyon bottom, and across to the other end of the canyon. It's a great view, but a lousy picture. Why? Well, when you're standing there, you can feel the space around you. You can look down at your feet, and then keep looking down and outward just a little, and the next horizontal surface is a long way down. If you're like me, you find yourself hanging onto the fence. If the picture is going to work, you need to find a way to provide some sense of "out there, back here." In other words, *perspective*.

When I was looking for the right shot, I got lucky. There was a tree kind of hanging out into space, just at the edge of the overlook. I moved over a few feet, got a branch from the tree in the corner of the picture and there it was, the difference that made the picture work. The branch was a little out of focus, but that just added to the sensation. One of the great benefits to digital cameras in this situation is that you're not wasting film, so you can keep shooting until you get the perfect picture.

There are a few things that digital cameras do very well. One of these is shooting in **low-light conditions**. Cameras that use film use one roll at a time, so you're stuck with the same kind of film all day until you use it up. There are "fast" films for low-light conditions and "slow" films for bright sunshine. When the light changes, you might as well put the camera back in its bag. A digital camera can adapt to the changes in light. You can go from dark to light, from indoors to outdoors, with only a couple of seconds to let the camera (and your eyes) adjust. Even when a photo looks dark, as the one in Figure 8.3 does, there's usually enough detail in it that you can save it.

Figure 8.3

The lighting was terrible, but my husband was autographing his newest book and I wanted a picture.

I didn't want to call attention to myself by using the flash, although it would have been helpful in this situation. So, I stood as still as I could, braced my elbows on my ribs to keep the camera steady, and took the picture. It's kind of dark, as you can tell at a glance, but there's plenty of detail in the shadows. A photo like this is easy to fix. Even though you should always try for the best possible photo, sometimes conditions are against you. Using a digital camera gives you a big advantage. Digital photos are much easier to correct.

I'm doing this in Photoshop Elements, but you can use any graphics program that has similar options. All this photo really needs is an increase in the **brightness** and **contrast**. (As you might remember, we talked about this in the last chapter also.) In Photoshop Elements, these two sliders are located in the same dialog box. From the Enhance menu, choose Enhance→Adjust Brightness/Contrast and move the sliders until the picture looks right, as I have done in Figure 8.4.

Figure 8.4

Now it's good enough for the family scrapbook.

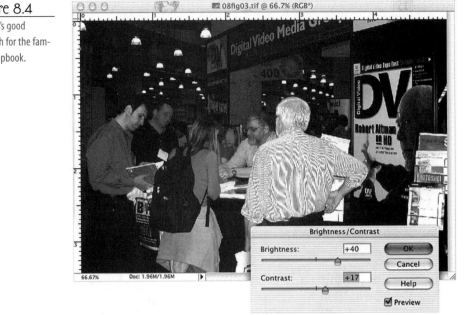

A Better Crop of Pictures

Nobody takes good pictures every time, not even the pros. One of the advantages of working with a digital camera and computer is that you're not wasting film and paper, never mind the cost of processing. You can simply throw away the unwanted photos. Just select them from the batch you've downloaded from the camera to the computer, and drag them to the trash bin or recycle bin on your computer's desktop. And say good-bye... But, if you're like me and hate to throw anything away, take a second look at the pictures before you trash them. There might be something good in there.

The picture might be a candidate for what I call *selective* **cropping**. Two friends of mine run an antiques/curiosities shop called *Oldies*, in Newburyport, Mass. Figure 8.5 is a shot of their parking lot. There's also a huge shed, with several tons more of the same. I took the picture because the scene was colorful, but I was too far away. There's too much to look at and nothing to see. But I think with the help of the cropping tool, I can find some good pictures in here.

Fortunately, this was taken with a **high-resolution** (5.1-megapixel) camera, so I can cut up pieces of it (figuratively, of course) and still have a good-quality photo. If you're going to enlarge a picture, as is the case here, always try to work with the best-quality image you can.

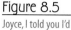

Figure 8.5

Joyce, I told you I'd put you in a book.

Beware of Lossy Compression

There's a file format called .JPEG, or sometimes .JPG. It's a very common and useful format, developed by and named after a bunch of photo experts who called themselves the Joint Photographic Experts Group (or JPEG). They developed this file format to use with photographs and the Internet. Photos, as you'll soon learn, can be very large files, especially with today's high-resolution digital cameras. Back in the good old days, maybe five years ago, average people didn't have high-speed cable connections to the Web. They often had dial-up modems, and they ran slowly. It often took several minutes to download a small picture. A big one took much longer. The only graphics file format was called GIF, or Graphics Interchange Format. It had a limit of 256 colors, so photos were blotchy looking and uneven. Not very good. The experts stepped in and developed a new way to compress photo files. It allowed millions of colors rather than the GIF's 256, and it shrank huge files into little ones, with very little quality loss—the *first* time you applied it. Of course, if you saved the same file as a JPEG again, the file went through the same file-compression process again, and was shrunk down more. After several saves, you often don't know what you're looking at. That's why JPEGS are also called *lossy* compression, because you lose some of the color detail each time you save them. The worst part of this is that there's no going back. Once an image has degraded, it's gone. Resaving it at a higher quality, or in another format, won't help. The picture data has been erased.

The main thing to remember about **cropping** is that, just as if you were doing it with scissors, after you cut something up and save the smaller piece, the big one's gone. What does that mean? It means work on a *copy* of the picture. Always save the original. When I download photos to the computer from my digital camera, before I even start to play with them, I make a CD-ROM of the entire folder. So should you. That way, you'll always have the originals to go back to. It's a very cheap form of **protection**. If you don't have a CD burner, you can designate a folder on your hard drive for the original picture files. Of course, hard drives can crash. I always figure nothing's really saved unless it's in two nonrelated places. A second copy on the same hard drive won't help if the drive dies. Consider buying a CD writer or a Zip disk drive if you don't have a second means of storage. (Zip disks are a higher capacity version of the now old-fashioned floppy disks folks depended on for years. Removable, reliable, and cheap...)

Artists often use a cardboard tool called a **cropping frame** to help work out a composition. It's simply two L-shaped pieces of heavy paper or cardstock. (See Figure 8.6.) You can use them to improvise differently shaped frames. Some pictures are square, some are rectangles. Some demand to be tall and thin or short and wide. Cropping frames help you see the proper shape of the picture. It's no coincidence that the cropping tool in every graphics program I've seen is shaped like the frame.

Figure 8.6

I've made a print of this picture and am using a cropping frame on it.

Using a cropping frame is a really good way to train your eye to pick out the best parts of a picture. I strongly recommend that you make one and try it, either on your own photos or on pictures from a magazine. You'll be amazed at how different things look when you train yourself to see "selectively."

You crop on the computer by using a **cropping tool** that drags a frame across your picture. You drag the sides or corners of the frame until it fits exactly around the part of the picture you want to keep, and then click inside the frame to make everything else disappear. Photoshop Elements makes cropping especially easy, because it darkens the part of the picture you're removing, making it much easier to see exactly what you've got. Figure 8.7 shows an example.

Figure 8.7

There might be a dozen pictures inside this one photo. The trick is finding them.

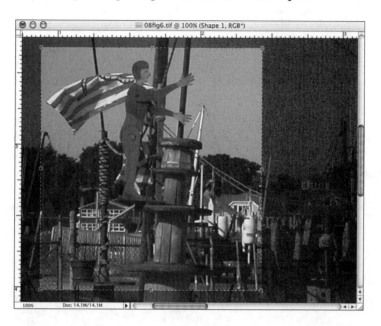

Cropping looks very similar in Paint Shop Pro. Photo Express My Scrapbook from ULead, though, does it differently. They call it **trimming** rather than cropping, and as you can see in Figure 8.8, they offer a collection of shapes you can trim the photo to fit into. The little squares at the sides and corners of the frame are called **handles**, and as with all the cropping tools, you drag them until the frame fits the part of the picture you want. Try experimenting with cropping in your own graphics program. Take a fresh look at some of your old photos and see what you can find in them.

Figure 8.8

Photo Express My Scrapbook calls this process trimming, rather than cropping, but it has the same effect.

About Face! Flipping Images

Most portraits seem to have the subject facing the camera. That's a good thing. You can see the face clearly. But, if you have someone who is looking off in another direction, you might also have a design problem. Our natural tendency, when we see someone else looking at something, is to look at it too. As discussed in Chapter 5, "Page Layout and Design," if you put a picture on a page that has someone looking away, you need to place it so that he or she is looking into the page, not away from it. Otherwise, anyone looking at the scrapbook will immediately look off in the same direction as the subject, and might not pay attention to the rest of the page. Because the point is to communicate, you have to bring the viewer's eye to the words you want him or her to read.

You have two options. You can arrange the page so the subject is looking at it, or flip the picture to make him look at it instead of away. Figure 8.9 is a quickie example I threw together to show what happens when the picture faces the "wrong" and the "right" ways.

Figure 8.9

Having the subject face the print makes you more likely to read it.

Most graphics programs let you **flip pictures**. They might call it **mirror** as Paint Shop Pro does, (see Figure 8.10) or hide it in the **Rotate** menu, as in ACD FotoCanvas and Photoshop Elements, but it's there somewhere. Some photos, of course, can't be flipped. If there are readable words, like a team name on a T-shirt, or a sign in the background, you're probably stuck. If you can't flip the picture, change the layout or put it on an opposite facing page.

Figure 8.10

Flipping in Paint Shop
Pro is only vertical.
Flipping horizontally
is called mirroring.

Image	
Flip	Ctrl+I
Mirror	Ctrl+M
Rotate	▶
Add Borders...	
Canvas Size...	
Crop to Selection	Shift+R
Picture Frame...	
Resize...	Shift+S
Arithmetic...	
Image Information...	Shift+I
Count Image Colors	
Palette	▶
Decrease Color Depth	▶
Increase Color Depth	▶
Greyscale	
Split Channel	▶
Combine Channel	▶
Delete Alpha Channel...	
Watermarking	▶

Resizing

Pictures are almost always either too big or too small for the layout. The nice thing—well, one of the many nice things—about using the digital camera and computer is that you aren't stuck with a wallet-size print, or a 4×5, or whatever format your film camera used.

Digital graphics programs like Photoshop Elements and Paint Shop Pro make it easy to change the size of the picture, or of anything in it. If you have one of the current multi-megapixel cameras, your picture can easily be 14×17 inches or more. That's not going to fit on a scrapbook page. So you have to make the picture smaller. In Photoshop Elements, the easy way to do this is to use a dialog box called **Image Size**. Choose **Resize** from the Image menu. As you can see in Figure 8.11, the current size of the picture is about 8 1/2×6 1/2 inches. That's too big for the page I want to put it on. The space I have is just about three inches wide.

All I need to do is make sure that **Constrain Proportions** box is checked, and enter the new width in the Document Size area. The computer does the arithmetic and scales down the picture to the right size. Constrain Proportions means that the ratio between height and width stays the same, no matter how the numbers change. Virtually every graphics program does this in a similar manner. Here's a screen shot of Microsoft's Picture It! resizing a photo. (See Figure 8.12.) There's very little difference.

Figure 8.11

Shrinking a photo is never a problem.

Figure 8.12

If you check Maintain Proportions, and enter one dimension, the computer determines the other one.

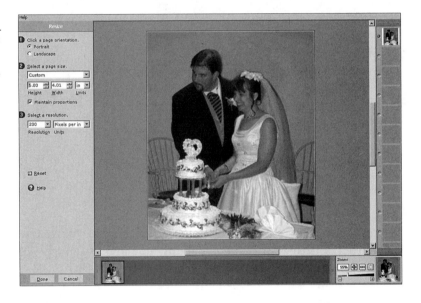

You can always shrink a digital picture, because you have lots of pixels worth of data. If you happen to have a small one that you want to make very big, you might not have enough data. In that case, you see the individual pixels as little squares. For scrapbooking, it's less common to have to make a photo larger, but you can do it if you have enough **resolution**. By resolution I mean dots or pixels per inch. (See Chapter 3, "Digital Tools: Hardware," for an in-depth explanation of resolution.) More dots means better resolution. To enlarge a picture, the program has to take a sample of the pixels in each area of the picture and find their average color, and then stick in more dots of the average color between the two sampled ones. If you overdo it, the image becomes fuzzy.

You can also **resize** a selected object. This is very helpful when you place a picture on a page, and then realize it's too big or not big enough. To resize a picture, first select the object or piece of an image to be resized. Use whichever selection tool is most convenient. In Photoshop Elements, with the Selection Marquee active, choose Image→Transform→ Free Transform. You can also right-click in the selection (Ctrl+click on the Mac) and choose Free Transform from the context menu. This places a **cropping box** around your selected object. See the example in Figure 8.13. Drag any of the **corner handles** on the box to change the size of the image while holding down the Shift key to maintain its proportions. If you drag the **side handles** of the box, you'll stretch the selection's height or width accordingly.

tip

If you enlarge an image by resampling it and it looks fuzzy to you, try the Unsharp Mask filter in Photoshop Elements to bring it back. Choose Filter→Sharpen→Unsharp Mask to access this filter. Paint Shop Pro and ACD FotoCanvas also have this capability. In both programs, you can find it on the Adjust menu, under Sharpness.

Figure 8.13

I happen to be using Photoshop Elements, but virtually all graphics programs do this similarly.

Blurring Backgrounds

How many times have you seen a good picture spoiled by a bad background? If you have the right editing tools available, you can get rid of it. Here's a picture I shot in Florida at a wonderful place called Big Cat Rescue. The subject, a Siberian Lynx named Natasha, is kept in an enclosure, but as you can see in Figure 8.14, we were allowed to go in and visit with her.

Figure 8.14

You can see we're on the same side of the fence.

I'm sure Natasha doesn't like the fence any more than I do, so let's get rid of it. There are several ways you can do it. The most effective, and most tedious, is to use the **Clone Stamp tool** and simply copy over all the lines with more grass and sand. That would take a while. The quicker and easier alternative is to select the background and **blur** it, as I'm doing in Figure 8.15. I can adjust the amount of blur that I add until the fence practically disappears. If I've done a good job of selecting the area around the cat, I won't risk blurring her.

There's a **Blur tool** in both Paint Shop Pro and Photoshop Elements. It's useful for blending small areas, but way too much work when you have something as big as the fence to remove. Working with the **Gaussian Blur filter**, the Blur tool, and a little bit of **cloning**, I've managed to de-emphasize the fence. Figure 8.16 shows the finished portrait, all ready for a big cat page. Be sure to see the before and after shots in the color section.

Figure 8.15

I'm doing this one in Paint Shop Pro, but most photo-editing programs have a Blur function.

Figure 8.16

The cage is still there, but it's not the first thing you see.

Anything that distracts you from the subject of the picture is worth the time it takes to get rid of it. Instead of blurring the fence, I could simply have traced around the cat with a **selection tool** and cut her out from the background. In Figure 8.17, I've done exactly that, and put her on a page with a couple of her friends. Please take a look at this page in color, too.

Figure 8.17

Notice how the three animals seem to focus on each other, leading your eye around the page.

There might be many times when the **Blur tool** comes in handy. It's good for hiding signs you don't want read and for removing details that don't help the picture communicate, or otherwise don't need to be there. It's always better to avoid the clutter when you shoot the picture, but sometimes you can't or don't want to take the time. In the digital world, you don't have to clean up the yard or sweep the floor until you're ready to do something with the picture.

Applying Color Correction

The last chapter talked about **color shift** as one of the things that can go wrong with an old picture. Well, new pictures aren't completely immune. If you shoot photos indoors with ordinary room light, you'll often find they look too yellow/brown. Or if you're spending a day at the beach, or skiing in bright sun and snow, all your photos look sort of blue. I could give you a whole lecture on the physics and color temperature of light, but you really don't need to know it.

Keeping it simple, have you ever noticed how a white T-shirt that looks really dazzling white in bright noontime sun can look sort of dingy at night in, say, the living room? That's because **daylight** is a very bright light with bluish tinge to it. Just like the bluing that Grandma used to put in her white laundry, it brightens whites. **Incandescent light**, however, the kind you get from a basic light bulb, isn't as bright. It has a sort of yellow tinge, and it makes colors look warm instead of cool like the blue sunlight. The camera records what it sees. If the shirt looks blue-white, fine. If it looks yellow-white, also fine. That's what it looks like. But we humans are apt to notice if the colors aren't what we think of as "right."

note If you're interested, photographers rate the color of sunlight as 5300 Kelvin, and ordinary Tungsten light as 3400 Kelvin. A candle is about 1000 Kelvin. Higher numbers are brighter, and therefore more blue.

The color we are most familiar with, and the one that's hardest to describe, is human skin. We humans come in flavors from vanilla to coffee to chocolate and licorice. But we know when **skin tones** are right and when they aren't. So, if there are people in the picture, use them as your benchmark. You know what their skin is supposed to look like, and if it's too green or too purple or too orange, you can fix it with your favorite photo-editing program.

Because I am sometimes rather lazy, I really like Photoshop Elements for **color correction**. Theirs is the easiest system to use. All you need to do is choose Enhance→ Adjust Color→Color Variations to bring up the dialog box in Figure 8.18. Then you choose the example that looks most right. You can adjust the amount of color change and whether it's applied to **shadows**, **highlights**, or **midtones**. You can also lighten or darken a photo as needed, and compare the changed photo against the original as you work on it.

Figure 8.18

You don't need to understand the physics of color to know what looks right.

A more complicated way to adjust color if you're working in Photoshop Elements (or any other program that offers color correction) is to use the Hue/Saturation dialog box, shown in Figure 8.19. Choose Enhance→Adjust Color→Hue and Saturation to access it. This dialog box lets you adjust either the entire color spectrum in the photo or a single color. Use the sliders to adjust the **hue**, **saturation**, and **brightness** as needed, after making sure that **Preview** is checked so you can see the results of your actions on the image in the workspace window. The pop-up menu lets you choose **Master**, which controls all the colors at once, or a single color channel (that is, red, green blue, magenta, and so on). This is more suited to making dramatic color changes, turning leaves from green to red, and so on.

Figure 8.19

This dialog box can be your best friend.

The dialog box in Paint Shop Pro, shown in Figure 8.20 (choose Adjust→Hue and Saturation→Hue/Saturation/Lightness), looks a little different, but serves the same functions. Instead of seeing the colors shift on a strip when you move the **Hue slider**, they rotate around the **color wheel**. But what you're doing in both cases is shifting the **spectrum**, so, for example, what was red is now bluer.

tip

In any of these dialog boxes, click on the piece of the picture in the window to slide it around so you can see the part of the image you need to adjust.

Figure 8.20

Because Paint Shop Pro doesn't have a simple Color Variations system, this is how you adjust colors.

Correcting Perspective

When you're looking up at a tall building from street level, you're not usually conscious of the sides of the building slanting in toward the top, but you see it all the time in pictures. It's a kind of **distortion** caused by the lens, and it's easy to fix, if you have Photoshop Elements. In Figure 8.21, you can see a picture I shot on a trip a few years ago. The building appears to be leaning backward, but in reality it wasn't.

To fix this, I need to stretch the top of the picture out so the edge of the building is **vertical**. First, I add a layer and draw a vertical line in an easy-to-see color. The Pencil tool, set to one pixel wide, is fine for this. If you hold down the Shift key as you drag, the line is constrained to vertical or horizontal, or any 45-degree angle. The line acts as a guide to show you when you've stretched the building far enough.

Figure 8.21

It's old but it's not ready to collapse yet.

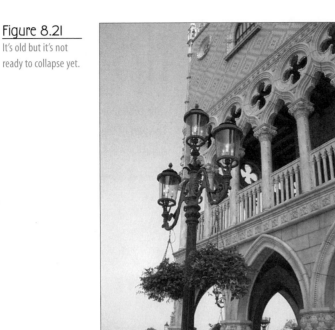

Figure 8.22

You might use this feature to straighten the Leaning Tower of Pisa, too.

From the Image menu, choose Image→Transform→Perspective. It places a cropping box around the picture, and then you simply drag the top handles outward until the wall is straight. Effectively, it has stretched the top of the picture and cropped away the excess. Then, you simply trash the layer with the guideline, and you have a perfect picture.

Removing Unwanted Items or People

One of the tricks I've found most useful over the years has been the capability to **rearrange people or other objects** in a picture. Sometimes there's someone who worked his or her way into the group shot and isn't part of the group, or maybe it's a former spouse whom you don't want in the family album anymore. Or your teenager's significant other with the spiked green hair and nose ring. Maybe you can't make them go away in real life, but you can usually do it digitally.

Here's one of my favorite examples: three happy couples out for a night on the town. Only problem is, one of the ladies is not the wife of the gentleman she's with. Can we make a "safe" version of this picture? Take a close look at the people in Figure 8.23. The one who's got to leave is the third from the left. But the background is very plain, so this will be easy.

Figure 8.23

His wife would not like to see him out with his secretary.

The first step is to draw a rectangle that covers as much as possible of her, and not much else. By the way, I'm working in Photoshop Elements here, but almost any graphics program can do this. See Figure 8.24.

In Figure 8.25, I've cut away most of the lady, and slid the right side of the photo over to cover the hole. The next step is to use the **Clone Stamp tool** to copy the background color to hide what remains of her.

Figure 8.24
Now that she's selected, I can cut her out and move the pieces together.

Figure 8.25
Some cloning and he's home free.

It's easy to do this when the background is as simple as this one. If you can't match the background, consider replacing the unwanted person with someone else. If I'd had a photo of the guy's wife, I could have put her head on the other body. Or I could have replaced her with some movie star from the same era; judging by the clothes, Marilyn Monroe would have fit in nicely. Figure 8.26 shows the final result.

Color Gallery

Figure I.2

Many scrapbookers keep a color wheel handy to help pick complementary background colors for their photos.

Chapter 1, page 10

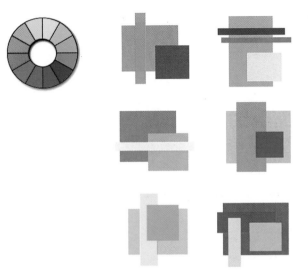

Sample Colors

Using a color wheel plus mixing different tints, shades, and brightness levels can yield amazing color combinations guaranteed to set your scrapbook pages apart.

Chapter 1, page 10

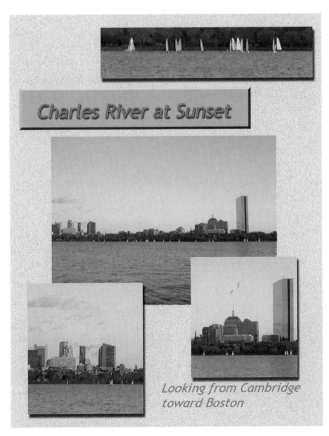

Charles River at Sunset

Looking from Cambridge toward Boston

Figure I.3

These are all the same pictures, cropped to show different scenes.

Chapter 1, page 12

Figure 1.5

I've made the pie and it's good.

Chapter 1, page 15

GRANDMA FIGG'S

MOCK APPLE PIE

- pastry dough for a 2-crust, 9-inch pie.
- 36 Ritz crackers, or other buttery snack crackers, coarsely crumbled
- 1 3/4 cup water
- 2 cups sugar
- 2 teaspoons cream of tartar
- 2 tablespoons lemon juice
- zest of one lemon
- 3 tablespoons margarine or butter
- 1/2 teaspoon ground cinnamon, and pinch each of nutmeg and powdered clove

1. Roll out half the pastry and line a 9-inch pie tin. Put the cracker crumbs in the prepared crust and set it aside.

2. Heat the water, sugar, and cream of tartar to a boil over high heat. Simmer for 15 minutes. Remove the mixture from the heat and add the lemon juice and zest. Let cool.

3. Pour the cooled syrup over the cracker crumbs. Dot it with margarine or butter. Sprinkle with cinnamon, nutmeg, and clove. Roll out the remaining pastry dough, arrange it over the pie as a lattice, or as one piece with slits to allow steam to escape.

4. Bake at 425° F for 30 to 35 minutes or until crust is crisp and golden. Cool.

Figure 4.1

HP Creative Scrapbook's interface is clean and understandable.

Chapter 4, page 53

Figure 6.8

Labelon on the left, Xerox on the right.

Chapter 6, page 104

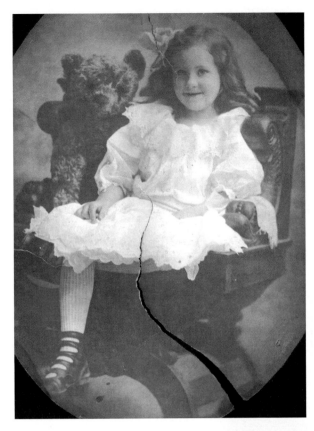

Figure 7.13
The photo has some bad damage, but it's all fixable.
Chapter 7, page 119

Figure 7.17
You need lots of patience to do this well.
Chapter 7, page 121

Figure 7.20
The final photo, restored to probably better than the original.
Chapter 7, page 122

Figure 7.27
Can this one be saved?
Chapter 7, page 129

Figure 7.28
ACD Photo Canvas at work. Color correction is easy with this program.
Chapter 7, page 129

Figure 7.29
I recommend that you skip Paint Shop Pro's automatic enhance function and do it yourself.
Chapter 7, page 130

Figure 7.31
Doing it yourself in Photoshop® Elements will give better results.
Chapter 7, page 130

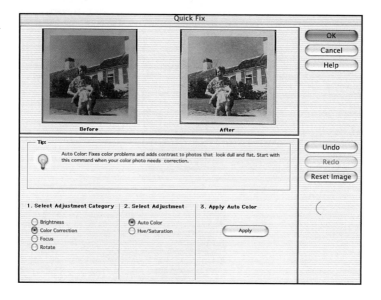

Figure 7.33
Better, but not there yet.
Chapter 7, page 131

Figure 7.36
Maybe the edited picture is not quite perfect, but considering how much better it is, I'm satisfied.
Chapter 7, page 133

Figure 8.1

Look for variety in your scenery shots as I did in these pictures from Nevada. **Chapter 8, page 137**

In the United States there is more space where nobody is than where anybody is. That is what makes America what it is.

Valley of Fire State Park

In the desert a fountain is springing, In the wide waste there still is a tree, And a bird in the solitude...

Figure 8.2

This is Red Rock Canyon, fifteen minutes from downtown Las Vegas, and a world away. **Chapter 8, page 138**

Figure 8.14

You can see we're on the same side of the fence. **Chapter 8, page 148**

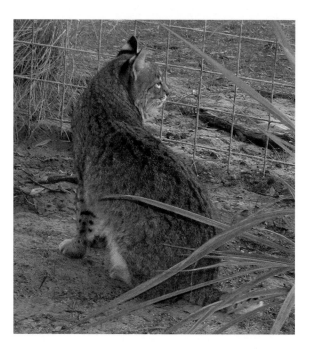

Figure 8.15

I'm using Paint Shop Pro on this image, but most photo editing programs have a Blur function. **Chapter 8, page 149**

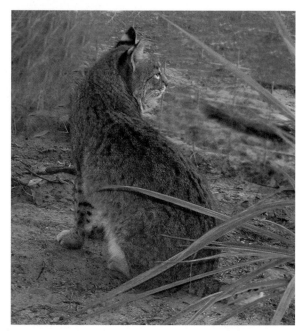

Figure 8.17

Notice how the three animals seem to focus on each other, leading your eye around the page. **Chapter 8, page 150**

Figure 8.18

You don't need to understand the physics of color to know what looks right.

Chapter 8, page 152

Figure 8.27

He's really a nice cat, not as evil as he looks here.

Chapter 8, page 158

Figure 8.30

Paint over it as much as you like with Photoshop Elements' Red Eye Removal tool, but it won't get any darker. **Chapter 8, page 160**

Figure 8.37
Bathing Beauties at Hampton Beach.
Chapter 8, page 165

Figure 8.39
All that swimming is paying off. They've lost several inches each.
Chapter 8, page 165

Figure 9.5

Photographers call this light "open overcast."
Chapter 9, page 173

Figure 9.7

The dry brush filter is a good way to make a watercolor with lots of detail.
Chapter 9, page 175

Figure 9.8

The original photo is on the left, the dry brush version on the right.
Chapter 9, page 175

Figure 9.10

Turning one of your
photos into an oil
painting lends an
interesting effect to
your scrapbook pages.
Chapter 9, page 178

Figure 9.15

Like the underpainting
filter, rough pastels apply
a texture to the photo.
Chapter 9, page 181

Figure 9.17

Notice how Find Edges picks up the detail of the sidewalk and the soda can collection. **Chapter 9, page 182**

Figure 9.18

Some of the color remains, but the background goes black. **Chapter 9, page 183**

Figure 9.22

This was done with Posterize set to four levels. **Chapter 9, page 186**

Figure 9.24

No animals were harmed in making this page (unless you count injured dignity). Photo art courtesy of Judy Blair. **Chapter 9, page 187**

Figure 10.10

There are two different kinds of drop shadow here. Under the type there's a hard edge shadow, under the picture a noisy one.
Chapter 10, page 206

Our Wedding

Figure 10.17

Metallic type effects can add shine to your scrapbook pages.
Chapter 10, page 210

Figure 10.21

Warped type is very effective, when you don't overdo it.
Chapter 10, page 212

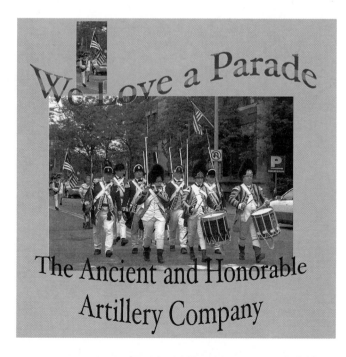

Appendix A.4

Soon, I will have a useful and pretty souvenir.

Appendix A, page 240

Appendix A.6

The Butterfly box.

Appendix A, page 242

Figure 8.26
It's as if she was
never there.

Figure 8.26
It's as if she was
never there.

Little Touches Mean a Lot

What we just did was a kind of "large-scale" **retouching**. I sometimes think that kind is easier than the little bits of things I have to do to make an ordinary snapshot look good. But retouching is worthwhile, and that makes up for the extra effort. There are lots of reasons to retouch a photo. Professionals do it all the time, and that's why the models on magazine covers look so perfect. It's not that they really *are* flawless. Someone has spent time covering up the tiny skin bumps and lines, and painting out the flyaway hair, and possibly doing some other tricks as well.

Fixing Red Eye

Let's start with something that plagues most amateur photographers: **red eye**. You've seen it, those glowing "devil eyes" in an otherwise great photo. People and Siamese cats get red eye. Figure 8.27 shows a particularly bad example. Other animals, the brown-eyed ones, are more likely to show green eye or yellow eye, but the "cure" for all is the same.

The strange eye color is caused by light reflecting off the back of the subject's eyes. It's worst when you're taking flash pictures in an otherwise dimly lit place, because the pupil (the black part of the eye) is wide open in **low-light conditions**.

Figure 8.27

He's really a nice cat; not as evil as he looks here.

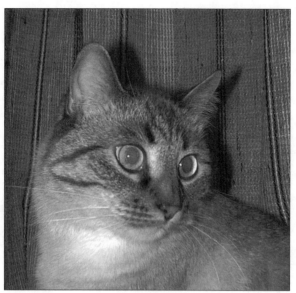

The easiest way to cure red eye is to prevent it in the first place. Most cameras with on-board flash, both digital and film cameras, have an **anti-red eye flash mode**. It uses one or more quick preflashes to close down the subject's pupils before the main flash goes off. The intention is to narrow the pupil enough to miss the camera lens entirely. It's usually at least partly successful.

The second way to avoid red eye is to increase the **ambient light**. Turn on all the room lights, rather than relying on the flash. Brighter lights narrow your subject's pupils and also allow the use of a dimmer flash setting to dim the reflex.

A less common problem is alcohol/drugs, although certainly alcohol and its results have affected a great many wedding pictures. Both alcohol and narcotics further dilate the user's pupils, and that makes red eye even worse. Besides, there's nothing attractive about being blotto. If that's what's going on, don't take the picture.

Try having your subjects look a few degrees away from the lens. If you know you've got a red eye problem, start by having the subject look at your shoulder instead of the camera, and increase the head turn if necessary. Get closer to your subject to widen the **flash-subject-lens angle** and thereby avoid the **reflection**. The longer the camera-subject distance, the greater the lens-flash distance must be to avoid red eye.

None of these methods is 100% effective, of course, so you'll eventually have to tackle **red eye reduction** yourself. Some scrapbooking programs, as well as the major graphics programs, have some form of red eye removal. Photoshop Elements has a **Red Eye Brush tool**, shown in the toolbox in Figure 8.28.

Figure 8.28

When you select this tool, the dot in the center of the eye turns red.

There's also a recipe for using it, which you can find under the Help menu. Choose Common Issues, and then choose Remove Red Eye to open the window shown in Figure 8.29.

Figure 8.29

Follow the steps to less scary eyes.

From there, you simply follow the directions, which tell you to do the following:

1. First, zoom in so the eyes are big enough to work on comfortably. Choose the **Red Eye Brush tool** and set it to a brush size close to the size of the pupil. (To do this, click on the brush options to open the brush palette or click and drag the size slider to change brush size.)

2. Set the **Sampling** option to First Click. (This selects the color to be replaced.) If necessary, reset the colors to Default.

3. Click the brush in the red part of the eye, and drag to paint over it. Don't worry about coloring outside the lines. It can't happen. The brush places paint only over the red, or green, or whatever color you have selected to replace.

As you can see in Figure 8.30, it doesn't do a perfect job. The replacement color, in this case, is much too light. This happens because the Red Eye Brush tool has a pre-determined blending mode and there's no way to change it. It might be fine for some cases of red eye, but not for this particular cat.

Figure 8.30

Paint over it as much as you like with this tool, but it won't get any darker.

There's another way to do it, of course. Instead of using the Red Eye Brush tool, use the **Magic Wand tool** to select the red part of the eyes, and then paint in a color that darkens them properly. I usually look for a color on the person or animal that I can copy with the **eyedropper**. If the color's already present in the picture, it seems to look more natural. Be careful not to cover the white highlights from the reflected flash. Those are called *catchlights*, and they make the photo look more natural. Figure 8.31 shows a close-up of this procedure. See it in the color section, too.

Figure 8.31

Figure 8.31

Leave the catchlights where they are.

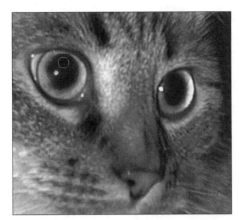

In ACD FotoCanvas, a **Red Eye Wizard** removes the red fairly well. You simply drag a selection box around one eye at a time, as in Figure 8.32, click in the Common Tasks window, indicate what color the eye is, and move the slider according to how dark you want the eye to be. When you click apply, the color goes on. You can't preview, so you might have to try several times before you get it right, but this is an easy and more or less foolproof system.

Figure 8.32

You can only do one eye at a time.

Paint Shop Pro has a very good system for red eye removal, shown in Figure 8.33. Make sure that there are no selections in the window, and then choose Adjust→Red Eye Removal. Then drag a box around the eye, and drag the handle on the circle inside it to make it fit the pupil. It can be stretched to an oval for the cat's eye or be round for a human eye. In addition, you can choose the **Auto Animal Eye**,

Auto Human Eye, or **Freehand Method** options, and select the proper pupil color from several choices. You can also add **catchlights** in any size you need, or have none.

Figure 8.33

This is probably the easiest method to use of all methods I tried.

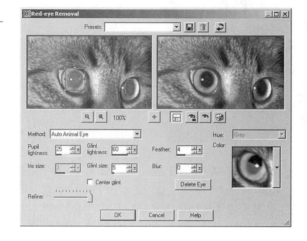

Eliminating Skin Problems

Even the best of the professional models and actresses have an occasional bad hair or bad skin day. Even on a good day, they might have a minor flaw or two. But you don't see those because they're retouched. Most professional graphic artists and retouchers use Photoshop, but you can use the same tools and techniques in Photoshop Elements or in any other graphics program that has some sort of rubber stamp tool.

Here's a fairly typical portrait. (See Figure 8.34, also in the color section.) It has a little bit of red eye, stray hair scattered across the guy's forehead, a few red spots, and he really needs a shave. Also there's dirt on the background, and a light switch that adds nothing to the picture. We'll fix this one, step-by-step in Photoshop Elements.

First, we'll do the **background**. In Figure 8.35, I've dragged a rectangular selection marquee over a matching section of the wall, a little bigger than the light switch, and **feathered** the selection by six pixels (found on the Select menu). The next step is to copy it and paste it. The selection appears on a new layer. I might also need to drag it to place it over the object I am hiding.

tip When you feather something, you are making the edges soft so they appear to fade out. The number of pixels refers to the distance from the unfeathered part of the object or selection, until its edges disappear. Feathering can make something that you have added to a photo, in this case, a copy of the clean background, blend in better.

Figure 8.34
It's not bad, but it could be better.

Figure 8.35
The Feather command is on the Select menu.

The **Clone Stamp tool**, or rubber stamp, is ideal for fixing hair and skin problems. Just find a clean bit of skin the same color and start stamping. In Figure 8.36, you can see a close-up view of the man before and after I cleaned up his face and enhanced his beard. It really only a takes a couple of minutes to do this kind of repair, and it makes a big difference to the people in the pictures, who might look at the scrapbooks in 30 years and not groan.

Figure 8.36

I even neatened up his shaggy eyebrows.

Going on a Digital Diet

What about those extra pounds we all put on as we get older? Can anything be done about those? The answer depends on a lot of factors, but mainly on what's in the background of the picture. In Figure 8.37, I caught a couple of girls spending the day at the beach. The photo isn't very flattering, I'm afraid. But we can help it a little.

As you can see in the figure, I've already used the **lasso** and **Magic Wand** tools to select both women. My next step, which you can see in Figure 8.38, is to copy them onto a **new layer**. Then I can drag a **Transform** box around them, and drag the box handles to make them taller and thinner.

Figure 8.37
Bathing beauties at
Hampton Beach.

Figure 8.38
They're not over-
weight, they're under
tall.

Now, I can make that layer invisible. (You do this in Photoshop Elements by clicking on the eye icon to close it.) Then I simply rubber stamp the background to cover the edges of the girls that stick out from behind their new shapes. When that's done, I make the layer with the cutout girls visible again, and after making sure I've matched the background behind them, I move the shadows down to line up with their feet. I then merge all the layers by clicking the More button in the Layers Palette and choosing Merge Visible or Flatten Image. See the final photo in Figure 8.39. They're looking a lot better now.

Figure 8.39

All that swimming is paying off. They've lost several inches each.

As you can see from these simple tricks, reality is what you choose to make it. Your teenager won't want to be reminded of her spotty face the night of the senior prom, but she will love the picture of herself and her boyfriend all dressed up if you just clean it up a little. Similarly, if Dad or Grandpa are sensitive about their receding hairlines, put a little back. They'll never hesitate to pose for pictures again, because you take such *good* ones.

How Much Change Is Enough?

There's a sort of moral question at stake when you're retouching photos. Is it right to do it in the first place, and how far should you go?

You can take people out of the places they've been, or put them into places or situations they haven't been in. You can turn that can of beer in the politician's hand into a harmless can of soda, or vice-versa, depending on your party affiliation. The question is not "can you," but "should you"?

There are certainly some ethical questions to be addressed if you're altering photographs for public display. It really depends on how the picture is to be used. Reputable newspapers and magazines tend to have strict guidelines about photo manipulation. The general rule seems to be that, if a change affects the *content* of the photo rather than its appearance, you can't do it. You can lighten a too-dark picture of the politician, but you can't change the soda can in his hand into a beer can (or beer into soda). That constitutes a change in content.

On the other hand, your scrapbooks are for your own use and pleasure, and to hand on to your kids and grandkids, or other family and friends. You want the people in them to look good because that's how you'll remember them.

Editing a picture to improve the composition seems entirely reasonable, if it's a picture for your own use, but this is precisely what got the esteemed *National Geographic* magazine in trouble some years ago. They were doing a piece on Egypt and sent a photographer to get pictures of the pyramids. The art director studied the pictures and decided the composition would be better if he moved one of the pyramids closer to the next. As soon as the issue was published, astute readers began calling and writing to the magazine to complain. An apology appeared in the following issue, but simply knowing that the manipulation was possible waved a red flag for many people, both inside and outside the publishing industry. The question has been debated ever since. How much change is okay? How much is too much?

It's clear that you can't always believe what you see. The supermarket tabloids frequently feature pictures that stretch the bounds of believability. Remember the one of the President shaking hands with the space alien? Or Bigfoot carrying off the scantily clad woman? (Why was she dressed like that in the snow anyway?) When a fashion model is having a bad hair day or her face breaks out, retouching is required and expected. Where do you draw the line?

To me, it depends on what's being done and its effect on communication. If it makes a better picture, it's worth doing. When I can make somebody look better than they did when I shot the picture, I'm happy to do so. If it changes the meaning of the photo, particularly in a way that might get me sued, I don't do it. Can anyone's reputation be harmed by it? Don't do it. If there's somebody you don't much like, take him or her out of the picture. But don't decorate them with zits and messy hair. That's just mean.

Summary—What You Need to Remember

The best way to have good color pictures for your scrapbook pages is to think about what you're shooting. Come in close to the subject, whether it's a person, a flower, or an animal. If you can't get too close physically, use a camera with a zoom lens to make the picture look like you're closer. If you're shooting distant scenery, find a tree or rock or something close by that you can use to give perspective. Otherwise, you can't tell whether something's far away or just small.

When you start to edit a photo, always work on a copy and keep the original untouched. Storing your raw photos on CD-ROMs guarantees that you can go back to them whenever you want.

Color photos and even digital photos can get just as messed up as the old black-and-white ones. Cropping can help by recomposing a cluttered picture or removing unnecessary objects. To make a picture fit a page layout, you can resize it and even flip it so the subject faces into the page instead of away from it. Blurring interfering backgrounds makes them less annoying and adds emphasis to the subject.

Color correction is sometimes necessary, even when you use a digital camera. Skin tones can look wrong, especially under indoor lighting. Some light turns things blue, some turns it orange, and color balancing corrects the off-colors.

Retouching can remove anything from a pimple to a person. The Clone Stamp tool makes it easy to cover up whatever you need to hide. There's no reason not to make your family and friends look good in their photos. It's simple and fun when you have the right tools.

Turning a Photo into Art

If you don't already have a good photo-editing program like Photoshop Elements or Paint Shop Pro, you need to invest in one to do the tricks and techniques you see in this chapter and the next. I think you'll find, when you flip through the examples on these pages and in the color section, that you will really want to add this extra dimension of art to your scrapbook pages.

Many of the tricks you're going to do rely on what are called **filters** or **plug-ins**. They are subprograms that "plug in" to the graphics software to add functionality—such as importing, exporting, special effects, graphics filters, and other options. Filters are a type of plug-in that allow you to apply many types of **visual effects** to images within photo-editing software. You can use different filters to change the lighting, add three-dimensional effects, or even make the image look like a mosaic tile surface. Photoshop Elements filters appear in the Filter menu. The ones used here are included with the full retail versions of Photoshop Elements and Paint Shop Pro. There are many others that you can find and buy online or at your local computer store. Photoshop Elements comes with about 100 filters. Not all of them are right for scrapbooking, but many can turn even a bad photo into a work of art that you'll be proud to display. I also like to use a filtered photo as a page background. You will learn how to do this at the end of the chapter.

Paint Shop Pro lists its **filters**, called *effects*, under the Effects menu, and has an **Effect Browser** that displays all 306 possible preset variations. Of course, each effect takes quite a while to apply. You might want to have another project handy while it's working. Figure 9.1 shows the Paint Shop Pro Effect Browser. One of the nice features about this tool is that it applies the effects to thumbnails of the photo you are working on, so you get a sense of what the effect will really look like when it's applied. Photoshop Elements has a sort of filter browser called the **Filters palette**, but it shows filters on a generic photo.

tip

Filters take a long time to apply because they are very math intensive. The computer has to do calculations to apply the effect to each pixel. One way is to speed this up is to add more RAM to the computer. Another, cheaper way is to tell the software to use more of the RAM in your computer, or *allocate memory*. In Paint Shop Pro, choose File→Preferences→General Program Preferences. In Photoshop Elements, choose Edit→Preferences→Memory & Image Cache and increase the percentage in the Memory Usage box. Keep in mind that you have to quit the program for these changes to take effect.

Figure 9.1

The Paint Shop Pro Effect browser shows its effects applied to whatever image you're working on.

Applying Filters and Effects

Most filters and effects have variable settings, which you apply via a dialog box. In Figure 9.2, you can see the dialog box for Paint Shop Pro's **Brush Strokes effect**. Use these settings to determine how big a brush to use, how much pressure to apply, and how the brush behaves in terms of hardness and the amount of "paint" it adds to the picture. The before and after windows show you the effect applied to part of your image, and you can also see it applied to the entire picture by clicking the **Proof button**. (It's the small icon that looks like an open eye.)

Figure 9.2

The Proof button shows you the filter applied to the whole picture, but it's not really applied until you click OK.

Photoshop Elements uses a slightly different dialog box, which you can see in Figure 9.3. I prefer the Photoshop Elements filter set for several reasons. First, the dialog boxes are less complicated. Adjustments are easier to make and easier to understand. Also, there are more "artistic" filters, including some that simulate particular painting media and styles. The Photoshop Elements filters are truer to the look and feel of the medium, be it oil paint, watercolor, chalk, or charcoal.

The Photoshop Elements Filters palette lets you see a great many filters applied to the same picture. But because it doesn't have to stop and calculate the effects of each filter on your art, it shows all 98 quickly—all at once if you have a big enough screen.

Figure 9.3

A less complicated dialog box is helpful.

Figure 9.4

Drag the scrollbar to see more filters. There are 98 in all.

However, if you compare the images in the Photoshop Elements Filters palette to those in the Paint Shop Pro Effect Browser in Figure 9.1, you can see that the Photoshop Elements filter set is more useful, at least for scrapbook photos. Superimposing an eyeball or Venetian blinds on your photos isn't going to improve them much.

Let's take an old photo, and see what we can do with it in Photoshop Elements, and then in Paint Shop Pro. Figure 9.5 shows the photo I'll be working on. (It's also in the color section, along with some of its variations.) This is a shot I took several years ago at Portland Head Light in Maine. It's not a bad picture, but it was a dull day, and the light was diffused and shadowless, making a generally dull photo.

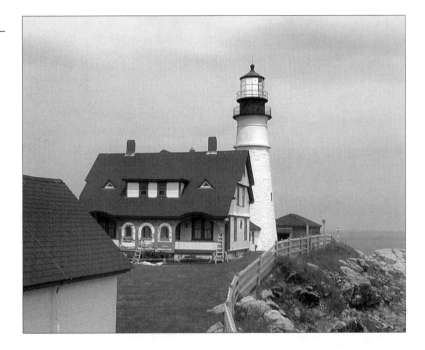

Figure 9.5

Photographers call this light "open overcast."

Faking Oil and Watercolor Painting

Artists who work in other media have a great deal of respect for those who can paint with **watercolors**. It's arguably the most difficult medium, because you have to work quickly, before the paint dries. But you also have to avoid working with your paint or paper being too wet, otherwise you'll end up with nothing but a puddle. Digital paint is, of course, much neater to work with. It doesn't get under your fingernails or leave a mess to clean up. And if you take your picture a step too far, you can always undo it.

Photoshop Elements has one specific **watercolor filter** (choose Filter→Artistic→ Watercolor). It gives you one style of watercolor, kind of dark and blotchy. There are ways to make this filter work better, and there are other filters that also create watercolors in other styles, but let's start with the official one. You can see its dialog box in Figure 9.6.

Figure 9.6
Use the plus and
minus symbols to
change the magnifi-
cation of the view in
the dialog box.

The Watercolor filter, like most filters, has a dialog box with several options. You can set the **Brush Detail, Shadow Intensity**, and **Texture**. Brush Detail ranges from 1–14, with greater detail at the high end of the scale. Shadow Intensity can be set from 0–10, again with much deeper shadows as the numbers get bigger. Texture ranges from 1–3, but there's not great deal of difference between the settings.

As with several other Photoshop Elements filters, you can end up with a muddy mess if you overdo the shadow settings. The filters have a tendency to darken a picture anyway, so if you intensify the shadows or add extra texture, the result is a lot of black on the screen. I'm actually quite pleased with the way this came out as a watercolor. You can see it in the color section.

Of course, there's more than one way to paint a picture. **Dry Brush** is a watercolor technique that, as the name suggests, uses less water, and more pure pigment. It's good for detail, and doesn't darken the picture the way the watercolor filter does. In Figure 9.7, I have applied it with a brush size set to 5, brush detail set to 9, and texture of 3. Because this is so close to the look I wanted, I spent an extra minute with the **Sponge** and **Dodge tools**, lightening the bushes, painting in some wild roses, and adding a little extra color to the rocks. Remember, just because you used one tool doesn't mean you can't go on and use others. The point is not to master perfect technique with only one kind of filter, but to make a picture that pleases you, no matter *what* you have to do to get there.

Figure 9.7
The Dry Brush filter is a good way to make a watercolor with lots of detail.

Using the Dry Brush filter on a portrait can be very interesting. When "lightly" applied, with the least radical settings, it softens the details just enough to hide lines and flaws without looking fake. Here it is, with a before and after in Figure 9.8. My settings were as follows: a brush size of 2, brush detail set to 10, and texture of 1.

Figure 9.8
The original photo is on the left; the Dry Brush version on the right.

The only way to learn what these filters do to a particular picture is to try them. Experimenting with the filters is fun, and it's the best way to master them. After you have used them a few times, you'll begin to learn the differences between **Brush Size** and **Brush Detail**. You'll know how to get a fuzzy effect, like I did in the previous portrait, or how to get a smooth, almost plastic, look from the same filter by using the opposite settings. Hint: Work with the Brush Detail settings.

Simulating Oil Painting

There are, of course, a great many styles of oil painting, from the Norman Rockwell or more recently Thomas Kincaid style of very realistic brush drawings, to big splashy abstract swoops of color. My own favorite school of painting is the Impressionists. I like soft, slightly fuzzy, but colorful paintings. Monet is my favorite artist, so let's turn the lighthouse into an imitation Monet.

Traditional painters begin a new canvas by creating an **underpainting**, which lays out the scene with a big brush in blocks of color showing little or no detail. After they have the basic underpainting done, the artists go back with smaller brushes and add detail.

In Figure 9.9, I'm applying the **Underpainting filter** to the lighthouse photo. Unlike some of the other filters that give you only a few adjustments, this dialog box includes textures that can be reset. The defaults are **burlap**, **brick**, **canvas**, and **sandstone**, but you can also load in any grayscale texture and use it instead. The textures can be scaled by **size**, and also by **relief** (or "lumpiness") and you can decide where to have the **light** strike them.

tip

If you like the general effect of the filter, but it's too dark, go back and lighten the picture before you apply the filter. In case you need to undo more than one step, remember that Photoshop Elements has an Undo History palette that lists your previous steps. Click on an earlier step to revert to that stage of your work.

tip

To create your own texture that you can load into a Photoshop Elements document, follow these steps. Create a New document, any size, set to grayscale (not color). Draw with different tools—brush, pencil, shapes, lines, and so on—and remember that high contrast works best to create texture, so draw in black on a white background. When you are done, save the file as a .psd file on your computer someplace where you'll know to look for it, perhaps in a folder named My Textures. Then you can load your custom-made textures whenever you want to use them with a filter in Photoshop Elements. Scanning textured paper or cloth works well, too. Save texture scans in the same way (high-contrast, in grayscale).

Figure 9.9

I like painting on sandstone. The default canvas is too rough.

The underpainting only takes one click. (You can see this step completed in the color section.) It's now time to actually pick up a brush and start painting. For this, I use a very small, hard-edged brush, and select colors either from the **Swatches palette**, or with the **Eyedropper tool**. Pressing the Option (Mac) or Alt (PC) key while any brush tool is active temporarily converts it to an eyedropper, for quick color selection.

In Figure 9.10, I've been working with the brush for a while, putting back detail and straight lines where the filter has softened the edges too much. If you have trouble **drawing straight lines**, try this trick. Press the Shift key while clicking the brush at the point where you want the line to start. Move the mouse to the point where you want it to end, and press Shift-click again. The line is drawn between the two points. You can also constrain a line to the vertical or horizontal by holding the Shift key down as you drag the mouse.

When you're **overpainting**, always do so on a new layer. That way, if you make a mistake, you can erase it without harming the picture. If you're not sure about the colors you're using, keep each one on a separate layer, so you can correct them later.

Figure 9.11 shows Paint Shop Pro's **Brush Strokes effect**. I worked with the settings for a long time, and this was the best I could manage. It's more like an oil painting than a watercolor, certainly, but I can't really say that I like the effect. Unfortunately, the Brush Strokes effect is the only one they have that even comes close to painting.

Figure 9.10

Be sure to see this in the color section.

Figure 9.11

I think it's a little too abstract.

Creating Line Art

Suppose, instead of painting, you wanted to try to turn the photo into a drawing? Photoshop Elements has a **Graphic Pen filter** (choose Filter→Sketch→Graphic Pen) that does the job very nicely. It uses the foreground color as the drawing medium and the background color, appropriately enough, as the background. You can set these two colors to anything you like, but I think the pen works best with black "ink" and a white or off-white background. I usually set the Light/Dark balance on this filter to 50%, so it's neither too light nor too dark. **Stroke Length**, the only other setting to alter in the filter dialog box, is a matter of personal taste, and what looks good with the picture. For this one (Figure 9.12), I chose the highest setting, 15, because I wanted dense blacks in the dark parts of the picture. I also tried it with a stroke length of 1, and discovered an interesting stippled effect, which you can see in Figure 9.13. To get this filter setting to "work" without having the picture look like a storm of black snow, I had to increase the brightness and contrast. You might often find that you need to adjust a picture before you filter it, and quite often have some cleaning up to do afterward. In this case, I had to Clone Stamp out some black dots in the sky where the filter noticed darker pieces of cloud.

Figure 9.12

This one has long strokes. The next example has short strokes.

Figure 9.13
I guess it's just a matter of "different strokes for different folks."

Can you do this in Paint Shop Pro? Well, not exactly. Paint Shop Pro has an effect called **Find All**. It's listed under **Edge Effects** on the Effects menu. When you apply it, it turns the background to black and highlights all the edges in the picture in white. To get something a bit closer to the Photoshop Elements Graphic Pen, I applied the effect and then applied **Negative Image** from the Adjust menu. This step, because we had white on black, reconverted it to black lines on white. I then used an eraser to clean up some of the spots the process left behind. You can see the result in Figure 9.14. You can also see why I like Photoshop Elements more.

Figure 9.14
If I had more patience, I might be able to get a usable picture from this.

Photoshop Elements has a very good selection of **drawing tools** in addition to the Graphic Pen filter. You can draw with **chalks**, **charcoal**, **colored pencils**, **pastels**, **Japanese brush painting** (called Sumi-e), **Conte crayon**, and even a **sponge**. One of my very favorite filters is called Rough Pastels. In Figure 9.15, I've applied it to the lighthouse. This is a filter that looks good with every photo I've ever tried it on.

Figure 9.15

Like the Underpainting filter, Rough Pastels applies a texture to the photo.

If you have a complex photo with a lot of details, you can really have some fun with some of the Photoshop Elements **Stylize filters**. Figure 9.16 shows a picture I shot in New York City. As you can see, it has a lot going on; all those cans of soda, and water bottles, and the signs... It's a very "busy" picture, which makes it a good choice for the **edge filters**: Find Edges, Glowing Edges, and Trace Contour. They're located on the Filter→Stylize menu. These three effects sound as if they look alike, and actually do look somewhat alike, with **Glowing Edges** and **Find Edges** being much more dramatic than **Trace Contour**.

The Find Edges filter removes most of the colors from the object and replaces them with lines around every edge contour. The color of the lines depends on the value at that point on the original object, with lightest points in yellow, scaling through to the darkest points, which appear in purple. The picture looks like a rather delicate-colored pencil drawing of itself. Find Edges works best, naturally, on photos that have a lot of detail for the filter to find. Find Edges sometimes becomes more interesting if you apply it more than once to the same picture. If you apply it once and don't like the result, try it again before you move on to a different filter, or increase the contrast in the original photo before you try again. Touching up areas afterward with the Sponge tool can bring out colors you hardly knew were there. This filter, applied to the right picture, can make a really outstanding page background or bit of art embellishment.

Figure 9.16

In the Big Apple, you're never far from a hot dog.

Figure 9.17

Notice how Find Edges picks up the detail of the sidewalk and the soda can collection.

Unfortunately, you cannot set the sensitivity of the Find Edges filter. In practical terms, this means that you have to prepare the picture before you trace it. Begin by running the **Despeckle filter** (in the Noise filter submenu) so that Photoshop Elements won't attempt to circle every piece of dust in the background. If you don't want the background to show, select and delete it, or select your object and copy it to a separate layer. You can lower the opacity of each separate layer too. Using this filter with different layer blending modes can produce some spectacular effects.

Glowing Edges is more fun because it's prettier, and because you can adjust it to have maximum impact on your picture. Glowing Edges turns the edges into brightly colored lines against a black background. The effect is reminiscent of neon signs. You can vary the intensity of the color and the thickness of the line. In Figure 9.18, I've applied Glowing Edges to the same picture. It works especially well with busy pictures with lots of edges. The more it has to work with, the more effective the filter is. Be sure to check these out in the color section. Black and white doesn't do them justice.

Figure 9.18

Some of the color remains, but the background goes black.

Trace Contours, like several of the previous filters, works better on some pictures if you apply it several times (see Figure 9.19). The Trace Contour dialog box has a slider setting for the level at which value differences are translated into contour lines. When you move the slider, you are setting the threshold at which the values (from 0–255) are traced. Experiment to see which values bring out the best detail in your image. Upper and Lower don't refer to the direction of the outline. **Lower Outlines** specifies where the color values of pixels fall below a specified level; **Upper Outlines** tells you where the values of the pixels are above the specified level. This also makes a nice background page.

Figure 9.19
The image was
traced several times
with different set-
tings.

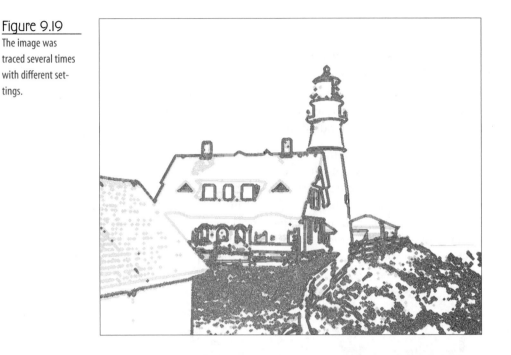

Figure 9.19
The image was traced several times with different settings.

I like to use the Trace Contours filter to place different tracings on different layers and then merge them for a more complete picture. To turn this into a scrapbook page background, I can put a second layer below the image with a pale color. But first I would convert the image layer to grayscale by choosing Enhance→Adjust Color→Remove Color. Then I'd reduce the opacity of the lighthouse layer to 20%. You can see this in Figure 9.20, and also in the color section.

Figure 9.20
This gives the effect
of a delicate etching
or pencil drawing—
very nice as a back-
ground.

Figure 9.20
This gives the effect of a delicate etching or pencil drawing—very nice as a background.

Posterizing

Posterizing is an easy and really awesome effect that can be used either as a scrap-book page background, as an "artistic" photo, or as a cover page with type. Posterizing, in effect, means reducing the numbers of colors available in the image. Instead of pixel-by-pixel full color, you see large flat areas in a photo, making it look rather like a **silkscreen print**. When you posterize an image in Photoshop Elements, the dialog box shown in Figure 9.21 lets you specify the number of **tonal levels** (or brightness values) for each of the three color channels (RGB) in the image and then maps pixels to the closest matching level. For example, choosing two tonal levels in an RGB image gives a total of six colors: two for red, two for green, and two for blue. By the way, posterizing is not found in the Filters menu because it is not a filter but a method of image (color) adjustment. Choose Image→Adjustments→Posterize to open the Posterize dialog box in Photoshop Elements.

Figure 9.21

Start with a low number of levels.

Figure 9.22 shows before and after views of a rather blah amusement park that has been posterized. Be sure to see them in the color section, too.

If you want a specific number of colors in your image, convert the image to grayscale and specify the number of levels you want. Then convert the image back to RGB mode, and replace the various gray tones with the colors you like. Note that posterizing can also be applied to an adjustment layer, making it a no-risk method for changing a picture. (If you don't know how to add an adjustment layer, the Photoshop Elements Help screens describe the process very clearly. Always check Help when you have questions about a program.)

Figure 9.22
This was done with Posterize set to four levels.

Posterization can be applied to both color and grayscale images, of course. Applying it directly to color gives a more random, but usually interesting, choice. As you play with it, you'll notice that lower numbers are apt to give you more satisfactory results. With too many levels of posterization, you can't really tell that much has changed.

Remember also that you're not stuck with what you get. You can change colors selectively, paint back the sky if it was lost in translation, use the Sponge tool to intensify small areas of color, and add a textured surface to the image. There's a whole arsenal of Photoshop Elements tools. Think about what they can do in combination.

Good news for Paint Shop Pro users: you can do this too. You can find it listed under Effects→Artistic Effects→Posterize. The posterizing levels setting works the same way. Again, fewer levels—three to seven—give the best results. Figure 9.23 shows the Paint Shop Pro Posterize dialog box. You can see the before and after versions of this photo in the color section. I shot this picture for a scrapbook about gardens I've visited and enjoyed. These rhododendrons come from Heritage Plantation in Sandwich, MA.

Figure 9.23
I found that three levels worked best with this picture.

Remember that you're not limited to using just one filter or only using it once. Sometimes a combination of several filters turns out to be exactly what you need. Other times, they have too much of an effect and you forget what the picture's about. But that's the good thing about working on the computer. You can always go back to your original picture, copy it, give it a new name, and start over as many times as you need to. And each time you do so, you learn a little more about how the program works and how to achieve the look you want every time you sit down to work with a new photo.

Drawing on Photos

You're certainly not limited to using the photo "as is". When you're working digitally, you can **draw** or **paint** on them. I belong to an online group of cat lovers. One of my friends, each year, designs Halloween costumes for some of the cats, and I thought that prints of those would be a fun page for my cat scrapbook. She works in Photoshop Elements, and paints the costumes on one or more layers—depending on how complicated they are—over the original photos. You can see her work in Figure 9.24, and also in the color section.

Figure 9.24

No animals were harmed in making this page (unless you count injured dignity). Photo art courtesy of Judy Blair.

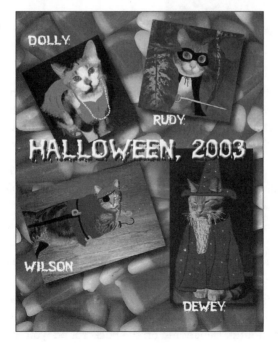

Making Composites and Collages

If you can't draw or paint as well as you want to, but still want to make some changes or additions to your pictures, consider **merging** a couple. I had a nice picture of my sons that I'd shot to prove Josh was still taller than Dan. Unfortunately, they happened to be standing in front of my very messy office bookshelves. The faces were great but the background was awful. So I looked through my travel pictures and found a view of the Golden Gate Bridge that I'd shot a year or two earlier. I used the selection tools to isolate the kids from the office wall, and posed them in front of the bridge. Now I have the classic "This is me in front of the bridge" photo, but at least it's a nicer background (see Figure 9.25). The trick with **composite pictures** like this is simple, as long as you work in a program that lets you work in layers.

Figure 9.25

They were never there.

Scrapbooking purists will probably have strenuous objections to doing this. It's changing history, and so on. You can't preserve a memory of something that never really happened. Nevertheless, I think it's a fun, and occasionally useful technique, so I'm including it here. If you don't approve, don't do it.

Let's take a couple of pictures and combine them step-by-step. Figure 9.26 shows two, selected at random. The first thing I have to do is to decide whether to colorize the couple or turn the railroad station into black and white. The latter is, of course, easier.

1. To remove the color from the train station photo, change the working mode from RGB color to **Grayscale**. In Photoshop Elements, Mode→Grayscale is on the Image menu. In Paint Shop Pro, simply choose Grayscale from the Image menu.

2. The second step is to prepare the couple to be moved from in front of their house to the railway platform. This requires selecting them and cutting them out of their background. Depending on the background, you might be able to select the subject with the **Magic Wand** or **Lasso tools**. Photoshop Elements has a tool called the **Selection Brush** that makes this task quite easy. Working

with the Selection Brush tool and a comfortably sized brush, paint around the inside edges of the couple. Then fill in the middle. It's easier if you enlarge the image to 200%, as shown in Figure 9.27. Then you can really see what you are doing. If you're working with the Lasso tool, this is especially true.

Figure 9.26

A couple of Don's relatives and the North Conway, NH railroad station. Photos courtesy of Don Maynard and Joshua Rose.

Figure 9.27

Bigger is sometimes better.

3. After they are selected, simply copy and paste them into a new layer in the other picture. You'll probably have to do some **resizing**, because the chances are good that they'll be too tall or short for the surroundings. In Figure 9.28, I've scaled them to fit.

Figure 9.28
I checked their height against the size of the train. They ought to be able to stand up inside it.

4. There's still one step left. If you look carefully, you'll realize that the day is sunny, but our couple isn't casting **shadows**. Rather than fool around with the drop shadow dialog box, I can simply paint in some soft shadows on another layer and then drag to move the new layer behind the old one. Figure 9.29 shows the finished picture.

Figure 9.29
I wonder where they're headed… maybe a Niagara Falls honeymoon?

Collages (an artist's word for any picture made by combining others) don't need to be fantasy, of course. You can combine any two or more pictures in any way you want. One that's often seen, and can be very effective, is the combination of a head-on portrait and a profile of the same person. Figure 9.30 is a double portrait of my daughter-in-law.

Figure 9.30

This is simply two pictures on different layers, trimmed to fit together.

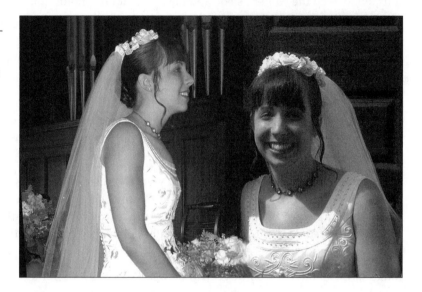

Making Panoramic Photos

People have been sticking photos together to create panoramic images for close to a hundred years, with varying degrees of success. The scissors and glue method rarely succeeded. Shooting a **panorama** all in one photo with a very wide angle lens almost worked, until you realized that the ends of the Grand Canyon were very fuzzy, or the two outermost bridesmaids in the wedding line-up appeared 50 pounds heavier than reality. **Distortion** is the main problem. Wide-angle lenses aren't that good. The more curve you apply to the front of the lens, the more glass the image has to pass through. Glass adds distortion. The more logical way to shoot a panorama that stays in focus from one end to the other is to take a series of pictures and splice them together. Prior to computers, that was exceptionally difficult, although it certainly was done. Now, thanks to clever software, it's easier than ever to get good results with panoramic photography. First, you must shoot the pictures, and that takes a bit of skill. Then you assemble the panorama.

Considerations When You Shoot a Panorama

Obviously, the main thing to consider when you shoot pictures for a panorama is to hold the camera steady at one height. Don't take it away from your eye while you're shooting. If you get interrupted mid-sequence, start again. Better yet, if possible, use a tripod to keep the camera steady. Remember, digital photos don't waste film. Stay away from the focus and zoom buttons. **Auto focus** the first picture and let that one dictate the rest.

Practice the panorama shuffle. Start shooting with your body aimed at one end of the scene. Take small steps circling to your right as you shoot your pictures from left to right.

Don't use a flash. Particularly, don't use **auto-flash**, because it throws varying amounts of light as it sees a need. These make the exposure all but impossible to correct.

Use a **"normal" lens** for best results. Set your zoom lens about halfway between zoom and telephoto, and leave it there. Don't use a wide angle, or a fisheye. They defeat the purpose of the panorama, which is to have everything in the same focus and not distorted. Nothing distorts more than a fisheye. That's how they got the name.

Make sure you have enough **overlap** between pictures, but not too much. Somewhere around 20% is good. As you pan across the scene, remember what was on the right side of each picture you take, and just cover it again on the left of the next shot.

Take a picture of something clearly different, even your foot, between shooting panorama sequences. That way you won't use **Photomerge** to try to assemble pictures that don't go together. Keep each set of pictures in a separate file as you download from the camera.

Once you have the pictures loaded into the computer and sorted out into separate folders, one per panorama, the rest is easy. You can either do the assembly yourself, or use software that does it for you. We'll look at both.

Photomerge

Photomerge is a Photoshop Elements plug-in that automates the process of assembling a panorama. After you've photographed the shots, you plug your camera or flashcard into the computer, and download the pictures. Then you open Photoshop Elements, choose File→Create Photomerge, and tell it where to find the pictures you want to use. The dialog box is shown in Figure 9.31.

Figure 9.31

It's easiest if you download your pictures to a single file. That way you don't have to go hunting around your hard drive for them.

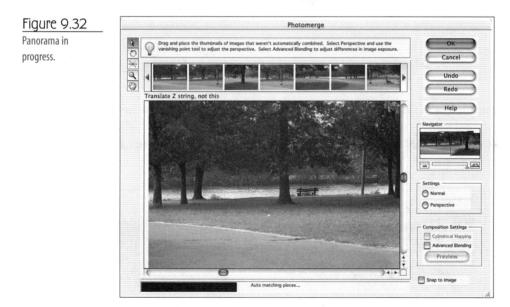

When you click OK, the magic begins. First, Photoshop Elements downloads all the photos you specified and opens a new page. Then it puts them down in order, matching the edges where images **overlap**. At this point, the window in Figure 9.32 opens, so you can watch the progress.

Figure 9.32

Panorama in progress.

The pictures appear to come in at 50% opacity, so the computer can easily line up areas of major **contrast**. In this series of pictures, tree trunks seemed to be the major point for matching. Pictures that can't be matched in are left at the top of the strip, so you can help drag them in and match them later. When all the pictures have been merged, **Photomerge** continues the process (in Figure 9.33) by adjusting the brightness and contrast of each pair of pictures so you have a **consistent exposure** from one end to the other. If the sun goes behind a cloud and emerges again, as it did for me, you have to do some extra tweaking. Apparently, it can only cope with *logical* changes.

Your final product is an untitled file (Figure 9.34) with all the pictures assembled and matched as well as possible. Unfortunately, when you get it, the image has already been **flattened**, making it difficult to adjust the exposure of one frame that's a little off.

Figure 9.34

The edges do help suggest that this is more than one photo.

It's still up to you to **crop** the picture, if you want to. Some photographers argue that the slanting edges and unevenness of the raw panorama somehow add to the experience. Others, myself included, prefer to crop. A lot depends on whether, and how, you intend to print the picture. The eight images I assembled for this test of Photomerge produced a strip four inches high by 36 long. At 300 dpi resolution, that's a 37MB file. I actually *can* print it at home, because one of my inkjet printers takes banner paper. But if I want a real panorama, I'd probably take it to a service bureau and have them print it 8 inches high by 6 feet long, and wrap it around the top of my office. That, of course, is much too big for a scrapbook, but if you have or can locate a printer that handles 11×17-inch paper (tabloid size), you can make a **foldout scrapbook page**. You need to size the photo up or down to a size that's no wider than 15 inches. Print the image centered on the page, as in Figure 9.35. Then, trim one inch off the right side of the paper, and after running a piece of Mylar tape up the left side, punch holes so it fits in the scrapbook. Make your fold precisely 8 1/2 inches from the left edge, so it fits right in.

Figure 9.35

Bring the cut side over and fold it so the edge of the paper is the same size as a regular page.

If this were a real page, I'd also add some journaling about where the picture was shot (Digby, NS), and some other smaller pictures from the same area.

What if you don't have Photomerge or some other panoramic photo program? (There are several panorama programs available online for Windows users including PTgui, free from www.ptgui.com and Easypano for Mac from www.easypano.com.) If you're working in Paint Shop Pro or an earlier version of Photoshop Elements that didn't include Photomerge, all you need to do is import the photos into a new document and place each one on a **separate layer**. Make sure you set up the page wide enough to hold all of the pictures. This also avoids the automatic flattening by Photomerge mentioned previously, so you can match **colors** and **brightness** of the individual pictures. Adjust the **opacity** of a layer to see "through" it to the next layer so you can more easily match the images. Then slide them as needed until you've matched the **overlaps** as closely as possible. Crop and save as usual. This method is also easier than Photomerge if you need to combine only two shots into a single picture.

If you need to scan something larger than your scanner can hold, like a full page of a newspaper or a calendar photo, use the same technique. Scan as many pieces as you need, and then import them to separate layers and match the overlaps.

Summary—What You Need to Remember

The main point of this chapter is to show you that you can do things to your pictures other than just cleaning them up and pasting them on pages. You can filter them, paint on them, and combine them in interesting ways. You can move people from one place to another, if you want. You can make collages and panoramic photos. The only limits are your creativity and your willingness to go beyond what's in the photo. Have fun!

Adding Type

To keep things simple, I'm calling it **type**. You might call it a title, text, a caption, a journal entry, lettering, or words on the page. Virtually all scrapbooking software includes the capability to set type. Some do it more flexibly and easily than others.

There are a lot of advantages to using the computer to set type. First, and most important, it's **easier to read** and **neater** than most handwriting. If you happen to be a master calligrapher, and really enjoy intricate Gothic script, go for it. But for the rest of us, the computer makes typesetting a lot easier. It's certainly **quicker**, and you don't mess up the page when the kids or dog jog your arm while you're writing. You don't have to deal with a clogged or leaky pen. Some programs even check your **spelling**!

The Language of Typography

Before you start working with type, there are a few terms you need to learn. The first is **point size**. This is a standard measurement based on the distance between the bottom of the lowest descender and the top of the highest ascender with a little bit added on. This is so that lines of type **set solid** (without any additional space between them) do not run into each other. Body text is typically somewhere around 12 points, and headings, titles, and so on, are set in larger type. A subhead might be 18 points high and a headline anywhere from 24 to 144 points high. Because a single point is 1/72 of an inch, 72-point type is normally about an inch high. However, certain fancy fonts have elongated **ascenders** and **descenders**. On such fonts, the point size is determined by a more typical letter such as lower case "n" or "o."

Alignment is the way the type is positioned on the page. You have three choices in most programs: **flush left**, **flush right**, and **centered**. Figure 10.1 shows some examples.

Figure 10.1

This typeface is called Helvetica.

Type set flush left is aligned to the left edge of the column.

Type set centered is equidistant to both sides of the column.

Type set flush right is aligned to the right edge of the column.

There's also an alignment style called *justified*. It forces each line in a column to be the same width. To achieve this, the spacing between letters and words is adjusted. Most graphics programs aren't that sophisticated, but if you need justified type, you can set it in most any word processor and paste the type onto your scrapbook page.

When you have multiple lines of type, you sometimes have to deal with **line spacing**, also called *leading* (rhymes with sledding). Back in the early days of metal type, the typesetter placed lead bars in between the lines of letters to separate them and make them easier to read. Both leading and type are measured by **point size**. If there's not enough leading between lines of type, it's hard to read, and makes the page look too crowded, and the block of type too black. Too much leading is also a problem. If the lines are spaced too far apart, the text seems disconnected, and your eye doesn't flow as it should from one line to the next. Type designers build into the font a suggested amount of leading, usually two points more than the height of a typical lowercase letter (They call it *x-height,* referring to the height of a lowercase x).

They also build in **kerning**, or kerned pairs. Kerning refers to the amount of space between two adjacent letters. Some letters look better and are easier to read if they are closer together. The combination "To," for example, looks best in larger point sizes if the letter O is moved closer to the T, even allowing the top of the T to extend over it.

If you set type in a word-processing or page-layout program, you can control the amount of leading yourself, or use **auto-leading**. Most graphics programs use auto-leading, and the type looks quite good. Only Adobe Photoshop (the full professional version, not Photoshop Elements) lets you control leading and kerning yourself.

Putting the Words on the Page

If you're working with Paint Shop Pro or most of the scrapbook-specific programs, you first choose your **type style**, **color**, and **size** in the Tool Options bar at the top of the workspace window. Then you place the type cursor on the page at the point where you want to start the line of type and click it to place a **type box**. Next, you usually enter your type in a separate window or box—either part of the toolbox, or one that pops up. Click OK, Apply, or whatever that program's particular procedure is, and wait for your type to appear on the page. Figure 10.2 shows Paint Shop Pro's pop-up Text Entry window. You can drag the type around on the page with the Move tool to reposition it if you decide it's not where you want it.

Figure 10.2

Enter your letters in the window.

The **Type tool** in Photoshop Elements works a bit differently. You simply place the type cursor on the page and start typing. There's no text box. To begin a new line of text, you must press the Enter (PC) or Return (Mac) key.

The Photoshop Elements Type tool is actually four tools in one: **Horizontal and Vertical Type tools** and **Horizontal and Vertical Type Mask tools** (see Figure 10.3). The regular Type tools set type on its own (vector) layer. Thus, you can **edit** the type and **apply layer styles** to the layer. You can change the type from horizontal to vertical and back again, change **display options** (discussed next), and **warp** the type into waves, flag shapes, or even fish. You can **move**, **copy**, and **change the position** or layer options of a type layer just as you can with a normal layer. However, filters and edits involving distortion or perspective can't happen until the type is *simplified*, or rendered into bitmap (raster) form.

The **Type Mask tools** allow you to do some very cool tricks with type and photos. When you use the Type Mask tool, you are making a mask in the shape of the letters you type. You can fill the mask with a picture, or cut the letters out of a picture. I show you how to do this later on in this chapter.

Figure 10.3

The Photoshop Elements Type tools.

Before you start entering your type, you probably need to adjust the settings on the Tool Options bar (see Figure 10.4). Other graphics and scrapbook programs have similar settings in a type dialog box or toolbox, although they might not have as many.

Figure 10.4

I had to cut the Type Options bar into two pieces so it would fit on the page.

The first four choices on the bar are the same as in the toolbox, namely which kind of type to set—**horizontal** or **vertical, masked** or not. Next, there's a pull-down menu of type styles. This menu changes according to the fonts you have installed, but generally you can choose from **regular** and **italic** styles, and often **light, bold**, or **demi-bold**, as well. The next pull-down menu displays a list of fonts installed, and the one after that offers a choice of point sizes. If you don't see the size you want, enter it into the window, or click the window and use the up and down arrows to adjust the point size up or down, by one point per click.

The next button determines whether to **anti-alias** the type. Anti-aliasing smoothes out "jaggy" type. It's important to apply anti-aliasing if readers will view your work on the screen. Few things look worse, or less professional, than jagged type. Figure 10.5 shows the difference. If your type is to be printed, however, turn off anti-aliasing. The same process that makes it look better on-screen adds a blur when the page is printed.

Figure 10.5

Notice the curves in the non-anti-aliased type. They appear lumpy, as if made of bricks.

Anti-aliased type
Not anti-aliased

The next choices give you false (or faux) **bold** and **italic**, and **underlined** and **strikethrough** type. You can use the bold and italic options to enhance a plain font or to increase the boldness and/or slant of already bold or italic faces. Strikethrough and underline have very limited uses, as far as I can see. Underlining was a way of indicating emphasis, back in the days of the typewriter, but it was always read as if it were italic. Because you now have lots of options for italics, underlining isn't typographically correct. Nor is strikethrough, because the invention of the Delete key. Use them if you think you must, but *please* don't tell me about it.

Those little stacks of lines indicate alignment: **flush left**, **centered**, or **flush right**. The **color swatch**, black by default, lets you choose a type color independent of the foreground and background colors. Just click it to open the usual color picker.

That sort of twisted letter with the curved line under it takes you to one of the more interesting aspects of setting type in Photoshop Elements, namely **Warp Text**. I'll come back to it in a later section, I promise. But first, let's finish discussing the options bar. The final icon lets you change horizontally set type to vertical type, or vice-versa. It's most useful if you tend to use type as a design element rather than as a means of communication. Simply click it to change a selected string of letters or symbols from reading left-right to up-down.

tip

If you learned to type on a typewriter rather than a computer, one of the rules you learned was that you always place two spaces after a period. Right? On the computer, it's wrong. Computer type, even in so-called monospaced fonts such as Courier, is designed so it leaves an appropriate amount of space between characters. You don't need to add the extra space, and when you do, it looks wrong.

One other no-no for computer users—never use those initials, abbreviations, and smiley faces you use in chat rooms and emails such as LOL, hw r u? and :-) for anything you want most people to understand. Your scrapbooks are going to be around for a lot longer than that online shorthand will. You don't want your grandchildren to think you were illiterate, do you?

If you happen to have ACD FotoCanvas, you have a clever option for type, perfect for making funny scrapbook pages. You can set type into a **"talk bubble"** or a **"thought bubble."** In Figure 10.6, I've added a comment to one of my favorite photos of Ari, shot through a fish tank. To add a talk or thought bubble, click Add Text in the Common Tasks window. Choose thought or talk bubble in the Text Style option, and then type your words in the box just below it. Change the font, color, and the point size and then choose bold, italic, or underline in the Font options area. In the Bubble option area, select colors for the **fill** and **border** (outline), as well as the **thickness** of the bubble's outline. While you make these choices, a generic bubble appears in the upper-left corner of the image window. If you can't see that part of your image, click on the **Pan tool** (the hand) in the toolbar to drag your image until you can see the bubble. You can also click and drag the scroll bars, shown on the right side and bottom of your image, to find the part of your image you need to view. Click the Pan tool again to return to your arrow pointer, and click and drag your bubble where you want it to appear. You can click on the yellow "handles" on the sides and corners of your bubble to stretch or squash it to the correct shape and size. Adjust the **angle** (direction) and the **length** of the stem for your bubble. When you have your talk or thought bubble just the way you like it, click the Apply button. If you are done adding bubbles to your image, click Done to return to the Common Tasks window and view your finished image.

tip Horizontal type is what we're used to seeing in the English-speaking world. Other cultures use many different alphabets and different typographic styles. Outside of short words on neon signs, we rarely see English, or French, or similar languages intended to be read vertically. It's unnecessarily difficult for readers to decipher, which doesn't mean you can't do it—just that you might want to think before you do. If you're featuring an old movie marquee, a theater, or hotel sign, some vertical type on the page might be a nice addition.

Figure 10.6
You can set the color of the balloon and the thickness of its outline.

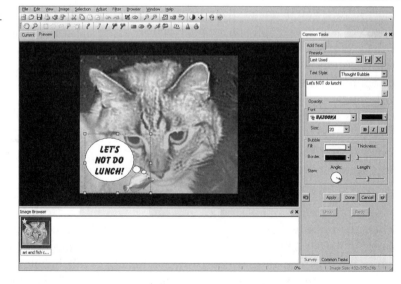

The thought balloon and talk balloons can also be hand drawn and filled in, if you use other graphics programs. Photoshop Elements has talk and thought bubbles available on the Tool Options bar, when the Custom Shape tool is selected. Don't forget that you can rotate or flip the bubble as needed, using the Image→Rotate or Image→Transform commands.

Choosing Fonts

There are literally thousands, if not millions, of fonts available. And, that's before you start adding styles and special effects to them. **Fonts** come in many styles but two basic categories, with **serifs** or without (**sans serif**, in typographer's terms). *Serifs*, if you're not familiar with the word, are those little strokes at the ends of letters. Serif type is supposedly easier to read, which is why it's used so much in children's books, and especially in reading primers. Here's an example in Figure 10.7.

Figure 10.7

Maybe it's easier to read because it's what we learned to recognize.

See Spot.
See Spot run.

There's also a distinction that needs to be made between **display type** and **body type**. What you're reading right now is body type. The chapter and section titles are in display type. The main difference is size. Body type is usually 12 points or less in size. Usually, but not necessarily—if you have a journal entry, and the space for it, set it in 14-point type to make it easier to read. Display type is always a bigger point size than body type. It can be precisely the same font, or not. Because it's bigger and placed more prominently on the page, it's easier to see, even if you're using a fancy or funky font. Fancy? Funky? Believe it. Figure 10.8 shows a few of the stranger examples.

Figure 10.8

Not all of these are right for all occasions.

Hello from
STRANGE THINGS
AND SILLY ONES
Hash House   Graduate
Phooey *Handsprings*
ORIENT *Sailor knots*

Your choice of font can either help convey the message, or interfere with it. These **"character" fonts** are good for setting a mood, and really help communicate what your scrapbook pages are about, as much as the words you apply them to. There are fonts that suggest **holidays**, fonts that relate to **sports** or places you've been, and fonts that look like **handwriting** or a **child's crayon printing**. The trick is choosing the right one for the right kind of page. Here's the same scrapbook title set in a bunch of different fonts (see Figure 10.9). Which one tells most about the subject?

Figure 10.9

The person in the next-to-last line stayed in a Left Bank bed and breakfast, the one in the last line, at the Ritz.

My Trip To Paris
MY TRIP TO PARIS
My Trip to Paris
My Trip to Paris
My Trip to Paris
My Trip to Paris
My Trip to Paris
My Trip to Paris
My Trip to Paris

You can find fonts all over the Internet, as well as in your local computer store, catalogs, and so on. Some you can get for free; others cost money. As mentioned in an earlier chapter, some scrapbooking programs come with dozens of free fonts. I've also found several CDs full of useful fonts at office supply stores and advertised in the back pages of computer magazines, at very reasonable prices. Start by checking out www.1001freefonts.com. They have an amazing collection, for both Mac and Windows users.

How many fonts do you need? That's going to depend on what you intend to use them for. Certainly, you already have some useful ones, probably Helvetica and one or two other sans serif faces like Arial or Verdana, and some of the classic serif ones like Palatino and Garamond. You have something like Courier, which imitates a typewriter, and you probably have one or two script fonts, such as Chancery or Dom Casual. Beyond that, why not wait and see what you need?

Tasteful Typography

With all those fonts waiting for you, it's hard not to get carried away and lose sight of the real reason for the type. Words mean something. You're putting type onto your page or picture for a reason, and most of the time it's to help communicate an idea. Maybe it's a title. Maybe it's a caption or a journal entry. Whatever it is, you want people to be able to read and understand it. Otherwise, why clutter up the art?

Using bizarre fonts and too many special effects gets in the way of communication. If the words are hard to read, only the most devoted readers will even try. If the message is "Get Well," but the font came from a circus poster, there needs to be a reason. Perhaps the recipient is a circus fan, or a part-time clown. Otherwise, you've just given him one more thing to make his headache worse.

Keep the type in proportion to the rest of the page, size-wise, as well as stylistically. Don't let one element overpower another, unless there's a reason to do so. However, don't make the type too small to read, either. Print a copy, and see whether you can read it from five feet away, without your glasses. If so, other folks probably can, too.

It's safe to say that every scrapbook or graphics program that sets type can do it in colors. **Colored lettering** looks really nice, if you've chosen the right colors, and it's a feature that you might as well make use of. To change the color of the letters, look for the color swatch on the Text window, options bar, or wherever your graphics or scrapbook program puts it. In Microsoft Picture It! Photo, there's a letter A underlined in the task bar. Clicking it leads you to a collection of color swatches and a color picker so you can choose a custom color, if none of the swatches are what you need. In Paint Shop Pro, your type comes out in whatever color is selected as the background/fill color. You can also use the foreground color swatch to make outlined type.

Adding Drop Shadows

Be sure that the color you choose for the type is enough different from the background that the letters will stand out. If you want to make the letters really stand out, add a **drop shadow** behind them. Drop shadows are so-called because they drop away behind the type or object you apply them to. Figure 10.10 shows part of a page I'm working on. (It's also in the color section.) It has several things going on, but one of the most obvious is the drop shadow behind the letters.

Figure 10.10

There are two kinds of drop shadow here. Under the type there's a hard edged shadow, and under the picture a softer noisy one.

Drop shadows are particularly easy to add in Photoshop Elements. You simply choose the one you want from the Layer Styles palette shown in Figure 10.11. After you have applied it, if you click on the script letter F that appears on the Layers palette next to the layer you have styled, you can adjust the way the effect is applied.

Figure 10.11

There are shadows, bevels, and lots of great special effects on this palette. Use the pop-up menu to view them.

You can add drop shadows in any program that works in levels, including Paint Shop Pro and even Picture It! Photo. Paint Shop Pro users need to set the type and rasterize it first, and then choose Drop Shadow from the list of **3D effects** under the Effects menu. This opens the dialog box shown in Figure 10.12, which lets you define the shadow by its **direction**, **offset**, **size**, **color**, and **amount of blur**.

Figure 10.12

The small device in the lower-left window controls the direction of the shadow.

You can also create reasonably effective drop shadows from scratch, if you don't have either of these programs available. You do need a graphics program that applies objects on separate layers. Figure 10.13 shows an example I did in Picture It! Photo. You need to set the type twice or copy the object that you're applying the shadow to, and fill it with a dark gray, or whatever color you want the shadow to be. Select the layer that becomes the shadow in the Stack and choose Effects→Edges→Soft Edges to blur it slightly. There's a command on the Format menu to enable to you move the shadow behind the type.

Figure 10.13

Notice how the shadow helps make the type stand out.

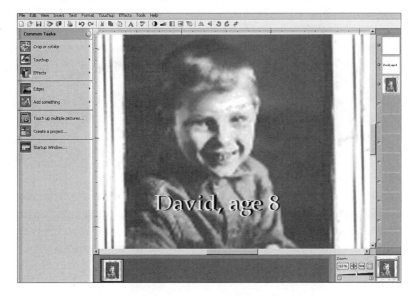

Using Masked Type

Now, go back and take another look at Figure 10.10. This time, notice the cut-out lettering. This is a trick that Photoshop Elements does really well. Choose a photo that you want to show through your type, and select the **Horizontal Type Mask tool**. The type tools are shown in Figure 10.14. Place the type cursor on the picture where you want to start typing. As soon as you do, the picture turns light red, telling you there's a mask on it. As you type, the letters are cut out of the background. After you're done typing, the mask disappears and you see the letters as "marching ant" marquees, as shown in Figure 10.15. You can then drag them wherever you want, even to a different page. To use the type marquee to copy a section of the photo, position it where you want it and then choose Layer→New and either make a Layer via Copy or a Layer via Cut. If you want to copy a section of the background with your type marquee and not make a hole in your background image, choose Layer via Copy. Layer via Cut cuts a hole in your image in the shape of the type you entered.

Figure 10.14

The Type Mask tool converts each letter to a little selection marquee.

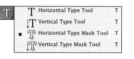

Don't forget that the Type Mask tool is essentially another selection tool, rather than a type tool, so you won't be working on a type layer. Your letters appear as a raster graphic shape on whatever layer is selected, and are not editable as regular text is. Therefore, you need to select your font, style, and size before you use the Type Mask tool. Don't forget to check your spelling, too.

Figure 10.15

Now you can drag the type wherever you want it or copy it to a new page.

Obviously, this only works with large bold type. Otherwise, your letters are so thin nothing really shows through from the background image well enough to be recognized. What you do with them from here is up to you. You can paste them into another picture, use them as a title, and add some layer effects.

Embossing and Other Special Effects

Traditional hand embossing requires tracing around the edges of pictures or type with a tool of some kind—either a stylus or ball-end burnisher, pressing a line into the paper and thus forcing it to sort of billow upward next to the impression. Press embossing uses brass dies and a combination of heat and heavy pressure to make raised images. Powder embossing uses plastic based powders applied to wet ink and heated so they melt and form raised lines. **Embossing** on the computer screen gives the same look, but a whole lot more easily. In Figure 10.16, you can see the **bevel and embossing styles** available in Photoshop Elements.

Figure 10.16

Bevels have angled or chiseled edges, whereas embossing gives a rounded edge.

You can vary the effect of these tools by changing the **blending modes**, by varying the **opacity**, and by changing **highlight** and **shadow** colors. As always, the best way to see what they do is to experiment with different settings. Paint Shop Pro, by the way, has most of the same tools. Check out your options under the submenus of the Effects menu. Tools in different graphics programs with similar names might produce very different effects when applied to any image. Be sure to make a copy of your original digital image before you experiment.

Creating Metallic Effects

There are lots of ways to create **metallic type** using the layer styles, particularly with the Bevel and Emboss options, and of course, Jack Davis's excellent Wow Chrome effects, which he's allowed Adobe to use along with his Neon and Plastic styles in Photoshop Elements. For many more tricks like these, take a look at his column in *Photoshop User* magazine.

Choose appropriately metallic colors, such as pale blues for silver and light yellows for gold. Remember to also set highlight or shadow colors to something appropriate, not necessarily black or white. Then just start experimenting. Try adding noise for a **brushed metal finish**. Figure 10.17 shows an example of liquid gold type. This example uses a combination of a drop shadow, simple emboss, and small outer glow, applied to yellow text. Remember, you can use as many layer styles as you want, not just one. If you go too far and make the type hard to read, just undo them and start again.

Figure 10.17

Be sure to see this effect in the color section.

Warping Text

Warped text is simply text that's set in a curve or along a wavy line or forced into a shape. It can definitely add interest to a page title, and can be a lot of fun, as long as it's readable. If your word processor happens to be Microsoft Word, you have pretty good collections of warping styles that you probably never knew about. Figure 10.18 shows the Word Art dialog box from Word (choose Insert→Picture→Word Art). After you choose a style, you see a window into which you enter your text. It's that easy.

Figure 10.18

You can set titles here and simply copy them to the Clipboard and paste them on your page.

Both Photoshop Elements and Paint Shop Pro have **type-warping tools**. Paint Shop Pro even lets you draw a path and place your type on it. In Photoshop Elements, you can select among 15 preset warp styles, and you can also drag and distort these until you have exactly the look you want. Figure 10.19 shows Photoshop Elements Warp Text styles. You can open this dialog box by selecting the Type tool and then clicking on the icon that has a warped letter T with a curved line beneath it in the Tool Options bar.

Figure 10.19

Some of these styles need multiple lines of text or large point size text to be effective.

None

○ Arc
○ Arc Lower
○ Arc Upper

○ Arch
○ Bulge
○ Shell Lower
○ Shell Upper

○ Flag
○ Wave
○ Fish
○ Rise

✓ ○ Fisheye
○ Inflate
○ Squeeze
○ Twist

The Warp Text dialog box settings, shown in Figure 10.20, are a little bit tricky at first. Use the sliders to increase the amount of **Bend** applied to the path. Moving to the right bends words up; to the left (negative numbers) bends them down. Distortion makes the line of type appear to flare out on one end (**Horizontal Distortion**), or from top to bottom (**Vertical Distortion**).

Figure 10.20

You need to experiment with the settings to really understand them.

In Figure 10.21, I've used two kinds of type warp. The first is **Flag**, and the second, used for the photo caption, is **Lower Arc**. The striped effect is the result of setting the type twice, once in red, and the same text on a layer over that, in blue. Then I warped both text layers exactly the same way, and dragged an eraser over the blue layer to let the red text layer show through, making the stripes. Be sure to see this in the color section.

Figure 10.21
Warped type is very effective, when you don't overdo it.

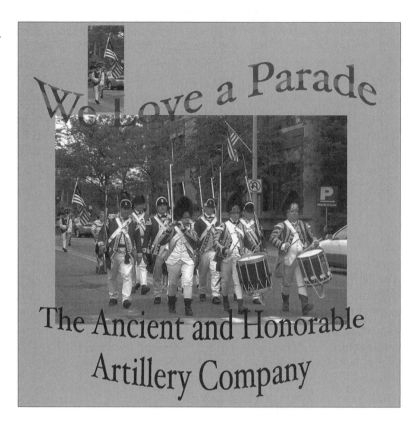

Journaling

Journal entries are a major part of many scrapbooks. Journaling can be loosely defined as any text that goes beyond a simple title or photo caption. Because journal entries tend to be at least a paragraph long, and sometimes several paragraphs or continued across multiple pages, it's generally much easier to write them in a word processor, rather than setting them directly in type on the page.

When you write for a scrapbook, consider who might be reading your words. This is a chance to tell your stories, relate your family history, and make daily happenings into memories your family will cherish. Write in your own voice. Don't use what Grandma Figg called "high-falutin' words" if that's not who you are. Just try to write concisely, clearly, and well, and say something worthwhile. When you want to use a journal entry, but don't know what to say, ask yourself what was the reason you chose the items you have put on the page, and then turn that concept into an explanation. Say what they mean to you, or what you remember most about the people in the pictures, or the place where they were taken.

Be sure to check your spelling, and always proof-read your words before you put them on a page. You can't trust the spelling checker to know whether you meant "to," "too," or "two" or "whether" or "weather."

Usually, after you decide which photos and other items to include on a scrapbook page, you'll have a specific amount of space on the page for your journal entry. One way to make sure that what you write will fit and be legible is to choose the font and type size that you think works best, and then set the page margins in the word processor to give you a block that size to fill.

There's a good deal of discussion in the scrapbook-ing forums on the Internet about what fonts to use for journal entries. I like to use "antique" fonts if I'm writing about family history. I use a font that gives the impression of handwriting when I'm journaling my own thoughts and ideas, and I often use a font that looks like comic book lettering if I'm entering something a child has said. Figure 10.22 shows some examples of different fonts.

tip

If you're not sure about questions of grammar or how best to say what you mean, there's a wonderful little book by William Strunk and E.B. White called *Elements of Style*. This is a book that should be in every home, and packed into every college freshman's suitcase. It's not just for writers or English majors, but for anyone who has to write anything that needs to be read and understood.

Figure 10.22

The first font is called Didot, the second is Hans Hand, and the third is called Gadget.

My great grandfather fought in the Civil war. He often said "There warn't nothin' civil about it."

I used to wonder what I'd be when I grew up. Now I wonder if I'll ever grow up...

"Mom, don't you think we need some ice cream?"

There are many handwriting fonts available online. You can even have your own handwriting turned into a font you can use for all your computer correspondence as well as your scrapbook. Do a Google search of handwriting fonts to find sources for free and shareware versions as well as companies that create your own handwritten font. This is a great gift idea, if someone you know wants to give you a very useful and personal present. Of course, you'd have to know about it, because you have to provide samples of your handwriting in capitals, lowercase, numbers, punctuation marks, and specific letter combinations.

Online Sources for Clips and Quotes

You know you want to say something, something significant. But you can't think of anything? The chances are fairly good that someone else already has said it, and there are many books of quotations that you can use, either as a source for quotes or to inspire your own messages. I used to keep a battered copy of Bartlett's *Familiar Quotations* on the shelf next to my desk. Then I discovered that the same excellent book is now available online. Go to www.bartleby.com/100/. You can search by author, alphabetically, chronologically, or by topic. Another good source is The Quotations Page (www.quotationspage.com). Finally, let me suggest two of my favorites, Quoteland (www.quoteland.com) and Quotations for Creative Thinking (www.creativequotations.com). Quoteland is organized with an alphabetical list of topics, as well as some quotes for special occasions, sports quotes, literary quotes, and a listing by author. They have many contemporary quotes from favorite TV shows. Quotations for Creative Thinking has proverbs, quotes from 3,000 or more famous people, and several indexing systems, all intended to help you find the words you want to use.

When you use a quotation, please don't forget to credit it to the person who said it first. Aside from being honest, it makes your pages more interesting and informative if quotes are attributed to their sources. Another idea, courtesy of my tech editor, Jennifer Burke, is to give credit to family and friends for their own "famous" quotes. People say interesting things all the time, and sometimes become known for always giving the same piece of advice or using a favorite phrase (such as "Button your jacket. I'm cold," or "Great galloping grapefruit," one of my dad's favorites). When you add a line that someone always says and place their name next to it on your scrapbook page near their photo, you are enhancing everyone's memory of that person as well as your page layout.

Summary—What You Need to Remember

There's obviously a great deal I can say about type. I could relate the history of type, from the first Sumerian script incised on clay tablets to Gutenberg and moveable type, and so on. But you don't need to know the entire history of typography to use it effectively. All you need to keep in mind when you use type is that the purpose of writing is to communicate. Anything that helps the communication is good. Anything that doesn't is bad.

Using fonts that relate somehow to the theme of the page helps get your message across. Using a delicate wedding invitation script font to caption the picture of your son's football team doesn't help the communication. Make sure your type is big enough to read easily, and is well spaced, so the reader can follow logically from one word or phrase to the next. Restrain yourself to a limit of two or three fonts per page or section. Type can help you tie related pages together as much as colors and styles can.

Using fancy type is fun, as long as it doesn't get in the way of the message. Warped type and other special effects add character. Drop shadows behind type make it appear to stand out from the page, just as a drop shadow behind a photo makes it look as if it's been stuck on rather than printed there.

Be sure to check your spelling and grammar before you print your pages. You don't want your family and friends to laugh at your work, and you certainly don't want to be embarrassed about showing it off.

Well-chosen words in legible fonts really help your scrapbooks tell their stories.

Creating Web/CD-Based Scrapbooks

You've probably heard about the "paperless" office of the future. The idea is that everything will happen on computer and cell phone screens. All the files will be stored on some kind of disks, either enormous hard drives or DVDs or memory sticks or whatever other storage medium the future brings. It's a good idea for a number of reasons. First, and most important to me, it saves trees, and I love trees. Tons of paper are copied on, scribbled on, and thrown away every day. True, some of the paper is recycled, but most of it is either burned, polluting the air, or dumped in a landfill, polluting the soil. Also, the paperless office means that important information can be shared by as many people as need to have access to it over the Internet or by distributing the material on a CD or DVD. If you're not at your desk, you can look at your cell phone or PDA, and call up the data you need, whether it's the babysitter's phone number or the company's annual report.

If you're at all like me, you enjoy the feel of the paper your scrapbook is made of, and the textures of the objects you have chosen to put in it. That's great, but suppose you want to show it to your mom and dad in another state, or give the same book to several grandchildren. With a paper scrapbook, that's difficult, if not impossible. This is when the computer becomes your working partner. You can put your scrapbook pages into a **digital album** that other people can look at on their computer screens or using an ordinary TV and DVD player. Sharing is easy, and you can send a disk for the same price as a letter.

Of course, there's also the **Internet**. Your family and friends don't have to wait for the mail carrier. They can look at your scrapbooks online whenever they're in the mood. With Internet access practically everywhere—from the public library to the corner coffee shop—the Internet is a simple and reliable place to store your memories. Your **Web pages** can be as public or private as you want to make them. You can share your scrapbook with other scrapbookers if you want, or password-protect them so that only the people who know your password can get in.

Understanding the World Wide Web

You've probably done some Web surfing, checked the weather report online, or found ideas for scrapbook pages from Web sites such as www.scrapbooking.com, but you might not understand the technology behind the Web. There are three things involved: the **Hypertext Markup Language** (HTML for short), **servers**, and **addresses**. You don't need to know how they work, but if you want to have your own Web pages, at least you need to know what they are.

HTML—You Can't Pronounce It but You Can Learn to Love It

Hypertext Markup Language controls how a page looks: which images are shown and where on the page they appear, what size a headline is and what it says, what color the background is, and anything else on the page. When you access a Web page, the information sent to your computer is not the collection of words and images you see on the screen. It's plain text—called the page's **source code**—that usually contains the words that appear on the displayed Web page, along with a bunch of *tags*. The tags are short pieces of **HTML code** that tell your computer what size or color to make the words, and where to find and copy other text or images.

The "hyper" in hypertext refers to *links*: underlined words on the screen that, when clicked, take you to other pages, play sounds, and activate other Web features. Making links is child's play: most Web page creation software does it for you automatically, or, if you're hand-coding your HTML, you can type a few words that serve the same purpose. **Web browsers** such as Internet Explorer, Macintosh Safari, Netscape Navigator, or the Web-viewing software in America Online understand HTML and use it to create an image of the page on your computer screen.

HTML is fairly simple and is based on English. Many people teach it to themselves by surfing to a page, and then using the View→Source command in their Web browsers. You'll look more specifically at HTML tags later in the chapter.

Are You Being Served?

Server? Let me explain. The second part of the equation that is the **World Wide Web** involves the **server**. When somebody looks at your Web page, they're not connecting directly to your computer. In fact, your computer can be turned off and the page still appears on their Web browser. Instead, they're contacting a *server*—a fast computer with lots of storage and a good Internet connection. The server stores your Web page's text and images in a folder, and transfers the Web page contents to anyone's Web browser on demand.

Big companies like car manufacturers and news media, or search-engine services like www.google.com, usually have their own servers. But there are plenty of companies that are simply in the server business. They maintain the computer and storage devices, and rent or, in some cases, give away space for individuals and businesses to store their Web pages. These companies are called **Web hosts**.

After you assemble your Web pages, you upload them to the server, and then other people can connect to them in exactly the same way they connect to any other Web site, by entering the address in their browsers. You'll look at finding a Web host later in the chapter.

The Right Address

People can't find you if they don't know where to look. That's why your **Web site** needs an address. Every Web site has a unique numeric address assigned to it, called an **IP address**. For example, the IP address for my site is 64.33.79.84. If you type that number into your browser, you'll see some of the digital photos I've taken. But all those numbers can be hard to remember, especially if you want to visit several sites. That's why each site also has a unique *domain name*. Internet registrars, such as verisign.com keep track of domain names for a fee and send lists of the names and their matching IP address numbers to your Internet service provider (ISP), where they're entered into a sort of giant phone book called the **Domain Name Server**. It's updated frequently because there are always new Web sites coming online. So if you enter my Web site's name, www.graphicalcat.com, into your browser, the Domain Name Server at your ISP translates that to my unique string of numbers (my IP address) and displays my Web page.

How To Get On the Web

If you have access to the Internet, you can have a Web site of your own. There are several ways to do it, depending on your budget and your tolerance for pop-up ads and flashing banners.

Free Web Sites

Companies like geocities.yahoo.com host your Web pages with simple **page-building tools**. Most make their money by putting ads on your pages or sending pop-under windows that appear when you close the original page, but these are generally unobtrusive and you can choose an appropriate category for the ads (such as "family," "cars," or "music"). Your Web site will have a **domain name** such as www.geocities.com/graphicalcat (a site I just set up to demonstrate some typical pages). There are plenty of others, including freeservers.com and free.pro-hosting.com. The list of hosts keeps changing, but if you enter "free Web hosting" in your favorite Internet search engine, you'll get hundreds of names. Check their terms. Some free hosts offer more storage space on their servers, so you can have more pictures on your Web page; others limit the size of file transfers, which can prevent you from adding sound or video to your Web site because the files would be too big.

America Online has a free Web site called AOL Hometown (hometown.aol.com). It comes with a page designer called 1-2-3 Publish, which is one of the easiest I've ever seen. It's also completely inflexible. However, they also allow you to upload pages you have created offline in some other program.

Your ISP might also have free Web space available. The disadvantage of using an ISP's server for your Web site is if you change providers, your Web address changes as well.

Web Sites for (Almost) Free

If you don't want to see ads, many free hosts can upgrade your account to a non-advertising version for as little as 5 dollars a month. Mac users might also want to look into mac.com, a $100/year Web-hosting service that also includes mail, an address book, online storage for important files, and other features. Actually, all these hosting sites are **cross-platform**—you can access them from Windows or Macintosh. However, some of the advanced mac.com features don't work with the Windows OS. Delphi Forums (www.delphiforums.com) has a low-cost Web-hosting service, along with related bulletin boards and chat rooms.

Be Master of Your Own Domain

If you sign up for a free Web host service such as Geocities, they'll assign you an address that takes visitors to your folder within their domain (such as www. geocities.com/graphicalcat). Similarly, if you have your Web site hosted by your phone company or cable company, your address might be something like www.cabletv.com/users/johndoe or users.cable.com/harpomarx. It's not quite as classy as having your own domain, but it's less expensive. For most scrapbookers, this isn't a problem. But if you also want to provide a service or run a small business or organization on the Web, it's a good idea to get your own **domain name**. It can also be a major ego boost. By the way, domain names are also used for email. If you want to contact me, I'm author@graphicalcat.com. Another advantage to having your own domain is that you can have as many mailboxes as you want. Perhaps there is one you only give out to family and friends, and one you use only as an address for signing up for freebies. (It'll fill up with spam.)

Web addresses don't have to be "dot-com," which is a good thing because almost all the good .com names have been taken. The dot-something is called a ***top-level domain***, and there are others available. Businesses can be a .biz, organizations can be .org, or individuals can be .name. There are even specialized top-level domains for museums and their managers, licensed professionals, and cooperatives.

To get a domain of your own, do a Web search for **"domain name registrar"**. There are dozens of registrars such as verisign.com and they're competitive—fees vary. Also, some might not have access to a particular top-level domain. The registrar will help you search for an available name, and make sure it gets properly registered. After you have a domain name, you'll still need a host. (It's possible to host a site on your own computer, but not recommended unless you're a serious computer geek.) Many domain name registrars offer low-cost hosting as well.

Assembling Web Pages

Unfortunately, there's no way to take your existing scrapbook pages and just post them as they are. You could, conceivably, take each page and scan it, and then save the scanned page as a JPEG. Or, if you created them entirely on the computer, you can simply save a low-quality JPEG version. In Figure 11.1, I've used the Adobe Photoshop Elements **Save for Web feature** to reduce a 9MB TIF page to a low-quality JPEG that's only 152KB. As you can see, the quality doesn't suffer too much.

However, that's still a fairly large file if you're on a dial-up modem. If you have a 28.8Kbps dial-up connection, loading the page takes 55 seconds. Some of your friends might not be willing to wait that long.

Figure 11.1

I also reduced the page size to 5×7" to save more file space.

The greater file size/more **download time** equation limits the usefulness of this technique for posting your scrapbook on the Web. That's why most people lay out their Web pages, in scrapbook form or otherwise, as HTML documents. You really don't need to be a computer whiz to make your own pages.

Sites that offer personal Web pages often have **wizards**, a kind of step-by-step, fill-in-the-blanks utility. With a wizard, you can choose from a variety of themes and backgrounds, select photos from your computer, automatically upload them to the Web site, and then add titles and captions. Figure 11.2 shows an example from the page wizard at Geocities.

Figure 11.2

Choose a style and then click Next to place your photos on the page.

The wizards make some rather boring and bland pages, but there are workarounds, of course. If you save your pictures with a block of color behind them, that's what appears on the Web page. If you set fancy type for a title and save it as a GIF, you can place it as if it were a photo and not have to deal with the limited fonts available in most wizards. Typically, these utilities restrict themselves to the two fonts everybody *has* to have on their computers: Times and Helvetica/Arial.

For the Do-It-Yourselfer

There's plenty of Web page design software available that doesn't require you to write your own HTML. ULead Photo Express has a $10 plug-in, called My Web Studio, which is shown in use in Figure 11.3. It adds another heading to the Photo Express Scrapbook builder. When you click the Web button, you see a selection of **predesigned Web pages**. Some even have **animations**. You add your own photos and text, as if you were building a scrapbook page, and the plug-in converts everything to uploadable HTML. This concept, by the way, is called WYSIWYG (wizzy-wig) and stands for What You See Is What You Get. As you add elements to the page, you see exactly what will appear on the finished Web page. **Page layout programs** like Microsoft FrontPage and Adobe InDesign use the same principle.

Figure II.3

There are lots of predesigned pages, divided into categories.

The MySoftware WebPage Creation Kit (from mysoftware.com) and Cool Page (www.coolpage.com) are both PC programs that will walk you through creating your own pages. These programs—for $30 or less—take you step-by-step through the process of designing a Web page or an entire site. One of the advantages of using Web design software, rather than the free wizards, is that you have more **design flexibility**. You can also work *offline*, designing and perfecting Web pages at your own pace, without needing a connection to the Internet. After you're happy with everything, you can upload your pages to your server. There are lots more page builders, all the way up to high-powered tools such as Microsoft Front Page and Macromedia Dreamweaver MX, which sell for $200 and $400 respectively. As you can tell by the prices, these last two are intended for professionals, and are probably overkill for the average scrapbooker. But if you have access to one of them, and the patience to learn it, you can turn out some amazing pages.

You can turn out some fairly amazing pages without any of these tools, if you have a recent edition of most any **word processor** or **text-editing program**. Many word processors and text-editing programs—including Microsoft Word, Microsoft Works, WordPerfect, and AppleWorks—save pages in **Web format**, complete with text styling and pictures. You simply design your pages in one of these programs, and when you save, the program writes HTML source code. Then, you can upload it to your server along with the images and other graphics you want to use. I was quite surprised when I started revising a page with Microsoft Word and found that I could apply graphics filters and add drop shadows and other effects right within the word processor. (This applies to the current version, not necessarily to earlier ones.) Check out Figure 11.4. You can even fix red eye, as well as crop and fix color on your photos.

Figure II.4

Who knew a word processor could do all this? I didn't.

Web Page Design Basics

There are a few things to think about when you create a Web page, as opposed to a normal scrapbook page. The first is to keep the graphics files small. You can save Web graphics in JPEG, GIF, or PNG format. Which one you choose depends on what kind of a graphic it is. Photos are best saved as JPEG or PNG, and they can be compressed to very small files. Line drawings, backgrounds, single or limited color blocks, or anything with fewer than 216 colors save smallest as GIFs.

When you choose type to add to a Web page, you have two options. You can set the type in a graphics program and save it as a GIF if you want a particular font. If "close enough" is good enough, just set your type in the Web page program, using one of the headline or text settings, and specify a common font that your viewers are likely to have installed, such as Times or Arial. Why? Well, suppose you want to use a character font like Chalkboard, or Rodeo, or your own handwriting font. The chances are good that the people who visit the page won't have that font available on their computers. So, their Web browser will choose a generic font instead, which probably won't even be close to what you wanted. If you set the type as a GIF, you can apply any special effects you like, and crop the block small, make the area surrounding the type invisible so the page's background or color shows through, or add a different background color behind it. Check the program's help files or manual for information on creating these effects.

Can This Page Be Saved?

When you save a Web page on the server, you have to give it a name ending in .htm or .html. People access your page by entering the **domain name** and your **folder**, followed by the name of the page. In the case of the site I just set up, it might theoretically be something like geocities.com/graphicalcat/MainScrapBookPage.html. (It's not.) But you can save your friends some typing by naming the main page **index.html**. That magic name is automatically used for the page name, when someone enters your Web site without specifying a page. That's why you can see my geocities page by just entering geocities.com/graphicalcat. It automatically takes you to the page I made called index.html.

tip If you want to put your email address on your Web page, so people can write to you, set it as a GIF, instead of as regular type on the page. They'll have to copy it, rather than just clicking on the address to send an email, but the search programs that crawl through the Web looking for email addresses for spammers can't find you this way.

How HTML Works

You don't have to know this. As you've seen, there are plenty of WYSIWYG page-building software and Web sites that translate your layouts into HTML, the universal language of Web pages. But if you have a basic understanding of how this authoring language works, you can better tweak your pages and make them look different from others.

Although HTML is a computer language, it's one of the simplest to understand. The commands (known as *tags*) are either abbreviations of English words, such as <b> to turn a font bold, or the words themselves. Many tags control **font formatting**, others let you put **multiple columns** on a page, but the most important ones tell the browser which **images** to put on a page, or where to go when someone clicks on a **link**. Links take you to other pages on your own Web site, or someone else's Web site, if you want. You might want to link to your favorite scrapbooking store or to your friends' pages. I have a link to Amazon.com so people who come to my Web site can buy my books. (And I make a few extra pennies per book from Amazon for providing the link.)

There are three important points to remember about HTML:

- **Tags** have to be enclosed in **angle brackets** < > (also known as lesser-than and greater-than symbols), which are found above the comma and period on a keyboard.

- Tags that affect formatting have to be **closed**, which you do by using another tag with a **slash mark**. For example, if you type <i> in front of a word to make it appear italic in the browser, every word that follows it will also be italic until you type the closing tag, </i>.

- The **source code** for your HTML pages—the **text files** that contain all the **tags** and **content**—in a Web site aren't formatted themselves. Everything's in the same dull typeface, and there are no colors or pictures. The magic happens after your browser downloads the page and interprets the tags.

Table 11.1 shows the HTML source code that displays the wedding scrapbook Web page in Figure 11.5, with an explanation of what the tags are doing.

Table 11.1 HTML Source Code for the Web Page Shown in Figure 11.5

Tag	Purpose
`<HTML>`	Tells browser this is an HTML document, so it should draw the page based on these tags.
`<HEAD>`	This is the beginning of the page's header. The `<HEAD>` tag can contain info for search engines, as well as style and script information.
`<TITLE>Josh & Melissa's Wedding</TITLE>`	The text contained within the `<TITLE>` tags is displayed in the browser's title bar.
`<META http-equiv="Content-Type" content="text/html;charset= iso-8859-1">`	Tells browser which version of code to interpret.
`</HEAD>`	End of page header information
`<BODY background="papertexture.jpg">`	...and beginning of the body of the page. The `background` command tells the browser to find an image called `papertexture.jpg` in the same folder as the HTML document, copy it as many times as necessary to cover the page, and put all the type and other images over it. The `<BODY>` tag always follows the `<HEAD>` tag in HTML documents.
`<TABLE border=2 bordercolor=#808080 bordercolorlight=#C0C0C0 bordercolordark=#404040 width= "90%" cellspacing="2" cellpadding="6">`	This places those nice embossed rectangles around the words on the left, and the picture on the right, by actually drawing a two-column table. The attribute `border=2` indicates that the border is two pixels wide. The text `bordercolorlight` gives the highlight color around the border, whereas `bordercolordark` gives the shadow color. The colors are represented by numbers as shown.
`<TR>`	Start one row of cells in the table.
`<TD>`	The `<TD>` tag defines the contents of a cell in a table.
`<H1 ALIGN=Center><FONT COLOR="#FF0000"> <BIG><I>Mr. and Mrs.  Joshua & Melissa  Rose </I></BIG></FONT></H1>`	H1 means "heading size 1," the largest the browser can display. `FONT COLOR` specifies the color, and `FF0000` means bright red. The `<BIG><BIG/>` tag obviously defines text that should be displayed in a larger font than usual. Text contained within `<I></I>` tags appears italicized. The ` ` tags force a break between lines of type. Note how all those formatting commands are closed with slash marks.
`<H3 ALIGN=Center><FONT COLOR="#FF0000"> September 1, 2001</FONT></H3> <FONT></FONT>`	Changes the font size and color, as shown in the source code at left. H3 is two sizes smaller than H1.
`<IMG SRC="palm2.gif" WIDTH=123 HEIGHT=114 ALIGN=BOTTOM>  <I><BIG><FONT COLOR="#FF0000">`	Find the palm tree image and make it the element after the previous text.

Table 11.1 Continued

Tag	Purpose
`<A HREF="message.htm">` `A Message in a Bottle </A>`	`<A HREF>` is a link to another page. When someone clicks on the words "A Message in a Bottle," they're taken to a different Web page (message.htm) that features a poem the groom wrote.
`   `	Adds some space…
`<A HREF="pictures.htm">` `To more pictures</a></FONT></BIG></I>`	…and then adds a link to the page that has more pictures.
`</TD>`	End of the first column in this row of the table.
`<TD>`	Start the next column.
`<IMG SRC="kiss.jpg" WIDTH=327` `HEIGHT=350 ALIGN=CENTER ALT="The Kiss">`	Finds the kiss image and put it here. The ALT attribute displays the words "The Kiss" while the picture is loading, or if the browser can't find the image.
`</TD>`	End of this column.
`</TR>`	End of this row.
`</TABLE>`	End of this table.
`</BODY>`	Okay, browser, you've displayed everything on the page.
`</HTML>`	End of HTML code.

Figure 11.5

Josh and Melissa's wedding page.

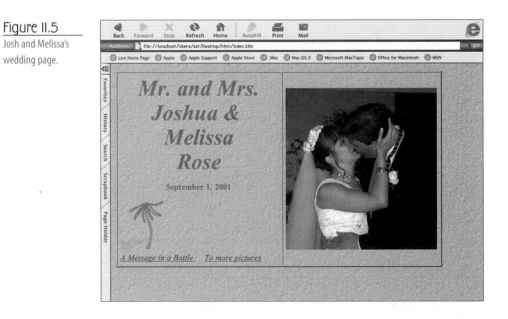

And that, in a nutshell, is very basic HTML source code. There are lots of good books about it, including one in the *Sams Teach Yourself in 24 Hours* series, and if you want to learn even faster, there's *Sams Teach Yourself HTML in 10 Minutes*.

Enhancing Your Site with Sound and Video

A Web site or CD can be an electronic version of a traditional scrapbook, with pictures and text arranged as they might appear on paper pages. But it can be more: **Electronic scrapbooks** can also include **sound** and **video**. Why just have a still picture of baby's first step, when you can hear and see him walking? Home movies and amateur sound recordings have been around for well over half a century, as a way to share family events and as a more personal communication than a letter. I still remember seeing my mother's movies of the 1939 New York World's Fair, and hearing a very early tape recording of my grandfather telling stories about his days as mate on a sailing ship. The film and tape are long gone, of course. Computers, CDs, and DVDs allow people to preserve these memories. Services exist for transferring old **home movies**, **photos**, **negatives**, and **VHS video tapes** to **digital data**. The biggest benefits are that digital data doesn't break down over time like film or video tape, and the digital format allows people to share these memories online easily.

File Formats and Sizes

Top-quality movies and sound can be extremely large. Full-screen movies eat 30MB per minute or more, depending on video quality; CD-quality sound needs about 10MB per minute. Sizes like this are impractical for a Web page—even at a paid host. They use up too much space on the server, and take too long to download.

Fortunately, there are ways to shrink the files. You can do it brute-force, getting small improvements in file size by drastically lowering the image or sound quality. Or you can use modern compression techniques that take advantage of the way we see and hear to significantly shrink the file without too much compromise in quality. The best known of these is **MP3**, the almost-universal format for compressed sound and music on the Web. Music files in MP3 format can be almost as good as a CD, yet use less than 1MB per minute; voice-only files can be a quarter that size and still sound acceptable.

Popular Web formats for video are Microsoft's **Windows Media Player** (.wma) and Apple's **QuickTime** (.qt). Both are **cross-platform**, so you can create and play either file format from a Windows PC or a Mac. Both can transfer **streaming video**, so viewers can start watching your movies without waiting for the whole thing to download. File sizes for video depend on a lot of variables, including image size, frame rate, and compression method, but a medium-small image without too much flicker can use as little as 3MB per minute.

These formats for sound or video are not part of the HTML specification. That means that a computer has to have Windows Media Player or QuickTime software installed to play them. They play directly in the browser only if the right **plug-in** has been installed. The plug-ins, in versions for just about any kind of computer, are available free from microsoft.com and apple.com.

Copyright Issues

It's illegal to put copyrighted music or video on your Web page without the owner's permission, and that pretty much rules out anything you can get at a music or movie store or over the air. Using even very short clips can be **copyright infringement**, no matter how appropriate they are to your pages. For more information, check loc.gov—the Library of Congress's Web site. They administer copyright law.

Unfortunately, the large music companies have convinced some Web hosts that all MP3 files are illegal copies of copyrighted music. They're not, of course. You can make perfectly legal MP3s of your daughter playing songs she wrote, or Grandpa talking about his war experiences. But these Web hosts refuse to let users post them, basically because they're scared.

The workaround is to turn your sound recordings into Windows Media Player or QuickTime files instead. These file formats can be used to shrink audio-only files as well as ones with video, and—as of now—don't make Web hosts nervous.

Creating Sound and Video Files

Sorry to say, this book isn't about how to make movies or sound files. There are lots of good ones that will tell you how and what to do. I liked *QuickTime for the Web: For Windows and Macintosh, Third Edition* (QuickTime Developer Series), but there are many others too. Software such as Apple's iMovie for the Mac is a good way to edit your movies, and it's included in Apple's OS X packages. Windows users, check out Magix Movie Edit Pro 2004 (at www.magix.com). It's under $100 and has some nice features for **video editing**. Microsoft offers Movie Maker software as a free download to Windows XP users. It's simple to use with **drag-and-drop features** and allows you to save to video tape for playback in a camera or VCR. Movie Maker is compatible with third-party software that allows you to make your movies into DVDs too.

Putting Your Audio/Video Creations on a Web Page

Better page-building software lets you select a **compressed movie** or **sound** on your desktop, upload it to your host, and generate the proper link. All the consumer-oriented software programs do this for pictures, but not necessarily for movies or sound.

If the wizard or software you're using doesn't let you select movies or sound, you have to follow a few extra steps:

1. Find the movie or sound file on your computer and upload it to your host. Most hosts have site-management tools that help you do this.

2. Decide where on your Web page you want that file to appear. Note what text is near it.

3. In the wizard or page-building software you're using, activate the Manual Edit feature. This shows you the page's source code and lets you type additional tags into it. Find the beginning or end of the text you noted in step 2.

4. Make sure the cursor is right next to the text, and not inside angle brackets. Enter the following: `<EMBED SRC="myFilm.mov" WIDTH="240" HEIGHT="195" CONTROLS="SMALLCONSOLE" AUTOSTART="FALSE">`.

The angle brackets (also known as greater-than and lesser-than) are important; they tell the Web browser that this is an HTML tag. You can get those characters by holding Shift and pressing the comma or period key. Of course, you should replace *myFilm.mov* with the name of whatever file you've just uploaded. Capitalization is important—it must match the actual filename exactly. So is the three-letter filename extension after the period. Windows users might have to manually view their file extensions. Choose View→Folder Options. Open the View tab and uncheck Hide File Extensions for Known File Types in your computer to see that extension. (In Windows XP, look in Folder Tools→Folder Options after you open a folder.)

`WIDTH` and `HEIGHT` indicate the size of the movie or sound player in pixels. You have to experiment to find the best numbers for your movie. If you change `Autostart="False"` to `Autostart="True"`, the movie or sound starts playing automatically when the page is loaded.

Finally, upload your new source code. Go to your Web site and see how it looks. It'll probably take some experimentation to make everything work perfectly.

Creating CD-ROMs and DVD-ROMs

If you have a **CD-ROM** or **DVD-ROM burner**, either built-in or plugged into your computer, you can make multiple copies of your scrapbooks, and send them to family and friends. The most reliable way to create them is to use what's now an old friend: HTML. That way, anyone with a Web browser can view them. Making a CD or DVD is often referred to as *burning*, because the mechanism in the drive uses a laser beam to inscribe the data on the blank disk. When you take it out of the drive, it's often still warm from the process.

If you want your work to be seen and enjoyed, be considerate. Organize your digital files before you burn the CD-ROM. Give the disk a title too. Don't make your viewers face a bewildering collection of files, as in Figure 11.6.

Your CD-ROM will be a lot more inviting if you organize it. Figure 11.7 shows how a properly organized CD-ROM should looks.

note In case you ever wondered, ROM is an acronym for read-only memory. After it's recorded, the CD-ROMs or DVD-ROMs can't be erased or reused. Thus, whatever you put on them is going to stay there. That's also why they're good for backing up your important files and photos. (You *do* make frequent backups, don't you? Many things can go wrong with computer hard drives, and a backup CD-ROM is cheap insurance.)

Figure 11.6

Faced with this mess, most folks would click at random or just give up.

Figure 11.7

Isn't this much easier to figure out?

The following are some easy steps to help organize the disk:

1. Before building the pages, **create a folder** on your desktop with a descriptive name such as Vacation Scrapbook or Lisa's First Year. Then create two folders inside it, one called **images** and the other **pages**. (If you or your viewers are using much earlier versions of the Windows operating system, instead of XP, be sure to use legal filenames, omitting spaces and most punctuation. Macs don't have that restriction.) Be sure to include those "dot-three" filename extensions, too, so your files are compatible with computers of all ages and operating systems, PC or Mac.

2. **Drag all the photos** you plan to use into the **images folder**. These can be copies if you want to keep the originals somewhere else, or you can move them there while building the scrapbook and then put them back after you've burned the CD-ROM.

3. Start building the **CD's home page**, using your favorite Web design tool. Give it a name such as welcome.htm and save it in the first folder you created in step 1 (perhaps Vacation Scrapbook).

4. When you select images to place on this page, be sure you choose them from the images folder you created in step 1—not from anywhere else in your computer. Your CD-ROM scrapbook page should link to images on the CD-ROM, rather than your computer. Your friends and family won't have your computer when they look at the finished CD-ROM scrapbook, and you don't want them to see **broken links**.

5. You can create **additional pages** that will be linked to the **Welcome page**. Save them in the pages folder, so they don't clutter the CD-ROM.

6. When you think the **electronic scrapbook** is complete, check it by opening welcome.htm in your browser. Make sure all the links work and the images display as they should. Check your spelling in any titles, captions, or journal entries, and if a link isn't working, check its spelling as well. Ensure that all the quotes and brackets are in their proper places. Save your .htm page.

7. Launch your **CD-ROM burning software**, and start a new CD with the same descriptive name you chose in step 1. Drag the welcome.htm file and the images and pages folders to it. You're now ready to burn as many copies of your digital scrapbook as you want.

There are just two things to be aware of. First, if your page-building software asks you to choose between **relative addressing** and **absolute addressing**, use relative. Otherwise, the links might not work. If it doesn't ask, don't worry about it. The software automatically does the right thing for your page.

Second, if your CD-ROM burning software lets you choose between **Windows and Macintosh formats**, select Windows—even if you know some of your friends have Macs. All modern Macs can open Windows CDs, but some Windows machines can't open Mac discs.

As a final touch, you might want to make a **custom label** and/or **jewel case insert** for your CD. You can find precut blanks at your local computer or office supply store and matching templates on the Web. I use Avery 8696, which has a CD label, CD box insert, and spine labels all on one sheet for easy printing. There's even a **downloadable template** for it at www.avery.com. Even though you can print nice round CD labels, don't try to label the disc without a special alignment tool: If it goes down wrinkled or off-center, the CD might not play. The label alignment tool is available wherever the labels are sold. You can also write on the top of a CD/DVD with a Sharpie permanent marker. Not as pretty, but it works.

Summary—What You Need to Remember

The stuff in this chapter is very technical, compared to the contents of the previous chapters. If there were things you didn't understand, ask a computer-savvy friend or family member for help. I am not a bit ashamed to admit that my husband takes care of my Web pages. He also helped out a lot with this chapter. (Thanks, Jay!)

What I really want you to remember is that wonderful things are possible, on the Web and on the computer, as well as on paper. You can take your scrapping to new levels with the techniques you've learned here. Go for it!

Above all else, HAVE FUN!!!

Appendices

A   Other Uses for Your Pictures

B   Glossary of Computer Graphics and Scrapbooking Terms

C   While You're Wandering the Web...

Other Uses for Your Pictures

You have all these beautiful scrapbooks now, and because you used the computer and a digital camera or scanner, you also have all the pictures digitized and ready to use for something else. What are the possibilities? Let's start with some simple projects.

Iron-On Photos

You can buy **iron-on paper** for inkjet printers. It's simple to use. Your regular inkjet ink is fine for fabric printing. All you do to print on a white or light-colored cotton or cotton blend fabric is reverse the original photo, either in your graphics program or as part of the page setup when you get ready to print. Then you print onto the special paper. Figure A.1 shows this step.

Iron your fabric and put a piece of cardboard under it so the ink won't bleed through and damage anything. Place the transfer paper on the fabric, design-side down, and iron according to the iron-on transfer package directions. Time and heat might vary with the material or brand of transfer paper, so I can't give you a definite direction. When it's done, let it cool and then peel off the transfer paper. Enjoy. Figure A.2 shows my finished T-shirt. You can also buy **transfer paper** to print pictures on a dark background, such as a black or dark blue T-shirt. These work a bit differently, so be sure to follow the manufacturer's instructions carefully.

Figure A.1

The transfer is ready to iron on. Note the backward lettering.

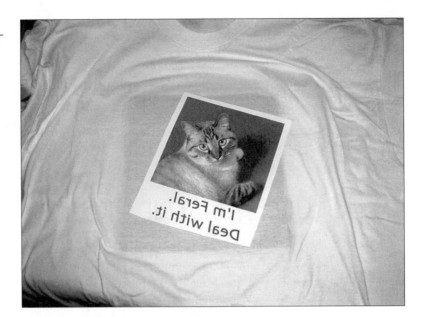

Figure A.2

He's definitely got "catitude."

Pictures can go on anything from a t-shirt, tote bag, or hat, to placemats, napkins, and curtains… Use your imagination. How about pictures of your prize-winning roses at the four corners of a linen tablecloth? Smaller photos on matching napkins? How about making a family photo quilt? Iron your photos onto squares of sturdy cotton cloth and alternate them with squares of brightly colored fabrics. Then, quilt as usual for a family heirloom that you'll be proud to display. In Figure A.3, I'm making beige linen napkins to go with my already decorated tablecloth. The transfers look a little different on a colored and textured background, but I think they work very well.

Figure A.3

Because these were small, I printed them four to a page and cut the transfers apart for easier ironing.

Printing on Fabric

If you have some **smooth all-cotton fabric** and a bit of patience, you can print directly on the fabric using your inkjet printer. First you have to prepare it. Cut the fabric to 8 1/2×11 inches, and either cut a piece of **freezer paper** to the same size, or use a full-sheet adhesive label. (You use these to stiffen the fabric so it can pass through the printer.) Freezer paper works well because it has a waxy coating that melts as you heat it, holding the fabric in place. Pretreat the fabric with an **ink fixative**. The best is Jenkins Bubble Jet Set 2000, which you can order from the Web site (www.cjenkinscompany.com) or find at some of the larger craft stores. Follow the directions for pretreating and drying, and then iron the fabric to remove any wrinkles.

If you're using freezer paper, place the fabric face down on a firm surface, like a sturdy table, kitchen countertop, or board, lightly padded with a couple of layers of old sheeting or something similar. An ironing board is too soft. Put the paper, shiny side down, on top of the fabric. Starting in the center, iron toward the edges with a hot iron, until the paper is bonded to the cloth. Use a dry iron and the cotton setting. Then turn the sheet over and iron out any wrinkles. Trim any uneven edges to prevent the fabric from snagging in your printer's guide rollers. Brush the fabric with a lint brush and you're ready to print on it.

If you are using adhesive labels, make sure to use the kind for printers and not for copiers. They use heavier paper that holds the fabric better. Be careful to avoid bubbles as you apply the peeled label to the fabric back. Use a cool iron or a roller if necessary to get rid of any wrinkles or bubbles.

If all this sounds like too much work, Jenkins also stocks **prepared fabric sheets** at a very reasonable price. A 10-pack of letter-size cotton sheets is less than 17 dollars. And here's a news flash. I just came back from my friendly local computer store (part of a national chain) where I bought a pack of **printable cotton fabric sheets**. They're about 3 dollars a sheet, so they're not cheap, but an enormous time-saver. They have an iron-on coating on the back, so all you do is print and press. Unfortunately, none of these comes in anything other than plain white cotton. If you want to print on something more interesting, you have to use the labels or freezer-paper backing.

In Figure A.4, I've printed a photo from my Nova Scotia trip onto a piece of cotton, and I'm getting ready to iron it onto a pillow cover. I can hold it in place with straight pins or a bit of tape, which I then remove after I iron the center part. After the picture's applied, I glue some moss green velvet ribbon around the edges of the photo to serve as a frame, and to hide the edges. The **iron-on fusing tape** called Stitch Witchery is very good for this, and less messy than the hot glue gun. Corners of the ribbon frame can either be mitered (cut at an angle) or hidden with a decorative button or embroidered rosette.

Figure A.4

Soon I will have a useful and pretty souvenir.

Printing on Frosting

Imagine a birthday cake with a photo of the guest of honor on it! Or cookies for baby's christening with her picture? There are lots of places that can turn your photos into edible images on **sugar sheets**. Last time I checked, even the local supermarket bakery could do so. If you've tasted supermarket cakes, though, you might prefer to bake your own. This, too, is feasible. Many online companies accept your emailed photos and send back an edible sheet printed with your photo in edible inks. You frost the top of the cake with flat white icing and place the sheet on it. Maybe add a few rosettes around the edges, and wait for the compliments. The frosting sheets are even kosher! Here's a cake I designed for a friend (see Figure A.5).

Figure A.5
Yummy! (Photo courtesy of Ali Williams.)

If you really want to get into this and have one of several specific models of Canon printer, you can buy the special, **edible inkjet ink cartridges** and **edible image sheets** and **nozzle cleaner**, and start your own cake business. For more information, visit www.photofrost.com. They can also make the icing sheets for you.

Trinket Boxes and Other Tchotchkes

Tchotchke is one of my favorite words. It's Yiddish for "little bits of decorative things." Some people buy their tchotchkes from places like the Franklin Mint or the Lillian Vernon catalog. I like to make my own. In Figure A.6, you can see a little **memory box** I put together. It has a photo of my pretty part-Siamese boy cat, Ari, on top.

I bought a simple papier-mache box at one of the craft stores, and covered it with bits of colored tissue and some torn Mulberry paper, all applied with thinned out Elmer's glue. (I use a scant tablespoon of water with a generous tablespoon of glue.) You brush the glue on the box first, and then slap on some paper and brush another layer of glue over the top. Don't worry about gluing the top onto the box. You can open it when it's dry by cutting along the seam with a razor blade or X-acto knife.

I tried printing the photo on Mulberry paper, but the printer didn't accept it. So I used a print on ordinary paper, which was still translucent after adding lots of glue. As a final touch, I applied some rub-on butterflies. Now I use it to keep track of the rabies tags, and of any medicines the vet prescribes for any of my three cats.

Figure A.6

The butterfly box.

Stationery, Calendars, and Cards

Many word processors and crafts programs, such as American Greetings Scrapbooks & More, include preformatted calendars. You can also find **calendar templates** online. Avery (www.avery.com) has a set in their Home Corner section, and there are many styles at the Calendar Template Web page (http://www.printablecalendar.ca/). Why not make your own personalized **business cards**, **note pads**, and **stationery**? You can have business cards, paper, envelopes, and note pads made up from your artwork at any instant print shop, usually for very little money, unless you choose a particularly expensive paper stock. Figure A.7 shows a few simple examples.

Figure A.7

The calendar template came from Avery. The other pieces were designed in Photoshop Elements.

If you just need a few business cards at a time, and not a thousand, you can buy blank business cards at most office supply stores. These come in standard letter size sheets with micro perforations so you can run them through your inkjet printer and then separate them easily and without shaggy edges. These are available in many colors and with preprinted designs as well as blank, so you can customize to suit your home business or your personality.

The End, or the Beginning?

In these pages, I've shown you just a few of the literally millions of possibilities. Now, it's up to you to put your computer and your visual skills to work. How many crafts can you combine in one piece? How many new ways can you think of to show off your favorite photos? The only limit is your own creativity.

If you have questions—or great ideas that you want to show off—you can always reach me at author@graphicalcat.com. Please send your files zipped or stuffed, make them as small as possible, and mention *Digital Memories* in the subject line.

Glossary of Computer Graphics and Scrapbooking Terms

Acid Migration   The transfer of acid from one source to another on your page through physical contact or acidic vapors. Placing acidic items, such as newspaper clippings, on a page can pass the acid from the source to your photo if you don't take steps to buffer and prevent this.

Acid-Free Paper   Paper that resists deterioration from age, and won't destroy items such as photos attached to it. Also called alkaline paper, archival paper, neutral pH paper, or scrapbook paper. Also, paper and other materials that have a pH balance between 7.0 and 7.5 are considered acid-free. Acid is neutralized during manufacturing. Acid-free papers and other scrapbooking supplies are labeled as such. Newsprint and construction paper are not acid- or lignin-free! (See also *Buffering* and *Lignin*.)

Acids   Acids weaken the cellulose in paper, which leads to its break down, causing discoloration and disintegration. Acid turns litmus paper red. To test the acid content of paper materials, purchase a pH test pen from a scrapbook, office, or archival supplier. A small mark in a corner will reveal acid content. (See also *pH* and *pH Testing Pen*.)

Acrobat   Acrobat is part of a set of applications developed by Adobe to create and view PDF files. Acrobat is used to create the PDF files, and the freeware Acrobat Reader is used to read the PDF files.

Adhesive The glue used to secure items in the scrapbook, including tape or glue. For scrapbooking, you should always use acid-free and lignin-free adhesives. Adhesives used in scrapbooking include double-sided tape, photo corners, photo splits, acid-free spray adhesive, and glue sticks. Rubber cement is an adhesive, but is not archival and not recommended for scrapbooking.

Airbrush Pen-shaped tool that sprays a fine mist of ink or paint to retouch photos and create continuous-tone illustrations. In most graphics programs, the paintbrush tool also can serve as an airbrush.

Album An album is a book typically used to protect and store photographs and other memorabilia items, also sometimes called a scrapbook album. (See also *Brag Book, Scrapbook,* and *Strap-Hinge Album.*)

Aliasing Aliasing occurs when a computer monitor, printer, or graphics file does not have a high enough resolution to represent a graphic image or text. An aliased image has jagged edges as if it were made from bricks, and is often said to have the "jaggies." (See also *Anti-Aliasing.*)

Alignment The positioning of a block of text. Text can be placed to the left, right, or center of a page, and can be justified, so both margins are even. Otherwise, type set flush left is also ragged right, and type set flush right is ragged left.

Alkaline The opposite of an acid; substances having a pH greater than 7.0 (between 7.5 and 14). (See also *pH.*)

Analogous Colors Any three colors that are side by side on a 12-part color wheel (one that includes tertiary colors), such as yellow-green, yellow, and yellow-orange. (See also *Color Wheel, Complementary Colors,* and *Tertiary Colors.*)

Anti-Aliasing The appearance of smoothing or blending the transition of pixels in an image. Anti-aliasing a raster graphic or text adds shading along the curves and diagonals, which the human eye interprets as a smooth edge rather than a serrated one.

Archival Products rated to last without changing chemically or fading for many years. There are currently no organizations defining or policing this rating, so check the manufacturer's reputation before you invest.

Bevel Adding a beveled effect to a graphic image gives the image a raised appearance. You do this by applying highlight colors and shadow colors to the inside and outside edges.

Binder A notebook cover, commonly found in office supply stores, with rings or clamps for holding and protecting sheets of paper. To use a binder as a scrapbook, make sure that it is not made with PVC or vinyl plastics. Also binder's board, a thick paperboard used to add stiffness to book bindings. Most binder's board has a high lignin content, although acid-free and lignin-free board is available. (See also *Acid-Free Paper, Lignin,* and *Three-Ring Binder.*)

Bitmap (.bmp) A graphic image stored as a specific arrangement of screen dots; the opposite of vector graphics. Web graphics are often saved as bitmap images. Also known as raster graphics. Common types of bitmap graphics are GIF, JPEG, Photoshop (PSD), PCX, TIFF, Macintosh Paint, Microsoft Paint, PNG, FAX formats, and TGA.

Bleed or Bleeding Edge   When a page or a cover design extends to and off the edge of the paper, it is called a bleed.

Bleed-Proof/Resistant   Adhesives and colorants that do not soak (or bleed) through to the reverse side of the material to which they are applied (such as a sheet of paper). This term also refers to coated or specially finished paper stock that prevents substances from soaking through to the opposite side.

Blow-Up   An enlargement made from an original image, normally used with graphic images or photographs.

BMP (Windows Bitmap)   The standard filename for Windows Bitmap graphics files, represented by the extension .bmp. (See also *File Extension*.)

Bond Paper   Category of paper commonly used for writing, printing, and photo-copying. Also called business paper, typing paper, copy paper, and writing paper.

Book Paper   General term describing a category of paper suitable for books, magazines, catalogs, advertising, and general printing needs. Book paper is divided into uncoated (also called *offset paper*) and coated paper (also called art paper, enamel paper, gloss paper, or slick paper).

Bookmarks   When using an Internet browser, electronic bookmarks are used to bring you to a Web site or other site you want to return to. The Netscape Navigator browser saves bookmarks in a file you can recall at any time. Microsoft Internet Explorer uses the term favorites instead of bookmarks for the same concept.

Brag Book   A small scrapbook or photo album that is easily transported. It usually contains photographs of children, pets, or grandchildren.

Browser   Short for Web browser. Software used to locate and access Web pages by interpreting hypertext and hyperlinks. The two most common browsers are Netscape Navigator and Microsoft Internet Explorer. Web pages often appear differently when viewed using different browsers, depending on the brand and version number of the browser intended to view them in. (See also *HTML*.)

Buffering   Process of adding alkaline substances to paper materials after production, removing the acids to protect the product against acid migration in the future. The most common buffers used are magnesium bicarbonate and calcium carbonate. (See also *Acid-Free Paper*, *Archival*, and *Lignin*.)

Calligraphy   Hand-written lettering created by using a quill pen, fountain pen, or other split metal nib that carries ink to the paper. Calligraphy is popularly used to decorate formal invitations to weddings, scrapbook pages, and photo albums.

Caption   The line or lines of text that provide information identifying a picture or illustration.

Card stock   Sturdy, solid colored, printed, or textured heavy papers commonly used in catalog covers, brochure covers, and business cards as well as in scrapbooking and rubber stamping.

Chalking   Using special artist's chalks to enhance edges and cutouts on scrapbook pages.

Circle Cutter   A tool designed solely for the purpose of cutting a perfect circle in different sizes.

Clip Art Simple graphics, both in color and in grayscale, that you can find online and in computer programs to print out and use. Clip art began as generic illustrations sold to newspapers and advertising designers, who would literally clip the picture they needed to drop into their layout. Computers, the Internet, and CD-ROMs have made finding the clip art you need for a specific theme very easy.

CMYK Abbreviation for cyan, magenta, yellow, and key (black), the four offset printing process colors.

Color Wheel The basic tool of color theory, a color wheel is a circle showing the relationship between colors in a logically arranged sequence of hues. Red, yellow, and blue are primary colors. They are separated from one another on a color wheel by the secondary colors. Tertiary colors are formed by mixing the secondary colors, and so on. (See also *Analogous Colors, Complementary Colors, Primary Colors, Secondary Colors,* and *Tertiary Colors.*)

Collage An artistic composition of materials, objects, or photographs layered together on a surface, often with a unifying theme or color. Also the method of combining borrowed images with original elements to create a new artistic creation. A montage of photographs is a type of collage. (See also *Montage.*)

Complementary Colors Any two colors that are directly opposite each other on any color wheel, such as red and green or orange and blue. Complementary colors create strong contrast when used together in images. (See also *Analogous Colors* and *Color Wheel.*)

Composition In graphic design, the arrangement of type, graphics, and other elements on the page.

Compression A method of storing data in a format that saves disk storage space or takes less time to transmit over a network such as the Internet. JPEGs are compressed bitmap graphics files. (See also *Lossless Compression* and *Lossy Compression.*)

Contrast The range of tones in an image from the brightest white to the darkest black. High-contrast photos have more pure blacks and whites. Low-contrast photos have many shades of gray but few strong highlights or shadows. Also called *contrast ratio.*

Copyright Copyright laws protect the originator of material to prevent commercial use without express permission or acknowledgement of the originator.

Corner Punch Similar to the corner rounder but these come in many decorative styles when you want something fancier than a rounded edge. Victorian, Snowflakes, Flowers, and Lace are examples of some different styles.

Corner Rounder A punch specially designed to round the 45-degree angles of photograph corners or paper.

Crop Trimming the photo to highlight a certain area or to remove unwanted background, or changing the photograph's shape. (See also *Cropping.*)

Cropping The elimination of parts of a photograph that are not required. Cropping can improve composition, and allows the remaining parts of the image to be enlarged to fill the space. Also, a scrapbooking workshop or party where people work on their own or a group project.

Cutout A photo from which the background has been removed to produce a silhouette.

Dauber   A kind of small stamp pad that can be dabbed onto a stamp to apply ink.

Dauber Duo   A dauber applicator with a different color or shade on each end.

De-acidification   The act of removing acid from newspaper clippings, certificates, and other scrapbook items using such products as Archival Mist, one brand of spray that neutralizes acid content.

Decorative Ruler   A normal ruler with a special edge used in designing scrapbook pages.

Decorative Scissors   Any kind of specialty scissors that cuts a decorative pattern when the blades are applied to paper. Some examples are Zigzag, Deckle, Victorian, and Waves.

Desktop Publishing   Technique of using a personal computer to design images and pages, and assemble type and graphics, and then using a laser or inkjet printer to output the assembled pages onto paper.

Die Cut   Shapes or letters cut from card stock by special machines. You can purchase precut paper designs or the cutting machine and a selection of dies to make your own.

Digital Image   Visual data stored electronically, as on a computer hard drive, rather than an image that is produced chemically or physically, as a photograph or a drawing. Digital images can be made using digital cameras, video recording devices, scanners, and other input devices that capture and store images without film. Digital images can be manipulated using computer software and transferred over the Internet. (See also *Scanner.*)

Dither   To create the illusion of new shades or tints of color by alternating the pattern of black and white dots within the image. For example, photos printed in newspapers are dithered. In computer graphics, dithering can occur if the color palette is too limited to show all of the shades and tints of color within an image. GIF files, limited to a 256-color palette, often show dithering. (See also *GIF.*)

Dot   A single point; the smallest identifiable part of an image. A dot is not synonymous with a pixel. (See *Dots per Inch, Pixel,* and *Resolution.*)

Dots per Inch   Measure of the resolution of an image. Abbreviated DPI. (See also *Dot* and *Resolution.*)

Drop Shadow   A black or gray patch "dropped" in place behind an object, photo, or type to give it depth by creating an apparent shadow behind the item.

Duotone   The application of two colors to provide a richer sepia or other colored tone than a single-color image, usually grayscale, can provide. A good duotone image can simulate a wider range of the color spectrum than two colors used separately.

Embellishment   Any extra decorative items used to enhance scrapbook pages. Examples include stickers, die-cut paper designs, punches, buttons, raffia, ribbon, and so on.

Embossing   Creating the effect of a relief image (actual or imagined). Embossing a graphic image adds dimension to it by making the image appear as if it were carved as a projection from a flat background. Also, creating actual raised edges or relief textures on paper by applying heat or pressure to the paper. (See also *Bevel.*)

Embossing Powder/Ink   Embossing powder is sprinkled on stamped images, and then heated using a craft heat gun to melt and create raised lines.

Encapsulation   Sealing memorabilia between two sheets of stable transparent polyester film (not to be confused with lamination) for the purpose of protection from handling, moisture, and acid migration. No adhesive is applied to the items being encapsulated. (See also *Acid Migration, De-Acidification,* and *Polyester.*)

Ephemera   Objects that have special meaning to you, but will not last without preservation. Ticket stubs, matchbook covers, postcards, and other souvenirs and memorabilia are considered ephemera.

Export   To save a file in a different format. For example, many Adobe Photoshop files (PSD) are exported to GIF or JPEG format for use on the Web. (See also *Import.*)

Eyelet   A round metal stud with a hole, applied by punching a hole in the page, inserting the two parts of the eyelet and flattening the back half of the eyelet. Used to durably attach objects or layers of paper or card stock to a scrapbook page, or sometimes as a decoration. Available in various sizes at sewing, craft, and hardware stores. Also called *grommets.*

Feathering   Feathering the edge of a graphic image gradually dissipates the edge, making the edge look blurry.

File Extension   Three or four letters separated from a filename by a ".", called a period or dot. Most computers use a dot-three standard, meaning that the file extension has three letters, such as .jpg, .gif, .htm, and .bmp. The dot-four extension is less common and not compatible with all computers or Web browsers. Examples include .jpeg and .html.

Fiskars   A very reliable scissors brand. They make both regular and decorative scissors and shears in many sizes. (See also *Decorative Scissors.*)

Flush Left   Text aligned along the left margin.

Flush Right   Text aligned along the right margin.

Focal Point   An element of page design where lines converge. The eye is naturally drawn to the focal point of an image or a page design.

Font   A complete set of characters in a particular size, design, and style. This includes the letter set, the number set, and all of the special character and diacritical marks you get by pressing the Shift, Option, or Command/Control keys. For example, Times New Roman Bold Italic is one font, and Times New Roman Bold is another font in the Times New Roman typeface family. (See also *Typeface.*)

Freeware   Copyrighted software distributed for free by the author. (See also *Shareware.*)

FTP   Abbreviation for File Transfer Protocol, the standard format on the Internet for exchanging files. An FTP Web site works the same way as HTTP for transferring Web pages from a server to a user's Web browser. FTP is commonly used to download from or upload to a server using an Internet connection. One example is to upload your scrapbook Web page to a server, so that you can share it with your family over the Internet. (See also *HTML.*)

GIF   Originally developed by CompuServe for use on its proprietary World Wide Web online service, GIF has become a popular file format for displaying graphics on Web sites. Pronounced "jiff" or "giff" (hard g), GIF is the abbreviation for graphics interchange format. Using the file extension .gif, a GIF is a bitmap graphics document that uses lossless compression to store image data. Because it uses a limited 256-color palette, GIF is better suited to simple logos and images rather than photographs.

Glow   The opposite of a shadow in that it creates a highlight around an image. A high radiance creates a soft, subtle glow and a low radiance creates a hard, bright glow, such as a neon glow.

Gradient   A gradient is a gradual transition of colors. Many metallic images are gradients. Web images that use gradient fills as a special effect need to be saved in a JPEG rather than a GIF format, to preserve the subtle transition without dithering. (See also *Dither, GIF,* and *JPEG.*)

Graphic Backgrounds   The bottom-most layer on a Web page, usually with either a design or color that highlights the copy above it. A small graphic can be tiled to create a background texture for a Web page.

Graphic Design   Arrangement of type and visual elements along with specifications for paper, ink colors, and printing processes that, when combined, convey a visual message.

Graphics   Visual elements that supplement type to make printed messages more clear or interesting.

Grayscale   An application of levels of black ink (for print) or shades of the color black (for the screen) that simulate a range of tones between black and white. Grayscale images have no hue (color). In print design, a grayscale graphic image appears to be black, white, and shades of gray, but only uses the black ink in your printer. Grayscaling assigns each dot within an image a specific shade of gray, using between 16 and 256 shades. Basically, the more levels the better, but with correspondingly greater memory requirements.

Grid   A systematic division of a page into areas to enable designers to ensure consistency. The grid acts as a measuring guide and shows text, illustrations, and page sizes.

Heat gun   Also called a thermal or embossing gun. A heat gun is a hobby tool that heats without producing air, unlike a hair dryer, which would blow your project away.

Heirloom   Used in regard to many aspects of scrapbooking. It can mean an old-fashioned looking page, or an actual antique photograph or object.

Highlights   Lightest portions of a photograph or piece of artwork, as compared to midtones and shadows.

Hinge Album   A plastic strap binding allows these albums to expand. These tend to lay more flat than the post bound albums. (See also *Post Bound Album* and *Strap-Hinge Album.*)

HTML Abbreviation for Hypertext Markup Language; a cross-platform page-layout system for creating Web pages, including copy, images, sounds, frames, animation, and more.

Hue The actual color of an object. Hue is measured as a location on a color wheel, expressed in degrees. Hue is also understood as the names of specific colors, such as blue, red, yellow, and so on.

Import To use data created by another program, such as a JPEG or GIF file. Many programs are capable of importing (reformatting) graphics in a variety of file formats. The opposite of export. (See also *Export*.)

Inkjet Printing Method of printing by spraying droplets of ink on to a sheet of paper or other print media. Inkjet printers are generally less expensive than laser printers. The print produced by an inkjet printer can be smudged or damaged by water unless special inks are purchased.

Japanese Papers Especially thin and strong art papers made in Japan from long fibers, such as mulberry. They are largely handmade, the fibers pulped by hand rather than acid; the lengths of the fibers give the paper exceptional wear capability. The edges tear with an attractive feathered effect. (See also *Mulberry Paper*.)

Journal entry Writings included in a scrapbook or journal describing a mood, feeling, scene, or event.

Journaling Process of writing journal entries.

JPEG (Joint Photographic Experts Group) The JPEG file format uses a method of lossy compression that reduces image file size by selectively reducing the amount of detail contained in the image and by transforming the image data into a format that is better suited for compression. Images with fewer details compress extremely well, whereas pictures with a high degree of random detail do not compress as well, or suffer some degree of image degradation. The relative amount of detail removed can be specified in most applications. At the default value of 75, relatively little picture degradation takes place, but a significant amount of compression is obtained. At lower values, you experience still better compression, but with a marked loss of image quality. JPEG images support up to 16 million colors and are typically RGB color or grayscale (256 shades of gray). The default file extension for JPEG files is .jpg. (See also *Grayscale*, *Lossy Compression*, and *RGB*.)

Justify The alignment of text along both the left and right margins. This is achieved by adjusting the spacing between the words and characters as necessary so that each line of text finishes at the same point.

K In computer terms, K or KB stands for Kilobyte, 1,000 bytes of data, as in 256K of RAM (Random Access Memory). In print design, the K stands for the ink color black in the CMYK (Cyan, Magenta, Yellow, and Black) color process. (See also *CMYK*.)

Kerning The horizontal spacing between the letters in a word. Some pairs of letters, such as AV, To, and Ta, look better and are easier to read when the space between them is closed up.

Laminate A thin transparent plastic coating applied to paper or board to provide protection and give it a glossy finish.

Lamination   Sealing an object between translucent plastic pieces for the same reasons as encapsulation, although lamination is not as safe for some photos and other scrapbook items because of heat exposure and pressure.

Landscape   Any page orientation in which the width used is greater than the height. Also used to indicate the horizontal orientation of tables or illustrations that are printed sideways.

Layout   A sketch of a page for printing showing the position of text and illustrations, exploring color options, and giving general instructions before final design decisions are made. Layouts also refer to groups of scrapbook pages that go together. Also the process of designing a page by placing elements in a harmonious and logical pattern. (See also *Graphic Design*.)

Latex Pages   Usually found in magnetic albums. They discolor anything that is placed on them in a very short period of time. Do not use for scrapbooking.

Leading   (Pronounced to rhyme with "sledding".) The vertical spacing between lines of text. In early typesetting, metal strips made of lead were placed between lines of metal type, thus the name.

Letraset   A proprietary name for rub-down or dry-transfer lettering used in page titles, and so on.

Library Picture   A picture taken from an existing photo or clip art library and not especially commissioned.

Light Box   A small light table used for viewing negatives or embossing.

Lignin   Substance found in trees that holds cellulose fibers together. Acid-free papers have most lignin removed; ground wood paper such as newsprint contains lignin.

Lossless Compression   In graphics programming, lossless compression refers to a data compression technique whereby the file quality is preserved and no data is lost. Lossless compression can reduce file size to about half of its original size. Lossy compression, by contrast, eliminates some data but can further decrease file size.

Lossy Compression   A term coined by graphics programmers to refer to a technique of shrinking file sizes by giving away some precision of detail. JPEG is an example of a file that is compressed this way. By reducing the so-called quality of a picture when you save it, you can make the file size smaller. Many photos can take some loss of fine detail before it becomes noticeable.

Magnetic Album   A widely available and inexpensive type of photo album not to be used for scrapbooking. It uses a special adhesive to hold photographs in place and creates static for the plastic page cover to cling to. These deteriorate over time and damage photos.

Mat or Matting   Placing a piece of acid-free paper behind the photo to accentuate it or act as a buffer between the photo and the page. Also, a cardboard frame around a piece of art.

Memorabilia   Anything that reminds you of an historical or family event or time in your life. Artwork, certificates, matchbooks, postcards, tickets, badges and medals, and brochures are all memorabilia.

Memory Book   Another name for a scrapbook.

Montage   A single image formed by assembling several images. A panorama is one kind of montage. Another type of montage is a scrapbook page formed entirely of photographs collaged or layered together. (See also *Collage*.)

Mount   To adhere a photo or other memorabilia to a piece of paper or card stock, such as the background page in a scrapbook. Also the wood or plastic handle of a rubber stamp.

Mounting Squares   A small square of double-sided tape-like adhesive generally dispensed from boxes.

Mulberry Paper   A type of handmade paper with long fibers that create a feathered edge when torn. Often acid-free due to a handmade process rather than an acid pulp production. Available in many textures, weights, and colors. (See also *Japanese Papers*.)

Neon Glow   Type of glow on a graphic image that gives the appearance of neon lighting.

Neutral   Having a pH of between 7.0 and 7.5; neither acidic nor alkaline.

Neutral Gray   Gray with no hue or cast, that is, neither warm nor cool.

Nonpermanent Mounting   Using photo frames, photo corners, or pocket pages to hold photographs and other items on or near a scrapbook page without permanently adhering them. (See also *Photo Corners* and *Pocket Page*.)

Opal Laminate   This is the film that is stuck to the top of opal stickers. It has a pearl look to it.

Origami   The Japanese craft of paper folding. Sometimes used to add embellishments to pages.

Outline   In graphic design, tracing the outer edge of text or a graphic image. If the outline is feathered, the effect is generally referred to as a glow.

Overalls   A shortcut used in scrapbook page layout, overalls are printed on card stock with a title and borders or pictures to cut out. It's an easy way to decorate a page because it comes with everything but your own photos. (See also *Page Toppers*.)

Page Protector   A PVC-free (photo-safe) plastic sleeve or cover used to protect and display your scrapbook pages. They can be sleeves that fasten directly into your album or covers that slide over your page, the latter are especially useful in spiral bound albums. Page protectors can be top- or side-loading and are generally available in 8.5"×11" or 12"×12" page sizes. Top loading page protectors are best for pages with glitter, beads, or anything that might come loose.

Page Toppers   Like overalls, a product that can be used as-is or cut up to create a title and die-cut paper accents on a scrapbook page. (See also *Overalls*.)

Paper Piecing   Die cuts and decorative punches used in multiple layers together to create an image for your scrapbook page.

PDF   Stands for Portable Document Format. Created by Adobe Systems in its software program Adobe Acrobat as a universal file format. Files can be downloaded via the Web and viewed page by page, provided the user's computer has the necessary plug-in, Acrobat Reader, which can be downloaded free from Adobe's own Web site. (See also *Acrobat*.)

Perforated Punches   Precut shapes that can be used as embellishments on a scrapbook page simply by punching out the precut perforations. (See also *Embellishment, Overalls,* and *Page Toppers.*)

pH   The measure used for acidity and alkaline. The scale runs from 0 to 14, with numbers over 7.0 being alkaline (and therefore scrapbook-safe).

pH Testing Pen   A pen used to test the acidity of paper or other scrapbooking materials. It contains an indicator dye that discolors the material it is applied to if the pH is highly acidic.

Photo Corners   Small paper corners with adhesive backs. Used to attach the four corners of photographs, postcards, or other items with four corners to pages of scrapbook and photo albums, without applying adhesives directly to the item. (See also *Nonpermanent Mounting.*)

Photo Splits   Squares of double-sided tape. Also called photo squares. Can be either flat or based on foam tape to add dimension to a pasted object.

Photo Tape   Double-sided tape on a roll with a paper backing. Good for sticking larger items like mats and frames.

Pixel   Also called *picture element,* refers to a single point in a graphic image. It has some attributes associated with it, for example, a certain color, texture, and so on, that are assumed to be constant over the whole area covered by it. All pixels are assumed to have the same shape and size. A pixel is the smallest element of a picture whose attributes can be controlled independently of the other pixels. Pixels refer to screen resolution, not print. The print equivalent of a pixel is a dot.

Plug-In   A software extension that works with a graphics program like Photoshop Elements to apply particular transformations to a photo or piece of art. Also, plug-ins can be designed to work with a Web browser, for purposes such as viewing, hearing, or saving especially formatted files such as audio or video. Most plug-ins are available via the creator's Web page for downloading.

PNG   Stands for Portable Network Graphics format, and is generally pronounced "ping." PNG is used for lossless compression and displaying images on the Web. The advantage of PNG is that it supports images with millions of colors and produces background transparency without jagged edges. The disadvantages are that PNG images do not show up on older browsers, do not support animation, and still can be comparatively larger in file size than GIFs. (See also *GIF* and *Lossless Compression.*)

Pocket Page   A scrapbook page with a built-in pocket. Useful for holding memorabilia you might want to take out and look at, such as programs or other booklets or two-sided postcards.

Point Size   A measurement of height used in typesetting. One point is typically equal to approximately 1/72 of an inch, although this can vary if the font has elongated ascenders and descenders. In general, a capital letter in 72-point type is about an inch high. (See also *Font.*)

Polaroid   A type of camera that prints a photo instantly. These photos cannot be cropped because they are made in layers, and have acidic chemicals inside that develop the instant photo. Cutting into them allows the chemicals to leak out and destroy both the photo and anything with which it comes in contact. If you need to crop a Polaroid, scan it and crop on the computer. Because Polaroids are small, you might want to enlarge them as part of the scanning process.

Polyester   The common name for Polyethylene Terephthalate (PET), a clear plastic resin safe for scrapbooking, not to be confused with polyvinyl chloride. (See also *Polyvinyl Chloride*.)

Polyethylene   A chemically stable, transparent plastic safe for storing photographs and other memorabilia, not to be confused with Polyvinyl Chloride. (See also *Mylar* and *Polyester*.)

Polyvinyl Chloride   Also known as PVC, this plastic is not stable and damages photographs and albums. PVC plastic page protectors, binders, photo enclosures, and other products, often found in office supply and discount stores, should never be used with photographs or in scrapbooks. (See also *Polyester*.)

Portrait   An upright image or page where the height is greater than the width. Opposite of a landscape.

Post Bound Album   This album type uses metal posts to bind the pages in the album. This gives you the most flexibility in size, because you can continually screw in extra posts to add more pages. (See also *Album*, *Strap-Hinge Album*, and *Three-Ring Binders*.)

PPI   Stands for pixels per inch. Pixels per inch is a measurement of the screen resolution at which a monitor displays image data. The number of pixels contained within one square inch of monitor space.

Primary Colors   In traditional color theory, the primary colors are red, yellow, and blue. They are considered primary because they cannot be made by mixing any other colors, and all other colors are derived from these three. (See also *Color Wheel*.)

Punch   A small gadget similar to a hole punch that creates die-cut shapes and comes in a variety of sizes and styles.

Punch Art   Similar to paper piecing but is art solely made up of punches.

Punches   The product made by using a punch; the "middles" of the die-cut holes. These embellishments can be used in paper piecing or pasted on to decorate scrapbook pages. (See also *Embellishment*.)

Quilling   A paper art featuring curls of long, slim pieces of paper, sometimes used as a scrapbook page decoration. Often curled and arranged to produce patterns and floral designs.

Raffia   A natural, grass-textured fiber that can be used to embellish scrapbook pages, providing a country or farm flair.

Rag Paper or Board   Any paper or board produced with a high content of long, cotton fibers. 100% cotton rag paper or board is considered safe for most scrapbooking because of its low acid content.

RAM   The acronym for Random Access Memory, the most common type of memory found in computers and printers. Computers and printers with more RAM perform tasks more quickly.

Raster   What your image is when using most paint programs; also called a bitmap image. They are composed of individual picture elements, or *pixels* that, when viewed from a distance, appear to form a complete image. You can tell if you are looking at a raster image by the extension on the filename. The extensions .bmp, .pcx, .gif, .tga, .jpg, .png, and .tif are common raster image filename extensions. (See also *Bitmap* and *Resolution*.)

Rasterize   To convert an image from a vector graphic to a bitmapped graphic. (See also *BMP* and *Vector Graphic*.)

Red Eye   An effect that happens when the flash of a camera hits the back of the eye and reflects. Human eyes literally look red in the photograph. Some animal eyes look green or yellow. Can easily be corrected on the computer.

Repositionable   A type of adhesive that holds photos and objects temporarily, but doesn't stick permanently. You can remove the object without damage and put it somewhere else. Sometimes called reversible adhesive. (See also *Nonpermanent Mounting*.)

Resolution   Refers to the sharpness and clarity of an image. Measured in dots per inch (dpi). The greater the numbers of dots, the more smooth and clean an appearance the image has. 300 dpi is generally enough resolution for small photos. (See also *Raster* and *Bitmap*.)

Retouching   A means of altering artwork or photographs to correct faults or enhance the image. Retouching is much easier on the computer than on an actual paper photo.

RGB   Abbreviation for red, green, and blue, the additive color primaries. In Web design and design for computer monitors, colors are defined in terms of a combination of these three colors.

Rubber Cement   An adhesive made from liquified rubber and solvents. It is not safe for scrapbooking, because it eventually stains your photos and any paper surface to which it is applied.

Sans-Serif   A style of typeface that means "without feet." Common sans-serif typefaces include Arial, Helvetica, Avant Garde, and Verdana. (See also *Serif*.)

Saturation   The color intensity of an image. An image high in saturation appears to be very bright. An image low in saturation appears to be duller and more neutral. An image without any saturation is also referred to as a grayscale image.

Scaling   A means of calculating the amount of enlargement or reduction necessary to accommodate a photograph within the area of a design.

Scanner   A device that attaches to a computer and scans or *digitizes* a page using light sensitivity to translate a picture or typed text into a pattern of dots that can be manipulated in software and stored by the computer. (See also *BMP* and *Resolution*.)

Score   To compress paper along a straight line so it folds more easily and accurately. Also called crease.

Scrapbook   An album used to display photographs and ephemera.

Scrapbooking   The craft of organizing your photos and other memorabilia into albums. Also the hobby of using photos, images, decorative papers, embellishments, and journaling to create archival memory albums.

Secondary Colors   The secondary colors on the color wheel—green, orange and purple—are formed by mixing the primary colors in pairs. (See also *Primary Colors* and *Color Wheel*.)

Self-Healing Mat   A mat used as a surface for cutting papers with a knife or razor blade. The cut edges reseal themselves, so the mat is good for many work sessions.

Serif   A type style that has "little feet." Also refers to the "foot" itself. Common serif typefaces include Times Roman, Garamond, and Palatino. (See also *Sans-Serif*.)

Setter   A tool used in attaching rhinestones, eyelets, or studs. It applies pressure to force the metal to bend and grip the paper or cloth.

Shade   Hue made darker by the addition of black; the opposite of a tint. (See also *Tint.*)

Shadows   Darkest areas of a photograph or illustration, as compared to midtones and highlights.

Shareware   Copyrighted software distributed by its creator using an honor system of payment. Most shareware is free of charge, but the author usually requests a small fee if you like the program or use it regularly. By paying the fee, you become a registered user, eligible to receive service help and updates to the shareware program. You can copy shareware and pass it to friends, but they are expected to pay the same small fee to the author if they use the product. (See also *Freeware.*)

Silhouettes   Just the shadow of an object or person. An old-fashioned practice of tracing the shape of one's shadow as a keepsake or form of art.

Spiral Bound   An album or notebook that is machine-bound by winding a metal wire or plastic rings through holes in the pages in a circular pattern.

Sticker   A self-adhesive cutout picture or tag. Often used to decorate scrapbook pages. (See also *Embellishment.*)

Sticker Art   Combining any number of stickers to create a larger project.

Straight Scissors   Regular straight-bladed scissors without any decorative edges used in cutting continuous lines. (See also *Decorative Scissors* and *Fiskars.*)

Strap-Hinge Album   A type of memory book, photo album, or scrapbook that is secured with plastic straps. The straps run through guides attached directly to the pages themselves and into guides on each cover. (See also *Album, Scrapbook,* and *Post Bound Album.*)

Template   Any predesigned page layout. Commonly used in computer scrapbooking programs, a template contains a page background, some art, and places for you to insert your pictures and titles. In traditional paper scrapbooking, a template is made of sturdy plastic and has shapes cut into it that you can trace onto your paper, such as circles, squares, and ovals.

Tertiary Colors   On a 12-part color wheel, the tertiary colors are formed by mixing the secondary colors in pairs, forming yellow-orange, red-orange, red-purple, blue-purple, blue-green, and yellow-green. (See also *Color Wheel, Primary Colors,* and *Secondary Colors.*)

Theme Album   An album in which all the photographs and memorabilia belong to a specific subject such as a birthday, holiday, wedding, or vacation.

Three-Ring Binder   A basic loose-leaf binder, which you can use as a cover for your scrapbook. Three-ring binders are found with office or school supplies. (See also *Binder.*)

Thumbnail   A small representation of a larger graphic image. Image browsers show thumbnail views of your photos. (See also *HTML.*)

TIFF (Tagged Image File Format)   Computer file format used to store bitmap images. Typically uses LZW, a lossless compression scheme, to decrease file size. TIFF files can be any resolution and support black and white, grayscale, and all color depths. The default file extension for TIFF files is .tif. (See also *File Extension* and *Lossless Compression*.)

Timeline   A spread containing one subject over a certain amount of time, such as your child's birthday parties, year by year.

Tint   A hue made lighter by the addition of white. (See also *Shade*.)

Typeface   A typeface is a family of fonts. For example, the typeface Arial includes the fonts Arial, Arial Bold, Arial Italic, and Arial Bold Italic. (See also *Font*.)

Value   The shade (darkness) or tint (lightness) of a color. Also called brightness, lightness, shade, and tone.

Vector Graphic   A graphic image drawn in geometric formulas visually represented by shapes and lines, called paths. Images created in Adobe Illustrator and Macromedia Freehand are vector graphics.

Vellum   A lightweight, translucent paper that is generally thicker than tracing paper. It can be plain, printed, white, or colored.

VersaMark   A brand of ink pad or pen that, when used on a solid color of paper, produces a subtle effect similar to a watermark. Other stamping effects can be created on many types of paper using the VersaMark Watermark stamp pad.

Vignette   Decorative design or illustration fading to the background color around its edges.

WYSIWYG   Pronounced "wiz-zee-wig". Abbreviation for "What You See Is What You Get." A popular feature in desktop publishing, a WYSIWYG program shows you onscreen exactly what you see when the document is printed.

X-acto Knife   A brand of precise, sharp hobby blades used to cut intricate designs. The #11 size blade is the most versatile for use in most crafts. Available in art, hobby, and office supply stores.

While You're Wandering the Web...

Be sure to check out some of the many **Web resources** for scrapbookers. You can use the following list, and you can also find a whole bunch of good sites by searching on Google (or whatever your favorite search engine is) for "scrapbook," "journal," and "scrapbooking." Of course, if you are looking for specific tools or items such as stickers, scrapbooking papers, and so on, try them as Google search terms, too.

I've also included a bunch of Web sites for **various scrapbooking and craft projects**. I'm not specifically recommending any of these. As always, buyer beware. Be especially wary of "companies" that only have email and Web site addresses, but no postal mailing address or phone number. This is common-sense advice that is found in many consumer guides. Also, Web sites come and go, so a year from now you might not find them. This list is correct as of February of 2004.

Here are some good scrapbooking sites to get you started:

- Avery Labels (www.avery.com/homecorner)
- Epson (www.epson.com/cgi-bin/Store/PrintLab/PrintScrap.jsp)
- HP Scrapbooking (h30039.www3.hp.com/scrapbooking/home)
- Learn2Scrapbook (www.learn2scrapbook.com)
- Scrap Circle (www.scrapcircle.com)

- Scrap Jazz (www.scrapjazz.com)
- Scrapbook Sites (www.scrapbooksites.com)
- Scrapbooking.com Magazine (www.scrapbooking.com)
- Simple Scrapbooks (www.simplescrapbooksmag.com)
- Stamping Links (www.rubberstampinglinks.com)
- Two Peas in a Bucket (www.twopeasinabucket.com)

Company Name	Products	Web Address	Phone
3L	Mounting corners, pockets, and adhesives	www.3L.dk	+45 63 76 86 00 (in Denmark)
7 Gypsies	Albums, paper, and tags	www.7gypsies.com	800-588-6707
A Stamp in the Hand	Stamps	www.astampinthehand.com	310-884-9700
Adobe	Software	www.adobe.com	800-833-6687
Agfa-Monotype	Type	www.agfamonotype.com	978-284-7201
All Night Media	Rubber stamps	www.allnightmedia.com	800-STAMPED
American Art Clay Co., Inc.	FIMO clay and embossing supplies	www.amaco.com	800-374-1600
American Tag Company	Eyelets, grommets, tags, tassels, and cords	www.americantag.net	800-223-3956
Anima Designs	Stamps, journals, and ephemera	www.animadesigns.com	
Art Gone Wild	Stamps	www.agwstamps.com	800-945-3980
Artchix Studio	Stamps, art bits, and more	www.artchixstudio.com	250-370-9985
Artisan's Choice	Make your own stamps and transfers	www.artisanschoice.com	877-7-ARTISAN
Artistic Wire	Colored wire and tools	www.artisticwire.com	630-530-7567
Avery Dennison	Paper goods, templates, and free clip art	www.avery.com	800-GO-AVERY
The Beadery	Plastic beads and rhinestones	www.thebeadery.com	401-539-2432
Bo-Bunny Press	Papers and stickers	www.bobunny.com	801-771-4010
Brown Bag Fibers	Natural fibers	www.brownbagfibers.com	
The C-Thru Ruler Company	Scrapbook pages, add-ons, and drafting tools	www.cthruruler.com	800-243-8419
Canson	Fine art papers	www.canson-us.com	
Carl Mfg.	Paper cutters and trimmers	www.carl-products.com	847-956-0730
Carolee's Creations	Papers, tags, and punch outs	www.carolees.com	435-563-1100
Chatterbox	Papers, frames, rivets, and nails	www.chatterboxinc.com	888-416-6260
Cheap Joe's Art Stuff	Art supplies	www.cheapjoescatalog.com	800-227-2788
Clearsnap	Inkpads, stamps, and stones	www.clearsnap.com	888-448-4862
Close to My Heart	Stamps	www.closetomyheart.com	888-655-6552
Club Scrap	Color-coordinated kits	www.clubscrap.com	888-634-9100

Company Name	Products	Web Address	Phone
Cock a Doodle Design	Pre-illustrated pieces, and a consultant program	www.cockadoodledesign.com	800-262-9727
Colorbök	Coordinated kits	www.colorbok.com	
Colors by Design	Cards and add-ons	www.cbdcards.com	800-832-8436
Craf-T Products	Chalks	www.craf-tproducts.com	
Crafts Etc!	Artists supplies	www.craftsetc.com	800-888-0321
Creative Imaginations	Papers and add-ons	www.cigift.com	800-942-6487
Daisy D's Paper Co.	Papers and themed pages	www.daisydspaper.com	888-601-8955
Daler-Rowney	Art supplies	www.daler-rowney.com	+44(0)1344 461000 (UK)
Darice, Inc.	Art supplies	www.darice.com	800-321-1494
Delta Technical Coatings	Stamping supplies and glass paints	www.deltacrafts.com	800-423-4135
Deluxe Cuts	Laser cuts and tags	www.deluxecuts.com	480-497-9005
Design Originals	How-to books and papers	www.d-originals.com	800-877-7820
Dick Blick Art Materials	Art and craft supplies	www.dickblick.com	800-828-4548
Dymo	Label makers and label tape	www.dymo.com	800-426-7827
Emagination Crafts EK Success	Punches, papers, corners, and scissors	www.emaginationcrafts.com	630-833-9521
Embellish It!	Jewelry findings and trims	www.boutiquetrims.com	248-437-2017
Epson	Ink jet printers, scanners, inks, and paper	www.epson.com	800-463-7766
European Papers	Papers, kits, and charms	www.europeanpapers.com	614-316-3948
Fibers by the Yard	Fiber, raffia, and hemp	www.fibersbytheyard.com	405-364-8066
Fiebing Company	Leather dyes	www.fiebing.com	414-271-5011
Fiskars	Punches, trimmers, scissors, and embossing tools	www.fiskars.com	800-500-4849
FoofaLa	Tags, envelopes, and charms	www.foofala.com	
Frances Meyer	Scrapbooking supplies and stickers	www.francesmeyer.com	
Funky Fibers	Yarns and fibers	www.funkyfibers.com	480-659-5616
Glue Dots International	Adhesives	www.gluedots.com	
Golden Artists Colors	Acrylic paints and archival varnish	www.goldenpaints.com	800-959-6543
Gone Scrappin'	General scrapbook supplies	www.gonescrappin.com	435-647-0404
Harbor Freight	Hand tools and craft knife sets	www.harborfreight.com	800-444-3353
Hero Arts	Stamps and supplies	www.heroarts.com	800-822-HERO (4376)
Hillcreek Designs	Hand-dyed buttons	www.hillcreekdesigns.com	619-562-5799

Company Name	Products	Web Address	Phone
Hot Off the Press	Templates	www.craftpizazz.com	800-227-9595
Inkadinkado	Rubber stamps	www.inkadinkado.com	781-938-6100
Inspire Graphics	Fonts and journaling art	www.inspiregraphics.com	801-235-9393
ITC (International Typeface Corporation)	Type	www.itcfonts.com	866-823-5828
Jacquard Products	Textile paints and dyes	www.jacquardproducts.com	800-442-0455
Jest Charming	Charms and embellishments	www.jestcharming.com	702-564-5101
JewelCraft	Beads, charms, and shaker kits	www.jewelcraft.biz	201-223-0804
Junque	Rubber stamps and supplies	www.junque.net	
K&Company	Papers, frames, and themed kits	www.kandcompany.com	888-244-2083
K&S Engineering	Metal tooling foils	www.ksmetals.com	773-586-8503
Karen Foster Design	Papers and stickers	www.karenfosterdesign.com	801-451-9779
Keeping Memories Alive	All kinds of scrapbooking supplies	www.scrapbooks.com	800-419-4949
Kolo	Photo albums	www.kolo-usa.com	888-636-5656
Kopp Design	Papers, cut-outs, and tags	www.koppdesign.com	801-489-6011
Kreinik	Iron-on metallic thread, yarns, and so on	www.kreinik.com	410-281-0040
Lazertran	Transfer papers	www.lazertran.com	800-245-7547
The Leather Factory	Leather goods, tools, and dyes	www.leatherfactory.com	
Limited Edition Rubber Stamps	Stamps, ink pads, ephemera, beads, tags, and die cuts	www.LimitedEditionRS.com	877-9-STAMPS
Linotype Library	Type	www.linotypelibrary.com	+49 (0) 1805 79 33 39 (Germany)
Ma Vinci's Reliquary	Rubber stamps	www.crafts.dm.net/mall/reliquary	
Magic Mesh	Decorative mesh	www.magicmesh.com	651-345-6374
Magic Scraps	Embellishments and supplies	www.magicscraps.com	972-238-1838
Making Memories	Scrapbook supplies	www.makingmemories.com	801-294-0430
Making Memories Unforgettable (MMU)	Scrapbooking supplies	www.scrapbookit.com	866-SCRAPIT
Marvy Uchida	Markers and art supplies	www.uchida.com	800-541-5877
McGill Inc.	Punches and craft tools	www.mcgillinc.com	800-982/9884
Memories of the Rabbit	Embellishments, papers, and kits	www.memoriesoftherabbit.com	505-479-9653
Michaels Arts and Crafts	Everything!	www.michaels.com	800-MICHAELS
Microsoft	Software	www.microsoft.com	888-218-5617

Company Name	Products	Web Address	Phone
Micro-Mark	Small tool specialists	www.micromark.com	800-225-1066
Midori	Handmade papers and ribbons	www.midoriribbon.com	800-659-3049
Mustard Moon	Papers, piercings, and tags	www.mustardmoon.com	408-229-8542
Nankong Enterprises, Inc.	Punch art and stamps	www.nankong.com	302-731-2995
Nature's Pressed	Pressed flowers and leaves	www.naturespressed.com	800-850-2499
Offray	Ribbons	www.offray.com	800-327-0350
Once Upon a Charm	Brass and pewter charms	www.uponacharm.com	763-684-0074
Once Upon a Scribble	Stickers and supplies	www.onceuponascribble.com	702-896-2181
P22	Type	www.p22.com	800-P22-5080
Paper Adventures	Papers and rub-on letters	www.paperadventures.com	800-727-0699
The Paper Loft	Stationery	www.thepaperloft.com	909-694-4420
The Paper Patch	Binder covers, papers, and stickers	www.paperpatch.com	800-397-2737
Patchwork Paper Design Inc.	Papers, die cuts, and patchwork pieces	www.patchworkpaper.com	239-481-4823
Pebbles In My Pocket	Papers and tools	www.pebblesinmypocket.com	800-438-8153
Plaid	Craft supplies	www.plaidonline.com	800-842-4197
Polyform Products	Polymer clay	www.sculpey.com	847-427-0020
Polyshrink	Shrink plastics	www.luckysquirrel.com	800-462-4912
Provo Craft	Scrapbooking supplies	www.provocraft.com	800-937-7686
Prym-Dritz Corporation	Sewing supplies and notions	www.dritz.com	
PSX	Papers, stamps, inks, and tools	www.psxdesign.com	866-779-9877
Ranger Industries, Inc.	Stamping inks and glitter glues	www.rangerink.com	732-389-3535
Red Castle	Templates and stamps	www.redcastle.com	
Rubba Dub Dub	Rubber stamps, supplies, and yarn	www.artsanctum.com	209-763-2766
Scrapworks	Embellishments	www.scrapworks.com	
Scrapyard 329	Embellishments	www.scrapyard329.com	775-829-1118
SEI	Albums, stickers, and embellishments	www.shopsei.com	800-333-3279
Shutterfly	Digital photo printing	www.shutterfly.com	
Sizzix	Die cutting machines, dies, embossing tools, and molds	www.sizzix.com	877-355-4766
Snapfish	Digital photo printing	www.snapfish.com	301-595-5308
The Stamp Doctor	Stamps and accessories	www.stampdoctor.com	208-342-4632
Stamp It!	Rubber stamps and accessories	www.stampit.com	757-425-0721

Company Name	Products	Web Address	Phone
Stampendous	Rubber stamps, stickers, and papers	www.stampendous.com	800-869-0474
Stampin' Up!	Rubber stamps and accessories	www.stampinup.com	800-STAMPUP
Tandy Leather Co.	Leather tools, stamps, and dyes	www.tandyleather.com	800-433-3201
Target	Craft and office supplies	www.target.com	800-440-0680
Therm O Web	Tapes and adhesives	www.thermoweb.com	847-520-5200
Tsukineko, Inc.	Inkpads and temporary tattooing supplies	www.tsukineko.com	800-769-6633
Two Busy Moms	Tags and embellishments	www.twobusymoms.com	480-497-9005
The Uptown Design Company	Stamps, inks, and embossing powders	www.uptowndesign.com	253-925-1234
Two Peas in a Bucket, Inc.	Papers, stamps, stickers, and glues	www.twopeasinabucket.com	608-827-0852
USArtQuest, Inc.	General craft supplies	www.usartquest.com	517-522-6225
Westrim Crafts	Embellishments, albums, and paper	www.westrimcrafts.com	800-727-2727
Winsor & Newton	Paints	www.winsornewton.com	
Wordsworth	Rubber stamps, stickers, and quotations	www.wordsworthstamps.com	719-282-3495
Young Bros. Stamp Works	Brass stencils and metal type	www.youngbrosstampworks.com	800-553-8248

Index

Symbols

3L Web site, 262
7 Gypsies Web site, 262
1001 Free Fonts Web site, 204

A

<A HREF> tag (HTML), 228
About Rubber Stamps Web site, 30
About Scrapbooking Web site, clip art sources, 93
ACD FotoCanvas
    color correction features, 129
    image flip options, 144
    noise options, 90
    Red Eye Wizard, 161
    talk bubbles, creating, 201-202
ACDSee PowerPack, 71-72
acid-fast paper, 22
acid-free paper, 22
Addicted to Rubber Stamps Web site, 30
adding drop shadows to type, 205-207
adhesive papers, 103

adhesives
  safe, 24-26
  Web sites
    3L, 262
    Glue Dots, 263
    Ranger Industries, 265
    Thermo O Web, 266
adjusting
  hue in old photographs, 132-133
  lighting in old photographs, 132
adjustment layers, 80
Adobe.com Web site, binding services, 69
Agfa-Monotype Web site, 262
AirPort wireless networking, 44
album Web sites
  7 Gypsies, 262
  Kolo, 264
  SEI, 265
<ALIGN> tag (HTML), 227
aligning type (Photoshop Elements), 201
alignment (text)
  centered, 198
  flush left, 198
  flush right, 198
  justified, 198
All Night Media Web site, 262
American Clay Art Web site, 262
American Greetings Scrapbooks & More
  background templates, 97
  free trial offer, 63
  image editing features, 62-63
American Greetings Web site, 63
American Tag Co. Web site, 262
Anima Designs Web site, 262

anti-aliasing type, 200
AOL Hometown, free hosting services, 220
AppleWorks, Web page creation features, 224
Art Explosion Scrapbook Factory Deluxe
  drawing tools, 56
  quality of art, 55
  quotations library, 57
  templates, 57
  user interface, 56
Art Gone Wild Web site, 262
art papers, 102
art supply Web sites
  Cheap Joe's Art Stuff, 262
  Crafts Etc!, 263
  Daler-Rowney, 263
  Darice, 263
  Dick Blick, 263
  Marvy Uchid, 264
  Plaid, 265
  USArtQuest, 266
Artchix Studio Web site, 262
Artisan's Choice Web site, 262
Artistic Wire Web site, 262
ascenders (fonts), 197
audio
  copyright infringement, 230
  formats, 229
  Web sites
    adding, 229-23
    file size drawbacks, 229-230
Avery.com Web site, 242-243, 261-262
  CD label templates, 234

B

backgrounds
blurring, 147-150
premade, 95-99
templates
American Greetings Scrapbooks & More, 97
Photo Express My Scrapbook, 96
Photoshop Elements, 97
textures
adding, 90-92
creating from scanned objects, 99
Bartleby Quotations Web site, 214
basis weight (papers), 101
batteries and digital camera usage, 40
BBEdit tool, Web page creation, 74
bead Web sites, 262
The Beadery Web site, 262
<BIG> tag (HTML), 227
bitmap images, 81
Blur tool (Photoshop Elements), 117
blurring backgrounds, 147-150
Bo-Bunny Press Web site, 262
<BODY> tag (HTML), 227
bolding type (Photoshop Elements), 201
book Web sites, 263
**
 tag (HTML), 227**
brightness levels in old photographs, adjusting, 110-111
Brown Bag Fibers Web site, 262
Brush Strokes effect (Paint Shop Pro), 177
Burn tool (Photoshop Elements), 113

burning
CD-ROMs, 232-234
DVD-ROMs, 232-234
burning tool, applying to old photographs, 111-113
business cards, online templates, 242-243
button Web sites, 263

C

C-Thru Ruler Web site, 262
cake frosting, printing on, 241
calendars, online templates
Avery.com, 242-243
PrintableCalendar.com, 242-243
Canson Web site, 262
canvas materials, printing on, 103-104
card Web sites, 263
Carl Mfg. Web site, 262
Carolee's Creations Web site, 262
catchlights, flash photography, 160
CD-based scrapbooks, 217-218
CD-ROMs
archival photo storage, 49
burning, 232-234
disk organization, 232-234
drives, 36, 49
labels, applying, 234

How can we make this index more useful? Email us at indexes@quepublishing.com

CD-RW drives, 49

center of interest and picture placement, 85-86

charm Web sites

Jest Charming, 264

Once Upon a Charm, 265

Chatterbox Web site, 262

Cheap Joe's Art Stuff Web site, 262

clay Web sites

American Clay Art, 262

Polyform, 265

Clearsnap Web site, 262

clip art

adding, 92

name terminology, 92

searching, 93

sources, 92

About Scrapbooking Web site, 93

Country Clipart Web site, 93

Gatherings Web site, 93

Leaves of Time Web site, 93

typical prices, 94

Clone Stamp tool (Photoshop Elements), 113-114, 155, 164

Close to My Heart Web site, 262

close-focus lenses (digital cameras), 41

cloth materials

Labelon, 103-104

printing on, 103-104

Xerox, 103-104

Club Scrap Web site, 262

Cock a Doodle Design Web site, 263

coherent page design, 87

collages, creating, 188, 191

color cast, repairing old photographs, 128-131

color printers, 47

color schemes in scrapbooks, 10-11

color shift, repairing old photographs, 128-131

Color Variations tool (Photoshop Elements), 114

color wheels, category divisions, 10

Colorbook Web site, 263

colors

complementary, 11

cool, 10

correction, applying, 151-153

fonts, selection guidelines, 205

grayed, 11

metallic type effects, 209-210

old photographs, correcting, 128-131

primary, 10

secondary, 10

temperatures, 10, 151

tertiary, 10

texturizing, 90-92

typography settings (Photoshop Elements), 201

warm, 10

Colors by Design Web site, 263

commercial photo services, scanning options, 45

complementary colors, 11

composing pages, 84

coherency of, 87

eye leading, 85

overview, 11-12

rule of thirds, 85-87

whitespace, 84

How can we make this index more useful? Email us at indexes@quepublishing.com

composites, creating, 188, 191

connecting scanners, 43

contrast levels, adjusting old photographs, 110-111

cool colors, 10

Cool Page Web site, 224

copyright issues
    audio/video infringement, 230
    image downloads, 46-47

correcting
    colors, 151-153
        old photographs, 128-131
    perspective in images, 153-154

Country Clipart Web site, clip art sources, 93

Craf-T Products Web site, 263

Crafts Etc! Web site, 263

creating
    templates, 82-83
    Web pages
        Macromedia Dreamweaver MX, 224
        Microsoft FrontPage, 224
        MySoftware WebPage Creation Kit, 224
        Ulead My Web Studio, 223
        via word processing applications, 224
        wizards, 222-223

Creative Imaginations Web site, 263

Creative Keepsakes, acid-free products, 22

Creative Thinking Web site, 214

cropping
    frames, 142
    images, 140-143

cut-out lettering, Type Mask tool (Photoshop Elements), 208

D

Daisy D's Paper Web site, 263

Daler-Rowney Web site, 263

Darice Web site, 263

DelphiForums.com, low-cost hosting services, 220

Delta Coatings Web site, 263

Deluxe Cuts Web site, 263

descenders (fonts), 197

Design Originals Web site, 263

designing
    scrapbook pages, 84
        clip art additions, 92
        coherency of, 87
        element additions, 88-89
        eye leading, 85
        fabric additions, 92
        rule of thirds, 85-87
        texture additions, 90-92
        whitespace, 84
    Web pages, guidelines, 225

Despeckle filter (Photoshop Elements), 118, 183

Dick Blick Web site, 263

digital cameras
    battery usage, 40
    convenience of, 38
    evolution of, 38
    flashcard memory versus internal memory, 38-39

How can we make this index more useful? Email us at indexes@quepublishing.com

images, capture process, 38

internal memory versus flashcard memory, 38

megapixel ratings, 37

one-use, 41

pictures, cropping, 140143

pixel measurements, 37

purchasing guidelines

built-in flash unit, 41

gray market warning, 40

macro lens, 41

name brand awareness, 40

recovery speeds, 40

zoom ranges, 41

resolution, 36

sensor dots, 37

shooting guidelines, 135

correction options, 139

flash usage, 139

low-light conditions, 139

scenery, 136-138

versus film cameras, 39-40

digital photos

share sites

ofoto.com, 46

Shutterfly.com, 46

Snapfish.com, 46

uploading to sites, 46

Dodge tool (Photoshop Elements), 111-112

dodging tool, adjusting old photographs, 111-113

domains

fees, 221

IP addresses, assignment of, 221

name registration, 219

obtaining, 221

downloading Web images, copyright restrictions, 46-47

dpi (dots per inch)

resolution measurements, 36

scanners and old photographs, 108-109

drawing on photos, 187

drawing devices

graphics tablets, 35

mouse, 35

trackballs, 35

drawn effects, applying, 179-184

drop shadows, type, adding, 205-207

Dry Brush filter (Photoshop Elements), 174-176

dust, old photographs, repairing, 118

DVD-RW drives, 49

DVDs

archival photo storage, 49

burning, 232-234

Dymo Web site, 263

E

Easypano application, panoramic photo creation, 195

Edge Effects (Paint Shop Pro), 180

edge trimmers, 28

edible frosting sheets, printing to, 241

editing

sound files, 230

text via Optical Character Recognition (OCR) technology, 45

Effect Browser (Paint Shop Pro), 170

effects

drawn, applying, 179-184

images, applying, 171-173

oil painting, applying, 176-177

Paint Shop Pro options, 170

watercolor, applying, 173-176

Elements of Style, **213**

Emagination Crafts Web site, 263

Embellish It! Web site, 263

embellishment Web sites

Magic Scraps, 264

Memories of the Rabbit, 264

Scrapyard 329, 265

embossing

powder style, 209

press style, 209

rubber stamps, 30

enlarging images, 146-147

Epson Archival Matte paper, 101

Epson CX 6400 scanner, 43-44

Epson Stylus Photo 1280 printer, 47

Epson.com Web site, 261

background images, downloading, 47

printer lines, 47

European Papers Web site, 263

eye leading, page design guidelines, 85

F

fabric

ink fixatives, 239-240

printing on, 239-240

texture effects, adding, 92

Web sites

Brown Bag fibers, 262

Fibers by the Yard, 263

Funky Fibers, 263

facing pages, design element coherency, 87

Fibers by the Yard Web site, 263

Fiebing Co. Web site, 263

fill layers, 80

film cameras versus digital cameras, 39-40

filters

drawn, applying, 179-184

function of, 169

images, applying, 171-173

oil painting, applying, 176-177

Photoshop Elements options, 169

watercolor, applying, 173-176

Filters palette (Photoshop Elements), 171

Find Edges filter (Photoshop Elements), 181-182

FireWire, scanner connections, 43

Fiskars Web site, 263

fixing

red eye effect, 157-162

scanned images of old photographs, 109-110

blurring effect, 117

brightness/contrast levels, 110-111

burning tool, 111-113

color variations, 114

despeckle filter, 118

How can we make this index more useful? Email us at indexes@quepublishing.com

dodging tool, 111-113

dust spot cleanup, 113-114

retouches, 114

severe damage, 118-122

sharpening effect, 116-117

smudging effect, 115

flash photography

old photographs, adjusting, 132

red eye, repairing, 157-162

shooting guidelines, 139

flashcard memory

capacities, 39

digital cameras, printing directly from, 43

versus internal memory (digital cameras), 38

flipping images, 144

<FONT> tag (HTML), 227

fonts

ascenders, 197

descenders, 197

display type versus body type, 203

handwriting style, 213

journaling entries, 213

libraries

CD-ROMs, 28-29

Web sites, 28-29

professional, 28-29

proper usage of, 29

readability of, 29

selecting, 203-205

serif, 203

sources, 1001 Free Fonts Web site, 204

tasteful use guidelines, 205

versus handwriting, 29

Web sites

design guidelines, 225

Inspire Graphics, 264

FoofaLa Web site, 263

Frances Meyer Web site, 263

free hosting services

AOL Hometown, 220

Freeservers.com, 220

Yahoo! Geocities, 220

Freeservers.com, free hosting services, 220

frosting (cake), printing on, 241

Funky Fibers Web site, 263

G

Gatherings Web site, clip art sources, 93

Gaussian noise, 90

glossy papers, 101

Glowing Edges filter (Photoshop Elements), 183

glue dots, 25

Glue Dots Web site, 263

glues

dots, 25

safe varieties, 24-26

Golden Artists Colors Web site, 263

Golden Number Web site, rule of thirds resources, 86

Gone Scrappin' Web site, 263

Graphic Pen filter (Photoshop Elements), 179

graphics, Web page design guidelines, 225

How can we make this index more useful? Email us at indexes@quepublishing.com

graphics tablets

as drawing device, 35

Wacom.com, 36

grayed colors, 11

greeting cards, online templates, 242-243

grids on pages, using, 82-83

guidelines on pages, using, 82-83

H

Hallmark Scrapbook Studio Deluxe, 61

handwriting fonts, 213

Harbor Freight Web site, 263

hardware

CD-ROM drives, 36

drawing devices

graphics tablets, 35

mouse, 35

trackballs, 35

PC components, 35

<HEAD> tag (HTML), 227

heavyweight textured paper, 23

Hero Arts Web site, 263

Hillcreek Designs Web site, 263

Horizontal Type tool (Photoshop Elements), 199-200

hosting services

free

AOL Hometown, 220

Freeservers.com, 220

Yahoo! Geocities, 220

low-cost

DelphiForums.com, 220

Mac.com, 220

Web servers, 219

Hot off the Press Web site, 264

HowStuffWorks.com Web site, virus resources, 50

HP Creative Scrapbook Assistant

drawbacks, 55

editing features, 54

effects, 54

user interface, 53-54

HP PSC 1350 scanner, 43-44

HP Scrapbooking Web site, 261

HTML (Hypertext Markup Language), 218

basic overview, 226

Sams Teach Yourself HTML in 24 Hours, 229

tags, 218

<A HREF>, 228

<ALIGN>, 227

<BIG>, 227

<BODY>, 227

*
, 227*

bracket syntax, 226

<FONT>, 227

<HEAD>, 227

<HTML>, 227

<META>, 227

source code explanation, 226-229

<TABLE>, 227

<TD>, 227

<TITLE>, 227

<TR>, 227

Web page code, viewing, 219

<HTML> tag (HTML), 227
hue, adjusting in old photographs, 132-133
Hypertext Markup Language. *See* HTML

I

---

images
    collages, creating, 188, 191
    color correction, applying, 151-153
    cropping, 140-143
    downloading, copyright restrictions, 46-47
    drawn effects, applying, 179-184
    filters
        applying, 171-173
        function of, 169
    flipping, 144
    iron-on transfers, 237-239
    JPEG format, lossy compression, 141
    layers
        bitmap, 81
        effect of, 77-78
        handling (Microsoft Picture It!), 78
        handling (Paint Shop Pro), 80
        handling (Photoshop Elements), 79-80
        raster, 81
        vector, 81
    making versus taking terminology, 52
    oil painting effects, applying, 176-177
    page placement
        coherency of, 87
        eye leading, 85
        rule of thirds, 85-87
    panoramic
        creating, 191-195
        shooting guidelines, 192
        software, 195
    perspective, correcting, 153-154
    posterizing, 185-187
    printing
        on cake frosting, 241
        directly to fabric, 239-240
    red eye, repairing, 157-162
    resizing, 145-147
    retouching, ethical issues, 167
    skin problems, correcting, 162-164
    sources
        Library of Congress Web site, 46
        NASA Web site, 46
        White House Web site, 46
    storage guidelines, 142
    taking versus making terminology, 52
    textures, adding, 90-92
    unwanted items, removing, 155-156
    watercolor effects, applying, 173-176
    weight problems, correcting, 164-167
iMovie, video files, editing, 230
ink fixatives in fabric printing, 239-240
Inkadinkado Web site, 264
inkjet printers
    color varieties, 47
    iron-on transfer paper, 237-239
    paper selection criteria, 100
    printing directly to fabric, 239-240

InkJetArt.com, art papers, 101

Inspire Graphics Web site, 264

internal memory versus flashcard memory (digital cameras), 38

IP addresses, 219

assignment of, 221

iron-on transfer paper, 23, 102, 237-239

Lazertran Web site, 264

italicizing type (Photoshop Elements), 201

ITC Web site, 264

J - K

Jacquard Products Web site, 264

Jenkins Bubble Jet Set 2000, 239

Jest Charming Web site, 264

JewelCraft Web site, 264

jewelry Web sites

Embellish It!, 263

JewelCraft, 264

journaling

grammar resources, 213

guidelines, 212-213

JournalTEK.com Web site, 64

JPEG (Joint Photographic Experts Group) format, 141

Junque Web site, 264

K&S Engineering Web site, 264

Karen Foster Design Web site, 264

Keeping Memories Alive Web site, 264

kerning, 198

kit Web sites, 263

Kolo Web site, 264

Kopp Design Web site, 264

Kreinik Web site, 264

L

Labelon canvas material, printable fabric, 103-104

labels

CDs, applying, 234

Web sites

Avery.com, 261

Dymo, 263

Epson.com, 261

lace paper, 21

laser printers, color varieties, 47

layers

adjustment, 80

bitmap, 81

effect of, 77-78

fill, 80

Microsoft Picture It!, 78

Paint Shop Pro, 80-82

Photoshop Elements, 79-80

raster, 81

vector, 81

How can we make this index more useful? Email us at indexes@quepublishing.com

Layers palette (Paint Shop Pro), 80-82

Layers palette (Photoshop Elements), 79-80

Lazertran Web site, 264

leading, 198

Learn2Scrapbook Web site, 261

Leather Factory Web site, 264

Leaves of Time Web site, clip art sources, 93

Library of Congress Web site

  copyright law resources, 230

  image downloads, 46

lighting in old photographs, flash adjustments, 132

lignin-free paper, 22

Limited Edition Web site, 264

line drawn effects, applying, 179-184

links in Web pages, 218

Linotype Library Web site, 264

lossy compression (JPEG), 141

low-cost hosting services

  DelphiForums.com, 220

  Mac.com, 220

low-light shooting conditions, 139

M

Ma Vinci's Reliquary Web site, 264

Mac.com, low-cost hosting services, 220

macro lenses (digital cameras), 41

Macromedia Dreamweaver MX, 224

Magic Mesh Web site, 264

Magic Scraps Web site, 264

Magix Movie Edit Pro 2004, 230

magnetic photo albums, 23

Making Memories Web site, 264

Marvy Uchida Web site, 264

McGill Web site, 264

megapixels, digital camera ratings, 37

Memories of the Rabbit Web site, 264

memory boxes, 241-242

<META> tag (HTML), 227

metallic inks, 104

metallic type effects, creating, 209-210

metallic vellum papers, 104

Michael's Arts & Crafts Web site, 264

Micro-Mark Web site, 265

Microsoft FrontPage, 74, 224

Microsoft Picture It!

  drop shadow options, 207

  pages, layering, 78

Microsoft Word

  text warping options, 210-211

  Web page creation features, 224

Microtek ScanMaker 5700, 42

Midori Web site, 265

mirror effect, applying, 144

monitors, resolution settings, 36

mouse as drawing device, 35

MP3 audio format, 229

Mustard Moon Web site, 265

MySoftware WebPage Creation Kit, 224

N

Nankong Web site, 265

NASA Web site, image downloads, 46

Nature's Pressed Web site, 265

newsprint paper, 22

noise

    Gaussian, 90

    options

        ACD FotoCanvas, 90

        Photoshop Elements, 90

obtaining domains, 221

offline photo storage, 49

Offray Web site, 265

ofoto.com Web site, photo sharing services, 46

oil painting effects, applying, 176-177

old photographs

    color correction, 128-131

    fill flash adjustments, 132

    hue adjustments, 132-133

    photo correction guidelines, 109-110

        blurring effect, 117

        brightness/contrast adjustments, 110-113

        color variations, 114

        despeckle filter, 118

        dust spot cleanup, 113-114

        retouches, 114

        severe damage, 118-122

        sharpening effect, 116-117

        smudging effect, 115

    scanning guidelines, 108-109

    tinting, 126-127

    vignetting, 123-126

Once Upon a Charm Web site, 265

Once Upon a Sticker Web site, 265

one-use digital cameras, 41

online photo storage, 49

Optical Character Recognition (OCR), 45

organization of scrapbooks, 8

overweight subjects, sliming effects, 164-167

P

P22 Web site, 265

page holders, 23

page layout software, selecting, 72-73

page sharing software

    BBEdit, 74

    Microsoft FrontPage, 74

    PDF format, 73

    selecting, 73-74

pages

    composition guidelines, 11-12, 84

        coherency of, 87

        eye leading, 85

        rule of thirds, 85-87

        whitespace, 84

    design guidelines

        clip art additions, 92

        element additions, 88-89

        fabric additions, 92

        texture additions, 90-92

How can we make this index more useful? Email us at indexes@quepublishing.com

grids, using, 82-83

layers

effect of, 77-78

handling (Microsoft Picture It!), 78

handling (Paint Shop Pro), 80-82

handling (Photoshop Elements), 79-80

saving in Web format, 225

Paint Shop Photo Album, 67

Paint Shop Pro

bit-mapped editing, 51

Blur tool, 147-150

Brush Strokes effect, 177

color correction features, 129

color variation options, 153

drop shadow options, 206

Edge Effects, 180

Effect Browser, 170

effects

applying, 171-173

filter options, 170

free trial version, 67

image flip options, 144

memory, reallocation of, 170

old photographs, vignetting, 123-126

pages, layering, 80-82

photo repair tools, 66

posterizing effects, 186-187

Red Eye Removal, 162

resizing options, 145-147

retouching tools, 114

templates, creating, 82-83

Wow Chrome effects, 125-126

paint Web sites

Golden Artists Colors, 263

Jacquard Products, 264

Winsor & Newton, 266

panoramic photographs

creating, 191-195

shooting guidelines, 192

software, 195

Paper Adventures Web site, 265

Paper and More Web site, 104

paper cutters, 28

The Paper Loft Web site, 265

The Paper Patch Web site, 265

papers

acid-fast, 22

acid-free, 22

adhesive, 103

art, 102

basis weight, 101

card stock, 20

commercial types

Epson Archival Matte paper, 101

HP, 101

Epson sample book, viewing, 102

glossy, 101

heavyweight textured, 23

inkjet printers, selection criteria, 100

iron-on transfers, 23, 102, 237-239

lace varieties, 21

metallic vellums, 104

newsprint, 22

photo, 101

premade backgrounds, 95-99

How can we make this index more useful? Email us at indexes@quepublishing.com

printers, handling, 48

safe adhesives, 24-26

selection criteria, 100-103

sizes, printer capabilities, 47

surface quality, 101

temporary tattoos, 103

text weight, 21

tissue, 21

transparency films, 102

variety packs, 101

vellum, 22

Web sites

    Avery Dennison, 262

    Bo-Bunny Press, 262

    Canson, 262

    Carl Mfg., 262

    Carolee's Creations, 262

    Chatterbox, 262

    Creative Imaginations, 263

    Daisy D's Paper, 263

    Emagination Crafts, 263

    European Papers, 263

    K&Company, 264

    Karen Foster Design, 264

    Kopp Design, 264

    Midori, 265

    Mustard Moon, 265

    Paper Adventures, 265

    The Paper Loft, 265

    Patchwork Paper, 265

    Pebbles in my Pocket, 265

    PSX, 265

    Westrim Crafts, 266

whiteness grades, 101

parallel ports, scanner connections, 43

Patchwork Paper Web site, 265

PCs

    connection options

        FireWire, 44

        parallel ports, 44

        SCSI, 44

        USB, 44

        wireless hubs, 44

    public availability, 49

    rental of, 49

    required components, 35

PDF (Portable Document Format) files, cross-platform distribution, 51, 73

Pebbles in My Pocket Web site, 265

photo albums, magnetic types, 23

Photo Express My Scrapbook

    background templates, 96

    cropping versus trimming, 143

    image editing features, 59

    multiple file formats, 60

photo papers, 101

photo-editing software, 64

    ACDSee PowerPack, 71-72

    Paint Shop Photo Album, 67

    Paint Shop Pro

        free trial version, 67

        photo repair tools, 66

    Photoshop Album

        image editing tools, 69

        user interface, 68-69

    Photoshop Elements

        cost, 66

        photo repair tools, 66

        user interface, 65-66

Picture It!
    templates, 71
    user interface, 70
PhotoFrost.com Web site, 241
photographs
    commercial scanning services, 45
    digital cameras, capture process, 38
    downloading, copyright restrictions, 46-47
    making versus taking terminology, 52
    old
        color correction, 128-131
        fill flash adjustments, 132
        hue adjustments, 132-133
        photo correction guidelines, 109-118
        scanning guidelines, 108-109
        severe damage correction guidelines, 118-122
        tinting, 126-127
        vignetting, 123-126
    online storage of, 49
    safe storage of, 49
    sequential pictures, 40
    share sites
        ofoto.com, 46
        Snapfish.com, 46
    stick-on corners, 25
    taking versus making terminology, 52
    uploading to sites, 46
Photomerge (Photoshop Elements), panoramic
  photo creation, 192-195
Photoshop Album
    image editing tools, 69
    user interface, 68-69
Photoshop Elements
    background templates, 97
    bit-mapped editing, 51

Blur tool, 117, 147-150
Brightness/Contrast levels, 110-111
Burn tool, 113
Clone Stamp tool, 113-114, 155, 164
color correction features, 130-131
color variation options, 151-153
Color Variations tool, 114
cost, 66
cropping features, 143
Despeckle tool, 118
Dodge tool, 111-112
drop shadow options, 206
filters
    applying, 171-173
    Despeckle, 183
    Dry Brush, 174-176
    Find Edges, 181-182
    Glowing Edges, 183
    Graphic Pen, 179
    options, 169
    Rough Pastels, 181
    Trace Contours, 183-184
    Underpainting, 176-177
    Watercolor, 173-174
grids, viewing, 82-83
Horizontal Type tool, 199-200
image flip options, 144
memory, reallocation of, 170
noise options, 90
old photographs, tinting effects, 126-127
pages, layering, 79-80
photo repair tools, 66
posterizing effects, 185-186
Red Eye Brush tool, 158-160
resizing options, 145-147

Sharpen tool, 116-117

Smudge tool, 115

Texturizer filter, 91

type

alignment options, 201

anti-aliasing options, 200

bold options, 201

color options, 201

horizontal/vertical options, 201

italic options, 201

strikethrough options, 201

underline options, 201

Type Mask tool, 199-200

Type tool, 199

user interface, 65-66

Vertical Type tool, 199-200

***Photouser Magazine*, 209-210**

Picture It!

templates, 71

user interface, 70

pictures

collages, creating, 188, 191

color correction, applying, 151-153

cropping, 140-143

drawing on, 187

flipping, 144

iron-on transfers, 237-239

panoramic

creating, 191-195

shooting guidelines, 192

software, 195

perspective, correcting, 153-154

posterizing, 185-187

printing

on cake frosting, 241

directly to fabric, 239-240

red eye, repairing, 157-162

resizing, 145-147

retouching, ethical issues, 167

skin problems, correcting, 162-164

unwanted items, removing, 155-156

weight problems, correcting, 164-167

pixels

digital cameras, picture quality, 37

dpi (dots per inch), resolution calculations, 36

placing

audio files on Web pages, 231

video files on Web pages, 231

Plaid Web site, 265

plug-ins. *See also* effects; filters

point size (text), 197

Polyform Web site, 265

Polyshrink Web site, 265

portraits

mirror effect, applying, 144

old photographs, vignetting effect, 123-126

skin problems, retouching, 162-164

posterizing images, 185-187

powder tyle embossing, 209

precut stick-ons, 27

premade backgrounds, 95-99

premade scrapbooks, 23

premade templates, 82

press style embossing, 209

primary colors, 10

Print Explosion Deluxe, clipart library, 57-58, 93

How can we make this index more useful? Email us at indexes@quepublishing.com

PrintableCalendar.com Web site, 242-243

printers

cloth materials, 103-104

drivers, 48

Epson Stylus Photo 1280

accompanying software, 47

paper sizes, 47

flashcards (digital cameras), direct print connections, 43

inkjet, color varieties, 47

laser, color varieties, 47

papers

sizes, 47

types, handling, 48

Web sites

Shutterfly, 265

Snapfish, 265

Provo Craft Web site, 265

Prym-Dritz Web site, 265

PSX Web site, 265

Ptgui application, panoramic photo creation, 195

punches, 27

purchasing digital cameras, guidelines, 40-41

Q - R

.qt format (QuickTime), 229

QuickTime, 229

quotation Web sites

Bartleby, 214

Creative Thinking, 214

Quotations Page, 214

Quoteland, 214

Quotations Page Web site, 214

Quoteland Web site, 214

Ranger Industries Web site, 265

raster images, 81

Red Castle Web site, 265

Red Eye Brush tool (Photoshop Elements), 158-160

red eye effect, removing, 157-162

Red Eye Wizard (ACD FotoCanvas), 161

removing unwanted items from pictures, 155-156

repairing old photographs, 109-110

blurring effect, 117

brightness/contrast levels, 110-111

burning tool, 111-113

color variations, 114

despeckle filter, 118

dodging tool, 111-113

dust spot cleanup, 113-114

retouches, 114

severe damage, 118-122

sharpening effect, 116-117

smudging effect, 115

resizing images, 145-147

resolution, 36

retouching

pictures, ethical issues, 167

tools (Paint Shop Pro), 114

skin problems, 162-164

weight problems, 164-167

Rough Pastels filter (Photoshop Elements), 181

Rubba Dub Dub Web site, 265

Rubber Stamp Club Web site, 30

How can we make this index more useful? Email us at indexes@quepublishing.com

rubber stamps

embossing effect, 30

Web sites, 30

rule of thirds

Golden Number Web site, 86

page design guidelines, 85-87

S

safe adhesives, 24-26

Sams Teach Yourself HTML in 24 Hours, **229**

saving pages in Web format, 225

scanners

benefits of, 44

commercial services, 45

connection options, 43

dpi settings, old photographs, 108-109

Epson CX 6400, 43-44

glass care, 44

HP PSC 1350, 43-44

image gathering process, 42

Microtek ScanMaker 5700, 42

object examples, 44

Optical Character Recognition (OCR), text editing features, 45

proprietary software, 44

resolution, 36

textured backgrounds, creating, 99

scanning

old photographs, 108-109

scrapbooks for Web page use, 221-222

scenery, shooting guidelines, 136-138

scissors

edge patterns, 26

recommended brands, 26

Web sites, 263

Scrap Circle Web site, 261

Scrap Jazz Web site, 262

Scrapbook Sites Web site, 262

scrapbook software

American Greetings Scrapbooks & More

free trialoffer, 63

image editing features, 62-63

Art Explosion Scrapbook Factory Deluxe

drawing tools, 56

quality of art, 55

quotations library, 57

templates, 57

user interface, 56

Hallmark Scrapbook Studio Deluxe, 61

HP Creative Scrapbook Assistant

drawbacks, 55

editing features, 54

effects, 54

opening, 54

user interface, 53-54

Photo Express My Scrapbook

image editing features, 59

multiple file formats, 60

Print Explosion Deluxe, clipart library, 57-58

YM Diary, journaling features, 64

Scrapbooking.com Web site, 218, 262

scrapbooks

binding systems, 23

color schemes, 10-11

composition overview, 11-12

How can we make this index more useful? Email us at indexes@quepublishing.com

organization of, 8

page holders, 23

premade, 23

purpose of, 7

scanning for Web use, 221-222

style of, 9

Scrapyard 329 Web site, 265

scratches in old photographs, repairing, 118

SCSI scanners, connecting, 43

search engines, 219

searching clip art, Web site sources, 93

secondary colors, 10

SEI Web site, 265

selecting

color schemes for scrapbooks, 10-11

fonts, 203-204

color guidelines, 205

tasteful use of, 205

page layout software, 72-73

page sharing software, 73-74

papers, 100-103

photo-editing software, 64-72

scrapbook software, 52-64

self-healing cutting mats, 27

sensor dots in digital cameras, 37

sequential pictures, 40

serif fonts, 203

servers (Web), 219

sewing Web sites, 265

Sharpen tool (Photoshop Elements), 116-117

shooting

panoramic photographs, 192

subjects, digital camera guidelines, 135-139

shrinking images, 146-147

Shutterfly Web site, 46, 265

Simple Scrapbooks Web site, 262

Sizzix Web site, 265

skin problems, correcting, 162-164

sleeve sizes, page holders, 23

Smudge tool (Photoshop Elements), 115

Snapfish Web site, 46, 265

software

overview, 51

page layout programs, selecting, 72-73

page sharing programs, selecting, 73-74

photo-editing programs, selecting, 64-72

scrapbook programs

American Greetings Scrapbooks & More, 62-63

Art Explosion Scrapbook Factory Deluxe, 55-57

Hallmark Scrapbook Studio Deluxe, 61

HP Creative Scrapbook Assistant, 53-55

Photo Express My Scrapbook, 59-60

Print Explosion Deluxe, 57-58

selecting, 52-64

YM Diary, 64

typical image editing features, 51

sound files, editing, 230

The Stamp Doctor Web site, 265

Stamp It! Web site, 265

A Stamp in the Hand Web site, 262

stamp Web sites

All Night Media, 262

Anima Designs, 262

Art Gone Wild, 262

ArtChix Studio, 262

Artisan's Choice, 262

Clearsnap, 262

How can we make this index more useful? Email us at indexes@quepublishing.com

Close to My Heart, 262
Delta Coatings, 263
Hero Art, 263
Inkadinkado, 264
Junque, 264
Limited Edition, 264
Ma Vinci's Reliquary, 264
Nankong, 265
Red Stamps, 265
Rubba Dub Dub, 265
The Stamp Doctor, 265
A Stamp in the Hand, 262
Stamp It!, 265
Stampendous, 266
Stampin Up, 266
Tandy Leather, 266
Tsukienko, 266
Uptown Design Co., 266
Wordsworth, 266
Stampendous Web site, 266
Stampin Up Web site, 266
Stamping Links Web site, 262
stationery, online templates, 242-243
stencil Web sites, 266
stick-on corners, 25
sticker Web sites
Once Upon a Sticker, 265
The Paper Patch, 265

stock, card type, 20
storing
images, 142
photographs
offline, 49
online, 49
supplies, 19-20
strikethrough type (Photoshop Elements), 201
styles for scrapbooks, 9
subjects
digital cameras, shooting guidelines, 135-139
overweight, slimming effects, 164-167
supplies, storing, 19-20

T

T-shirts, iron-on transfers, 237-239
<TABLE> tag (HTML), 227
tag Web sites
American Tag Co., 262
FoofaLa, 263
Two Busy Moms, 266
tags (HTML), 218
<A HREF>, 228
<ALIGN>, 227
<BIG>, 227
<BODY>, 227

, 227
bracket syntax, 226
<FONT>, 227
<HEAD>, 227
<HTML>, 227
<META>, 227

source code explanation, 226-229

<TABLE>, 227

<TD>, 227

<TITLE>, 227

<TR>, 227

talk bubbles, creating (ACD FotoCanvas), 201-202

Tandy Leather Web site, 266

<TD> tag (HTML), 227

templates

creating, 82-83

premade, 82

Web sites, 264

temporary tattoo papers, 103

tertiary colors, 10

text

editing via Optical Character Recognition (OCR) technology, 45

warping, 210-211

text weight paper, 21

textures

backgrounds

adding, 90-92

creating from scanned objects, 99

fabric, adding, 92

images, adding, 90, 92

Texturizer filter (Photoshop Elements), 91

Thermo O Web Web site, 266

thought bubbles, creating (ACD FotoCanvas), 201-202

three-dimensional gold lettering, 104

tinting old photographs, 126-127

tissue papers, 21

<TITLE> tag (HTML), 227

tools

edge trimmers, 28

font libraries

CD-ROMs, 28-29

Web sites, 28-29

fonts

proper usage of, 29

versus handwriting, 29

paper cutters, 28

punches, 27

rubber stamps

About Rubber Stamps Web site, 30

Addicted to Rubber Stamps Web site, 30

embossing, 30

Rubber Stamp Club Web site, 30

safe adhesives, 24-26

scissors

edge patterns, 26

recommended brands, 26

seal-healing cutting mats, 27

storing, 19-20

Web sites

C-Thru Ruler, 262

Harbor Freight, 263

K&S Engineering, 264

McGill, 264

Micro-Mark, 265

Sizzix, 265

X-acto knives, 27

<TR> tag (HTML), 227

Trace Contours filter (Photoshop Elements), 183-184

trackballs as drawing device, 35

transparency films, 102

trinket boxes, 241-242

How can we make this index more useful? Email us at indexes@quepublishing.com

Tsukineko Web site, 266

Two Busy Moms Web site, 266

Two Peas in a Bucket Web site, 262

Type Mask tool (Photoshop Elements), 199-200, 208

Type tool (Photoshop Elements), 199

typography
  alignment, 198
  drop shadows, adding, 205-207
  embossing styles
    powder, 209
    press, 209
  fonts
    display type versus body type, 203
    handwriting style, 213
    selecting, 203-205
    sources, 204
    tasteful use guidelines, 205
  kerning, 198
  leading, 198
  metallic effects, 209-210
  Photoshop Elements
    alignment options, 201
    anti-aliasing options, 200
    bold options, 201
    color options, 201
    Horizontal Type tool, 199-200
    horizontal/vertical options, 201
    italic options, 201
    strikethrough options, 201
    Type Mask tool, 199-200
    Type tool, 199
    underline options, 201
    Vertical Type tool, 199-200
  point size, 197
  Type Mask tool, 208
  warping effect, 210-211
  Web pages, design guidelines, 225
  Web sites
    Agfa-Monotype, 262
    ITC, 264
    Linotype Library, 264
    P2, 265

U - V

Ulead My Web Studio tool, 223

underlining type (Photoshop Elements), 201

Underpainting filter (Photoshop Elements), 176-177

Uptown Design Co. Web site, 266

USArtQuest Web site, 266

USB scanners, connecting, 43

vector images, 81

vellum paper, 22

Verisign.com Web site, domain registration and fees, 219-221

Vertical Type tool (Photoshop Elements), 199-201

video
  copyright infringement, 230
  formats
    .qt (QuickTime), 229
    .wma (Windows Media Player), 229

Web sites
  adding, 229-231
  file size drawbacks, 229-230
video files, editing tools, 230
viewing Web pages, HTML source code, 219
vignetting old photographs, 123-126
viruses, 50

W

Wacom.com Web site, graphics tablets, 36
warm colors, 10
warping text, 210-211
watercolor effects, applying, 173-176
Watercolor filter (Photoshop Elements), 174
Web (World Wide Web), 218
  HTML
    basic overview, 226
    links, 218
    source code explanation, 226-229
    tags, 226-228
Web browsers, HTML source code, 219
Web pages
  audio files, placing on, 231
  creation
    Macromedia Dreamweaver MX, 224
    Microsoft FrontPage, 224
    MySoftware WebPage Creation Kit, 224
    overview, 221-222
    Ulead My Web Studio, 223
    via word processing programs, 224
    wizards, 222-223

design guidelines
  graphics, 225
  typography, 225
file formats, saving, 225
HTML source code, viewing, 219
links, 218
server storage, 219
video files, placing on, 231
Web servers, 219
Web sites
  3L, 262
  7 Gypsies, 262
  1001 Free Fonts, 204
  About Rubber Stamps, 30
  Addicted to Rubber Stamps, 30
  Adobe.com, binding services, 69
  Agfa-Monotype, 262
  All Night Media, 262
  American Clay Art, 262
  American Greetings, 63
  American Tag Co., 262
  Anima Designs, 262
  Art Gone Wild, 262
  Artchix Studio, 262
  Artisan's Choice, 262
  Artistic Wire, 262
  Avery Dennison, 262
  Avery.com, 234, 242-243, 261
  Bartleby, 214
  The Beadery, 262
  Bo-Bunny Press, 262
  Brown Bag fibers, 262
  C-Thru Ruler, 262
  Canson, 262

Carl Mfg., 262

Carolee's Creations, 262

Chatterbox, 262

Cheap Joe's Art Stuff, 262

Clearsnap, 262

clip art sources

    About Scrapbooking, 93

    Country Clipart, 93

    Gatherings, 93

    Leaves of Time, 93

Close to My Heart, 262

Club Scrap, 262

Cock a Doodle Design, 263

Colorbook, 263

Colors by Design, 263

Cool Page, 224

Craf-T Products, 263

Crafts Etc!, 263

Creative Imaginations, 263

Creative Thinking, 214

Daisy D's Paper, 263

Daler-Rowney, 263

Darice, 263

Delta Coatings, 263

Deluxe Cuts, 263

Design Originals, 263

Dick Blick, 263

Dymo, 263

Easypano, 195

Emagination Crafts, 263

Embellish It!, 263

Epson.com, 47, 261

European Papers, 263

Fibers by the Yard, 263

Fiebing Co., 263

Fiskars, 263

FoofaLa, 263

Frances Meyer, 263

free hosting services

    AOL Hometown, 220

    Freeservers.com, 220

    Yahoo! Geocities, 220

Funky Fibers, 263

Glue Dots, 263

golden Artists Colors, 263

Golden Number, 86

Gone Scrappin', 263

Harbor Freight, 263

Hero Arts, 263

Hillcreek Designs, 263

Hot off the Press, 264

HowStuffWorks.com, virus resources, 50

HP Scrapbooking, 261

Inkadinkado, 264

InkJetArt.com, 101

Inspire Graphics, 264

IP addresses, 219

ITC, 264

Jacquard Products, 264

Jest Charming, 264

JewelCraft, 264

JournalTEK.com, 64

Junque, 264

K&Company, 264

K&S Engineering, 264

Karen Foster Design, 264

Keeping Memories Alive, 264

Kolo, 264

Kopp Design, 264

Kreinik, 264

How can we make this index more useful? Email us at indexes@quepublishing.com

Lazertran, 264

Learn2Scrapbook, 261

Leather Factory, 264

Library of Congress
  copyright law resources, 230
  image downloads, 46

Limited Edition, 264

Linotype Library, 264

low-cost hosting services
  DelphiForums.com, 220
  Mac.com, 220

Ma Vinci's Reliquary, 264

Magic Mesh, 264

Magic Scraps, 264

Magix.com, 230

Making Memories, 264

Marvy Uchida, 264

McGill, 264

Memories of the Rabbit, 264

Michael's Arts & Crafts, 264

Micro-Mark, 265

Midori, 265

Mustard Moon, 265

MySoftware, 224

Nankong, 265

NASA, image downloads, 46

Nature's Pressed, 265

Offray, 265

ofoto.com, 46

Once Upon a Charm, 265

Once Upon a Sticker, 265

P2, 265

Paper Adventures, 265

Paper and More, 104

The Paper Loft, 265

The Paper Patch, 265

Patchwork Paper, 265

Pebbles in My Pocket, 265

PhotoFrost.com, 241

Plaid, 265

Polyform, 265

Polyshrink, 265

PrintableCalendar.com, 242-243

Provo Craft, 265

Prym-Dritz, 265

PSX, 265

PTgui, 195

Quotations Page, 214

Quoteland, 214

Ranger Industries, 265

Red Castle, 265

Rubba Dub Dub, 265

Rubber Stamps Club, 30

Scrap Circle, 261

Scrap Jazz, 262

Scrapbook Sites, 262

Scrapbooking.com, 218, 262

Scrapyard 329, 265

SEI, 265

Shutterfly, 46, 265

Simple Scrapbooks, 262

Sizzix, 265

Snapfish, 46, 265

sound files
  adding, 229-230
  editing, 230

The Stamp Doctor, 265

A Stamp in the Hand, 262

Stamp It!, 265

Stampendous, 266

How can we make this index more useful? Email us at indexes@quepublishing.com

Stampin Up, 266
Stamping Links, 262
Tandy Leather, 266
Therm O Web, 266
Tsukineko, 266
Two Busy Moms, 266
Two Peas in a Bucket, 262
Uptown Design Co., 266
USArtQuest, 266
Verisign.com, 219-221
video additions, 229-230
Westrim Crafts, 266
White House, image downloads, 46
Winsor & Newton, 266
Wordsworth, 266
YM (Young Miss Magazine), 64
Young Bros. Stamp Works, 266

Web-based scrapbooks, 217-218

weight problems, correcting, 164-167

Westrim Crafts Web site, 266

White House Web site, image downloads, 46

whiteness grades (papers), 101

whitespace, page design guidelines, 84

Windows Media Player, .wma format, 229

Winsor & Newton Web site, 266

wire, Artistic Wire Web site, 262

wireless hubs, AirPort/AirPort Extreme, 44

wizards, Web pages, creating, 222-223

.wma format (Windows Media Player), 229

word processing applications, Web page creation, 224

WordArt (Microsoft Word), text warping options, 210-211

WordPerfect, Web page creation features, 224

Wordsworth Web site, 266

World Wide Web. *See* **Web**

Wow Chrome effects (Paint Shop Pro), 125-126

WYSIWYG (What You See Is What You Get) principle, Web page creation, 223

X - Y - Z

X-acto knives, 27

Xerox canvas material, printable fabric, 103-104

Yahoo! Geocities, free hosting services, 220

***YM* (Young Miss Magazine) Web site, 64**

YM Diary, journaling features, 64

Young Bros. Stamp Works Web site, 266

zoom settings on digital cameras, 41

Want to learn more?
Check out these other books
by Carla Rose!

You know how to use Photoshop Elements for scrapbooking. Now see what else it can do! In *Sams Teach Yourself Adobe Photoshop Elements 2 in 24 Hours*, Carla digs deeper into this popular photo-editing software, teaching you how to fix red eye, create original digital images, and build customized patterns and brushes to reuse.

Taking the next step? Learn to use the more advanced Adobe Photoshop CS with the *Sams Teach Yourself* series. Work through 24 proven one-hour lessons and learn everything you need to know. With Carla's friendly, conversational style and step-by-step instructions, you will be up and running in no time.

Sams Teach Yourself
Adobe Photoshop
Elements 2
in 24 Hours
ISBN: 0-672-32430-X, $24.99

Sams Teach Yourself
Adobe Photoshop 7
in 24 Hours
ISBN: 0-672-32388-5, $24.99

Sams Teach Yourself
Adobe Photoshop CS
in 24 Hours
ISBN: 0-672-32592-6, $24.99